# Rebels and Reformers

# Rebels and Reformers

*Christian Renewal in the Twentieth Century*

Trevor Beeson

SCM PRESS

0 334 02792 6

This edition first published 1999 by
SCM Press
9–17 St Albans Place London N1 0NX

SCM Press is a division of
SCM-Canterbury Press Ltd

Typeset by Regent Typesetting, London
and printed in Great Britain by
Biddles Ltd, Guildford and King's Lynn

# Contents

# Contents

# Contents

# Contents

# Preface

Christianity was born in rebellion. The Jewish religion out of which it came was, and remains, a noble faith, but the prophet Jesus saw clearly the need for radical change in the lives of individuals and in the ordering of society. Thus his announcement of the dawning of the Kingdom of God, based on the law of love, was accompanied by a call to repentance – to a change of direction that would bring to the world new life and hope, not least to the poor and the marginalized.

For the greater part of his three-year mission Jesus appears to have seen himself as God's agent in the reforming of the ancient religion of Israel. It was to Jews that he addressed his message, and the Sermon on the Mount includes the declaration, 'Think not that I have come to abolish the law and the prophets; I have not come to abolish them but to fulfil them.' But the religious establishment rejected his call because they discerned, correctly, that it had revolutionary implications. So Jesus came to realize that new personal and corporate expressions of God's abiding love for his people were needed and that this required first his own sacrificial death.

There is, in my view, little evidence to support the idea that Jesus was a Zealot and therefore committed to overthrowing the Roman occupying power. But the secular rulers were astute enough to discern the direction in which the Jesus movement was pointing and they executed its leader because they feared it might, if allowed to grow, create trouble and begin to threaten the stability of the established, albeit enforced, social order. Church and state combined to protect the *status quo*. It was to become a familiar pattern.

The New Testament account of the life of the Christian community indicates that for some years its members saw themselves as forming a reform movement, or even a sect, within Judaism and it was not until the momentous conversion of Saul of Tarsus that the radical character of the life and teaching of Jesus came to be fully recognized. He had offered a new vision of God's loving will and purpose, and under the guidance of the divine Spirit this vision was to be taken to the ends of the earth and lived out until the end of time. The Jews living in the Greek city of Thessalonica were aware that Paul, as he had now become, was not proposing minor modifications to their inherited tradition for, after listening to his sermons for three weeks, they complained to the civil authorities that he and his followers were intent on turning the world upside down. They were.

From those early days until the end of the second millennium Christian history has been enlivened and the life of the church renewed by a long line of men and women who have been seized by the life and teaching of Jesus and, in the power of the Spirit, have challenged the set ways of religious institutions or the inhumanity of unjust social orders. Sometimes their witness has brought about early change; more often the change has come much later, and too often the rebels and reformers have endured great suffering or even death. It is an inspiring and challenging story.

The twentieth century has had an ample share of such witnesses and in the following pages I offer brief biographies of a hundred or so of them. The choice is a personal one and represents those I find interesting and believe to be significant. Their contributions to the renewal of church and society have not been equal and, had space permitted, many more could have been included. I am sorry to have left out Alan Ecclestone, whose combination of Christian faith and Communism sustained a remarkable ministry in inner-city Sheffield and who, in his later years, wrote classics of spirituality. I wish that I could have discovered more about the Abbé Michonneau, whose work in Paris, described in *Revolution in a City Parish,* inspired me and many others in the 1950s. Chad Varah not only founded the Samaritans but also won a battle to install a Henry Moore stone altar in his City of London church and then turned to belief in reincarnation. That would have made an interesting entry. Colin Winter's courageous battle against apartheid in Namibia and concern for the oppressed everywhere merited attention, as did the leadership of Cardinal Raul Silva Henriques in Chile during the dark days of Pinochet rule. There was a foolhardiness about the decision of Camilo Torres to abandon the priesthood in order to join the freedom-fighting guerrillas in Colombia, only to be killed in his first engagement with government forces, but his heroism continues to inspire those still seeking liberation in Latin America. Tomislav Sagi-Bunic lost his position as head of the Catholic theological faculty in Zagreb in 1977 because the bishops objected to his encouragement of Christians to share in the development of a socialist society in Yugoslavia at the end of the Tito era. They also failed to heed his warnings against the dangers inherent in the religious alliances with Croat and Serb nationalism – at great cost in human life during the 1990s. So one could go on.

Broadly speaking, my rebels and reformers fall into three categories. There are those whose primary concern was with the changing of secular society, and here pride of place must go to those who witnessed against the great evils of Communism and Fascism. The injustice and repression experienced in Southern Africa and Latin America also drew a heroic response, and both Britain and the USA needed rebels against injustice. This was the century, too, when the need for the Christian faith to be re-stated in the language and thought forms of the modern age became very urgent. There were some attempts to do this, but by no means enough, and the unwillingness of the churches to take seriously the work of rebellious theologians was specially disappointing, even if predictable. As indeed was the retreat of many theologians into the academic world where the Holy Spirit seems to find it specially difficult to operate. An important exception to this emerged in Latin America from the 1960s onwards, when some of the most able theologians lived among the poorest of the poor in shanty towns and slums and produced a liberation theology which began with the desperate human condition and discovered God at work within it. This new approach to theology was, I believe, one of the most significant happenings in the twentieth century, which makes it all the more regrettable that a series of conservative appointments to Latin American bishoprics hindered the assimilation and further development of its insights.

Many of those included in this book were concerned with the reform of the church. As the century advanced, the inability of the church to carry out its mission effectively through inherited forms of worship and organization became so evident that over the course of three decades, 1960–1990, the churches in many parts of the world embraced changes comparable in scale with those experienced in Northern Europe during the sixteenth and seventeenth centuries. But society was changing even faster, and the 'New Reformation' initiated in the 1960s was not sufficiently sustained to enable the church to enter into the process of continuous reformation which marks a true community in the Spirit. Once again, however, there was an important exception, related in this case to a new understanding of the role of women in the church, expressed in some non-Roman denominations by their ordination as priests or ministers. Much more remains to be done in this crucial area, but the courageous work of rebels such as Maud Royden and Una Kroll bore some fruit.

Often enough there was overlap in the call for change in society, Christian thought and the organization of the church. And in every case the motivation was provided by a new or renewed vision of the faith as originally preached and lived by Jesus Christ. There is, of course, no possibility of reproducing exactly in the modern world that which is described in the pages of the New Testament. The Word is made flesh in many very different situations, which makes it all the more important that there should be constant reference to the original pattern. Rebels and reformers provide a vivid reminder of this essential element in Christian discipleship and of its renewing power, so I hope that the examples in this book may challenge and inspire its readers to look again at the roots of their own faith.

I have included a number of Christian artists – musicians, painters and writers – whose vision of reality has taken them in new directions. Often enough they were initially misunderstood and their work was rejected by the various establishments of their day, as well as by the public at large. But looking back over the century it is possible to see how great a contribution these and other artists made to the renewal of the wellsprings of human existence. I hope that the coming century will see a new partnership developing between the church and the artist, for they share a common mission.

Esmé Parker has yet again – three times in three years – placed her high secretarial skill and infinite patience at my disposal. I am exceedingly grateful to her, and also to the Librarian of Heythrop College, London and the Archivist of Keston Institute, Oxford for providing access to biographical material which would otherwise have eluded me. My dear friend Nadir Dinshaw – the unfailing supporter of many rebels and reformers – read the proofs and a word of gratitude goes to him, too.

TB

# Alfred Loisy

## (1857–1940)

Alfred Firmin Loisy – 'the Father of Catholic Modernism' during the early years of the century – was a French priest and biblical scholar who believed that the church would survive the assaults of modern learning only if it broke free from the constraints of mediaeval scholastic theology and allowed the Holy Spirit to adjust some of its doctrines and practices in the light of new insights and discoveries. 'Our aim,' he said, 'must be to substitute the religious for the dogmatic spirit.' But although he sought to defend the church, he was believed to be attacking it and in consequence he was excommunicated.

Loisy first emerged as a fierce opponent of the German liberal Protestant theologian Adolf von Harnack, who argued for a return to the historical Jesus, disclosed in the Gospels and freed from the accretions of Christian tradition. In his *The Gospel and the Church* (1902), Loisy responded, 'The essence of Christianity is not to be sought only in its beginning but also in the fullness and totality of its life. This life shows vitality and movement just because it is life.' He went on to argue that the gospel did not enter the world as an unconditional, absolute doctrine, summed up in a unique and steadfast truth, but as a living faith, concrete and complex. The Pope at the time, Leo XIII, was by no means a liberal but he encouraged scholars with liberal ideas and did not intervene when they strayed from traditional orthodoxy. However, his successor, Pius X, who had just become Pope when Loisy published *The Four Gospels* (1903), was of a very different stamp and placed this and his other books on the Index of forbidden reading 'for their very grave errors'. He perceived that Loisy's views undermined not only Harnack's plea for simplicity but also the Catholic Church's claim to be the sole repository of revealed Christian truth.

Loisy was born at Ambrières in Burgundy, and after some years of preparation for the priesthood at the seminary at Chalons-sur-Marne completed his training at the Institut Catholique in Paris. The Institut was then the chief centre of the Modernist Movement in France and, having spent a couple of years as a country priest, Loisy returned in 1881 to teach Hebrew and biblical exegesis. Increasingly he questioned the adequacy of the traditional approach to the Bible, believing it to be in need of radical renewal. By 1886 his faith in traditional Catholicism was wavering, but he stayed in the church in the hope that the Modernist Movement would bring about changes in its teaching, and in 1890 he became Professor of Holy Scripture at the Institut Catholique. Three years later, however, he was dismissed from this chair and told to confine himself to the teaching of oriental languages. This providing nothing like full-time employment, he became chaplain to a community of nuns and their school at Neuilly-sur-Seine.

In 1900 Loisy began to teach in the School of Practical and Higher Studies at the Sorbonne, but he gave this up in 1904 and two years later ceased exercising his priesthood. When Modernism was condemned in 1907 he responded with a combative book on the papal encyclical and the decrees of the Holy Office and in 1908 he was excommunicated. In the same year he published a two-volume study *The Synoptic Gospels*, which is generally regarded as his greatest work. The starting point of all his teaching is that 'God is before everything else a mystery that transcends us. And to claim to express in human language the last word about him is, in effect, to blaspheme him . . . Absolute truth is not revealed.' This being so, truth is always contextual and therefore changeable in the light of new circumstances and knowledge. The New Testament documents are to be seen as the product of faith, not its cause, and the church should not therefore merely repeat what has been taught by Jesus and the apostles: 'Jesus foretold the Kingdom, but it was the church that came . . . enlarging the form of the Gospel.'

In 1909 Loisy resumed his academic career as Professor of the History of Religions at the Collège de France and remained there until 1930. He wrote, in all, over thirty books, including a three-volume *Memoirs of a Servant of the History of Religion in our Time*. His work as a biblical critic became increasingly radical and he came to believe that all religions were alike in their quest for justice. At one stage he asserted that the ultimate end of religious and moral evolution would be what he called 'a moral religion of humanity', but in old age he seemed to return to his earlier Catholic faith.

A. R. Vidler, *The Modernist Movement in the Roman Catholic Church*, Cambridge University Press 1934.

# John Clifford
## (1836–1923)

John Clifford was one of Britain's best known 'political parsons' during the early years of the century when the Free Churches were still strong and had considerable political influence. He was a Baptist minister who combined evangelical fervour with wide social and political concerns and a liberal approach to Christian doctrine. He was said to be the most powerful orator in the country.

For several years his chief preoccupation was education, and what he believed to be a grave injustice arising from the government's attitude to church schools. An Education Act in 1902 permitted these schools to be financed on the same basis as those of the state. This was stoutly opposed by Clifford and other Free Church leaders, partly because it was seen as giving the Church of England and the Roman Catholic Church an unfair advantage over other churches, but chiefly because it sustained church schools in many areas where Free Church children had no alternative but to attend them. For Clifford this was a denial of liberty – always for him a grievous disability.

A National Passive Resistance Committee, with himself as President, was formed, and before long there were 648 local Leagues consisting of people who refused to pay the portion of local government rates that was applied to the financing of schools. Many of the defaulters were prosecuted, their possessions were seized by bailiffs, some were struck off electoral rolls, others were imprisoned. A series of articles by Clifford in the *Daily News* brought a response pamphlet from the Prime Minister, Arthur Balfour, who accused him of being Jesuitical. Some 7–10,000 people took part in this resistance movement and, although government policy remained unchanged, the defeat of the Conservatives in the Liberal landslide in 1906 owed much to Clifford's influence over Free Church voters. Later it was said that no Liberal government minister would move if he knew that Clifford was against him.

Clifford was born in Sawley, Derbyshire, where his father was a factory worker. At the age of eleven he was sent to work a twelve-hour day in a Nottingham lace factory but he had a conversion experience when he was fourteen and in 1855 entered the Midland Baptist College,

Leicester. Three years later he became Pastor of the Praed Street Baptist Church in Paddington, London – a post he accepted on the condition that he could continue his studies – and he took degrees in arts, science and law at London University. This did not prevent him from building up a large congregation or from raising a large sum of money to erect the Westbourne Park Chapel to accommodate the increased numbers. His own early experience gave him a lasting concern for the poor and a hatred of injustice. He became a member of the Fabian Society, opposed the Boer War, and denounced all forms of privilege. He favoured Home Rule for Ireland but called for the immediate retirement of Charles Parnell, the Irish Prime Minister in waiting, because of his adultery with the wife of an MP. In doctrinal matters Clifford said that the church 'made too much of theology' and claimed freedom to interpret the gospel in the light of advances in human knowledge. He regarded Charles Darwin as a fellow worker in the quest for truth, he welcomed biblical criticism, and although he insisted on the unique character of Christianity he was sympathetic to other religious faiths.

None of this endeared him to the strong conservative element in his church, and C. H. Spurgeon, the famous preacher, withdrew his South London Tabernacle from the Baptist Union of Great Britain and Ireland because of what he described as 'the downgrade tendencies' in theology and biblical interpretation then prevalent in this church. Clifford, who was Vice-President of the Union at this time, claimed that the church was being faithful to its long tradition of defending individuals against coercion in their quest for the truth contained in the gospel. He opposed the idea of church unity on the grounds that it would inevitably involve the sacrifice of truth and freedom and thus enfeeble the Christian witness.

Clifford's social and political conscience sprang from a high doctrine of the state, which he believed to be 'more sacred than any church . . . for the state stands for the whole people in their manifold collective life; and any church is but a fragment of that life, though one of the most important fragments'. This did not inhibit his criticism of government policies and, besides his public speaking and preaching, he wrote ninety-nine books and pamphlets. Although he was known to the general public for his outspoken views, often expressed in colourful terms, he was a kindly, loveable man who was revered throughout the Baptist world. In 1921 he was made a Companion of Honour.

# Octavia Hill

## (1838–1912)

Most of Octavia Hill's reforming work was undertaken during the nineteenth century, but she was active for a dozen years in the twentieth and a leading figure in the realm of social work until the time of her death. Her ideals were those of a Christian Socialist and, although her concern for the underprivileged was wide, her special skill and lasting contribution was in the field of housing. She was also one of the founders of the National Trust.

Hill was born in Wisbech in the year following the accession of Queen Victoria and in company with her sisters was educated at home by her mother. The greatest influence on her early years, however, was her grandfather, Dr Thomas Southward Smith, who was an authority on sanitation and fever epidemics and told her how the health of the poor was adversely affected by their squalid housing conditions. When she was in her early teens she also came under the influence of F. D. Maurice, the theologian–social reformer, who put her in charge of a branch of the Ladies' Guild – a co-operative association founded by Christian Socialists. She taught poor children to make toys. In 1853, when still only fifteen, she met John Ruskin, who helped her with her artistic training and encouraged her to spend her spare time copying pictures. He proved to be another powerful influence in her life.

In 1856 she became secretary of classes for women held at the Working Men's College in London's Great Ormond Street, and a few years later she and her sisters started a school in a house in Nottingham Place in the West End. This increased her awareness of the housing problems of the poor and in 1864, having aroused Ruskin's interest, got him to provide money for an improvement scheme involving three houses. This was so successful that she expanded her aim and proved to be such a good manager that other property owners put their houses in her hands for improvement. The Ecclesiastical (later the Church) Commissioners, who owned the land on which many notorious London slums had been built, took her on to their staff, and when leases fell in replaced the old, decayed, back-to-back houses with their own new estates. Hill advised on the type of housing needed and also persuaded the Commissioners to embark on projects which involved planning over a large area, rather than permitting piecemeal development by individual housing associations. A model estate of cottages was completed at Walworth, in South London, in 1903 and by the time of her retirement in 1912 she was responsible for the management of most of the Commissioners' property in South London and supervising some 6,000 London houses and flats. When she first started, virtually every family occupied just one, rented room, but by the end of her life a high proportion were living in two- and three-bedroomed houses and flats.

Her reputation soon became widely known and, besides training housing managers for other British towns, she was called upon to advise on schemes in America and other parts of Europe, including one in Berlin which was named Octavia Hill-Verein. The secret of good management, she emphasized, was no overcrowding, carefully-supervised cleaning, prompt repairs, and strictly kept accounts. She also stressed the importance of dealing with tenants kindly and sympathetically. More than this, jobs should be found for the unemployed, help given in times of illness and other misfortune, and opportunities provided for families to have holidays in the country. All of which required the development of community and a spirit of self-help; thus tenants should be encouraged to treat each other with respect and, where possible, placed so that they might be helpful to one another. It was a broad, humane vision which first found expression in her book *Homes of the London Poor* (1875), and, although not everything she advocated was always realized, she transformed the living conditions of many thousands of society's poorest and revolutionized the concept of social housing.

Linked to this was a deep commitment to the preserving and securing of open spaces in towns and cities for common use. It was as a result of her persistence that Parliament Hill Fields in North London and other spaces were saved from development and made available to the public. Looking beyond London, she was a member of the Commons Preservation Society and in company with Canon H. D. Rawnsley and Sir Robert Hunter founded the National Trust in 1895. Again, this represented the realization of an earlier analysis and dream, expressed in *Our Common Land* (1878). But she had no political concern and refused to join a Royal Commission on Housing in 1889, though she did become a member of one on the Poor Laws in 1905.

Gillian Darley, *Octavia Hill*, Constable 1990.

# George Tyrrell

## (1861–1909)

George Tyrrell was a Roman Catholic theologian of considerable depth and originality who was expelled from the Jesuit Order because of his beliefs and his outspoken criticisms of ecclesiastical authority. He was the leading figure in Britain of a 'Modernist' movement in the Roman Catholic Church which was condemned in 1907 by Pope Pius X, who described it as 'the compendium of all heresies'.

Tyrrell drew a sharp distinction between theology as embodied in abstract, static doctrinal statements and theology as a dynamic, personal experience of and response to divine revelation. He also believed that the truth of religious belief is to be tested by its effects on the believer's way of life – 'by their fruits you shall know them' – though he did not confine these effects to ethical behaviour, for he was a man of deep spirituality and greatly valued Catholic worship and devotion. He did not, however, hesitate to describe the doctrinal system of the church as 'a pseudo-science begotten of dogmatic fallacy', and he went as far as saying that the refinements of Scholastic metaphysics on the Trinity, the Incarnation and the Real Presence were 'even further from the truth than the simple faith of the peasant'.

He was born in Dublin, where he had an evangelical upbringing, but later came under the influence of Dr Maturien, a moderate Church of Ireland high churchman. He became a Roman Catholic in 1879 and in the following year entered the Jesuit Order. After serving his novitiate at Roehampton, Stoneyhurst College and in Malta, he had four years' theological training at St Beuno's College, North Wales, before his ordination to the priesthood. He then lectured in philosophy at Stoneyhurst for a short time and after this undertook mission work in Salford, Oxford and St Helena.

His next move was to the Jesuits' principal London church at Farm Street, where he established a friendship with Baron Friedrich von Hügel, a distinguished lay theologian, and was influenced by the writings of the activist philosophy of Maurice Blondel, the vitalist Henri Bergson, and the French Catholic modernist Alfred Loisy. His own first three books were, however, of a devotional character and fairly orthodox, and it was not until 1899, when he contributed an article on Hell to the *Weekly Register* under the title 'A Perverted Devotion', that he became involved in controversy. He was banished to the Jesuit Mission House at Richmond, Yorkshire, where he lived in seclusion, but continued to write. *Lex Orandi* (1903) was the last of his books to receive an official imprimatur and in 1905 he asked to be released from his priestly vows. This was refused.

In 1906 a Milan newspaper printed some extracts from a privately printed but widely circulated *Letter to a Professor of Anthropology* in which Tyrrell argued that, since man can rest only in a conscious relation to the Universal and Eternal, the truth of revelation cannot be conveyed in theological statements, but only in fact and experience. The dogmatic decisions of church councils could therefore only protect revelation in its original form and purity. They could re-assert but not amplify. The position of conservative Catholics was, he asserted, untenable, and he contrasted living faith with 'dead theology'. The newspaper attributed the material to Tyrrell, which he could not deny, and he was forthwith expelled from the Jesuit Order. The same year saw the publication of *Lex Credendi*, an exposition of the Lord's Prayer, with a strong emphasis on the experiential, and also *A Much-abused Letter*, which indicated complete estrangement from the church. He was by this time living in Storrington, Sussex and devoting his life completely to literary work.

Pope Leo XIII was largely tolerant of the Modernist movement in the church but his successor Pius X saw things very differently and the condemnatory encyclical *Pascendi* was published in 1907. Tyrrell replied to this and its accompanying decree *Lamentabili* in two highly critical letters to the London *Times*, as a consequence of which minor excommunication was imposed on him, pending a decision in Rome. Tyrrell responded in some anger with a book *Mediaevalism*, and began writing his most significant book, *Christianity at the Cross-Roads*. In this he argued that he was being faithful to the basic 'idea' of Christianity, but believed that it was not the final religion. Because it has the potential for indefinite development and inexhaustible symbolism, Christianity contains the germ of a coming universal religion.

Having completed his book, Tyrrell became seriously ill and died in 1909 shortly before its publication. The Roman Catholic Bishop of Southwark refused him burial with Catholic rites, so he was interred in the Anglican churchyard at Storrington. His friend the Abbé Brémond paid tribute to the qualities of his mind and character and blessed the grave.

# Walter Rauschenbusch
## (1861–1918)

Walter Rauschenbusch was the leading exponent of the social gospel in America during the early years of the century and exercised great influence not only in the churches but also among politicians and others in public life. Woodrow Wilson, Theodore Wilson and David Lloyd George were among those who consulted him. Although he was essentially a church historian and held a chair in this subject at Rochester Theological Seminary for more than twenty years, his chief concern was with the interaction between theology and social action. He found the clue to this in the doctrine of the Kingdom of God, which he interpreted in terms of social and economic life in this world, rather than in spiritualized or eschatological ideas. In his *A Theology for the Social Gospel* (1917) he wrote:

> The Kingdom of God is the first and the most essential dogma of the Christian Faith. It is also the lost social ideal of Christendom. No man is a Christian in the full sense of the original discipleship until he has made the Kingdom of God the controlling purpose of his life, and no man is intellectually prepared to understand Jesus Christ until he has understood the meaning of the Kingdom of God.

The book in which he first adumbrated this concept, *Christianity and the Social Crisis* (1907), was only seven chapters long, but it became an immediate best-seller, was translated into several languages and eventually ran to seventeen editions.

Rauschenbusch was the son of German immigrants, and his father, who was originally a Lutheran, became a Baptist and taught for some years at Rochester Theological Seminary. Young Walter studied in Germany, where he was awarded a First in classics at Gütersloh University before returning to America to prepare for ordination at Rochester. On completion of his training he offered for overseas missionary work, but was turned down because his views on the Old Testament were considered to be too liberal. Instead he became Pastor at the Second German Baptist Church in a district of New York City known as Hell's Kitchen, where there was said to be 'an endless procession of men out of work, out of clothes, out of shoes, and out of hope'. This had a profound effect on him, as did a book *Progress and Poverty* by Henry George, and he felt challenged to relate his individualistic evangelical faith to the social needs of those to whom he was ministering.

In 1888, however, he had an illness that caused permanent deafness, and three years later he left his parish in order to undertake further study. This included a visit to London to inspect the conditions under which the poor were living, and to meet people involved in Fabian social-ism and other social movements. He also studied New Testament in Germany and returned to America with a liberal approach to the Bible and a vision of the Kingdom of God as something to be realized on earth. For him this integrated science and faith, ethics and theology, culture and the church, dogma and the social gospel. He joined the teaching staff of Rochester Theological Seminary in 1897, and although he taught church history, by this time he was much more interested in social ques-tions. In *Christianizing the Social Order* (1912) he was severely critical of American capitalism which he regarded as only 'semi-Christian', and he prescribed various remedies, mainly of a mild socialist character. *Dare We Be Christians?* (1914) was a commentary on I Corinthians 13 and *The Social Principles of Jesus* (1916) was a study book which had a large readership.

Rauschenbusch's wide influence undoubtedly owed something to the fact that he lived at a time of widespread disillusionment with the character of American society, which he said had been corrupted by 'the lust for easy and unearned gain'. He offered a vision and a hope, and his distrust of philosophy and dogma also won the support of pragmatic Americans. But although some of his followers virtually abandoned all serious theological understanding of the basis of social reform, Rauschen-busch himself remained a deeply devout man, who never lost touch with his evangelical roots and was driven to propound the concept of a 'King-dom of Evil' to account for the many obstacles to the early realization of the Kingdom of God. He also retained a high doctrine of the church which, although subordinate to the Kingdom of God, was nonetheless a vital instrument in the realisation of the kingdom.

During the 1914–18 war he was a pacifist and this, combined with his German origin, led some to question his loyalty. Thus he became less popular, and the destruction and suffering of war raised a serious ques-tion mark over his optimistic vision.

# Charles de Foucauld

## (1858–1916)

Charles de Foucauld was a French cavalry officer who resigned and became a hermit in the North Africa desert, where he lived a life of intense spirituality. This attracted no followers during his lifetime but, after his death, his example led to the formation of fraternities of Little Brothers and Little Sisters committed to contemplation, poverty and the service of the poor. There are now about 200 Brothers of 20 different nationalities living in 30 countries and over 1,000 Sisters of 50 different nationalities, living in communities among the poor of Marseilles, Algiers, Latin America, Africa and India. There are also many more associations of priests and lay people living according to the ideals of de Foucauld.

He was born into an aristocratic family in Strasbourg and as a young lieutenant used his inherited wealth to live a dissolute life. Matters came to a head when he was posted to Algeria and failed to obtain permission to take his mistress with him. He left the army. During 1883–84 he undertook a dangerous journey of exploration in Morocco, accompanied by a Jewish rabbi as his guide. His report on this journey *Reconnaissance au Maroc* (1888) won him the Gold Medal of the French Geographical Society, and he also came back much impressed by the faith of the Jewish and Muslim communities he had encountered. A period of spiritual uncertainty followed, but in 1886 he returned to the Catholic faith of his childhood.

He believed that his love for Jesus required him to identify with Jesus in poverty and insecurity and in 1890, after undertaking a pilgrimage to the Holy Land, he entered a Trappist monastery in Syria. Severe though the life of this austere Order proved to be, it was not severe enough for de Foucauld, who felt that his membership provided a security which was unknown to Jesus and still denied to the poorest of the poor. He was also anxious because his superiors wished him to study theology. 'Theology may be admirable,' he told them, 'but how much did St Joseph know of it?' Having obtained release from the Trappists, he went to live in a simple hut alongside Poor Clare communities, first in Nazareth and then in Jerusalem, undertaking menial duties for the nuns.

He returned to France in 1901 for ordination to the priesthood, then set off to Algeria to live as a hermit, settling for a time at an oasis not far from the border with Morocco. There he had the company of a French army garrison and ministered to the many slaves in the area, at one point appealing to the French authorities to abolish slavery in their colonies, but to no avail. Eventually he settled at Tamanrasset, a community of no more than twenty homes in a mountainous area at the heart of the Sahara. 'I choose this abandoned place,' he wrote, 'and here I stick', which he did for the remaining years of his life. He spent long hours in prayer ('Praying to the Lord for those I love is the chief business of my life'), did some elementary medical and social work, and studied the language of the Tuaregs. At this time the language had no written form, but de Foucauld compiled a dictionary and a grammar and made various translations, including portions of the Bible.

Although few people were within easy reach, he started to receive visitors, and began to exert a noticeable influence simply by the character of his life. It had been his hope that he might form a community which should 'lead the life of our Lord as closely as possible, living solely by the work of their hands, without accepting any gift . . . giving to all who ask . . . adding to this work much prayer . . . forming small groups only . . . scattered, above all, through infidel and neglected lands'. But no one ever joined him and in the end, and to his great joy, the Vatican gave special permission for him to celebrate the eucharist with no one present but himself.

In 1916 de Foucauld was killed – whether deliberately or accidentally has never been certain – during a disturbance in the desert caused by the 1914–18 war. On the day of his death he wrote in a letter to his cousin Marie: 'Our annihilation is the most powerful means we have of uniting ourselves to Christ and doing good to others'. Seventeen years later René Voillaume and four other priests who had been inspired by his writings went to live a monastic life on the edge of the Sahara and a small community of Little Sisters was founded near Montpellier in France. The 1939–45 war hindered development, but when the war ended the number of fraternities grew steadily.

Elizabeth Hamilton, *The Desert My Dwelling Place*, Hodder and Stoughton 1968.

# Charles Péguy
## (1873–1914)

Charles Pierre Péguy was a French poet and writer who combined patriotism, socialism and a deep Christian mysticism. He could have lived only in France, to the history and culture of which he attributed an almost mystical significance. And he had a deep attachment to the memory of Jeanne d'Arc whose response to the prompting of her 'inner voices' spoke to him powerfully of the way of Christian obedience, and in particular of the unbreakable link between prayer and action.

His best-known, but usually misunderstood, saying, 'Everything begins as a mystique and ends as a politique', provides an important clue to his understanding of life and of his own vocation. For him 'mystique' embraced the whole of the Christian life – prayer expressed in social and political action in the cause of justice. But 'politique' meant the rejection of Christianity and the pursuing of political ends for their own sake – turning politics into a form of idolatry.

Péguy believed that France in his day had forsaken its rich Christian past and turned in an idolatrous direction, with destructive consequences. For this he blamed the leaders of church and state, and he had many harsh criticisms of the Roman Catholic clergy, whom he accused of complicity in a social and economic system which created division between rich and poor, and also of being so wedded to past tradition that they lacked the freedom to make the leap of faith into the God-given future. He saw himself as engaged in a battle to restore a new sense of mystique that would give spiritual force and direction to political effort in the modern world, and he was not afraid to make enemies or lose friends in this struggle, for he was a man of independent mind who expressed himself vehemently.

Péguy was born in Orléans and brought up in poverty by his widowed mother and grandmother, who eked out a living by repairing chairs. He won a scholarship to the Lycée and went in 1894 to the Sorbonne in Paris to study philosophy, with the intention of becoming a teacher. By the time he arrived at the university, however, he had been converted to socialism, seeing this as the only way to overcome poverty. At this point he abandoned his traditional Catholicism, but retained a deep religious faith and shared the belief of Jesus and the Old Testament prophets that the indifference of the rich to the poor constituted sin. By the beginning of the twentieth century he had become an unbeliever, but this did not last long, and in 1907 he returned to faith, though not to the church, declaring that this did not amount to a conversion, since it was the discovery at the deepest level of his life of something that had always been there in embryonic form.

Meanwhile in 1897 his Jeanne d'Arc trilogy was published – a long mystical poem which expressed his devotion to the 'Maid of Orléans' and embodied a statement of his religious and socialist principles. It also included a number of blank pages, designed to encourage pauses for reflection. About this time he became caught up in the Dreyfus affair and fought to prove the innocence of a young Jewish officer who had been accused of selling military secrets to a foreign power. He recruited other socialists to the cause and set up a bookshop in Paris which became the centre of the Dreyfus battle. He also began publishing, in 1900, *Cahiers de la Quinzaine* (Fortnightly Notebooks). This never achieved a large circulation but nonetheless became highly influential over the next fourteen years, not least on French literature. The journal contained a commentary on current issues, outspoken editorials and essays by leading writers such as Anatole France, Henri Bergson and Romain Rolland.

Besides this journalism he published several collections of essays. One of the themes to which he often returned was the de-Christianization of France – a development he attributed to the negligence of the clergy, who had not been alive to the profound changes taking place in French society during the nineteenth century. His most important work, however, was his poetry: his *magnum opus, Le Mystère de la charité de Jeanne d'Arc* (1910) was an enlargement of his earlier trilogy. *Mystère des Saints Innocents* (1912) spoke of God's delight in the purity of life expressed in his original creation, renewed by the child Jesus, and continued in the birth of every child, while *Eve* (1913) consisted of many thousands of lines expressing his view of the human condition in the perspective of the Christian revelation.

On the outbreak of war in 1914 he enlisted as a lieutenant in the army and was killed in the First Battle of the Marne in September of that year.

M. Villiers, *Charles Péguy*, Collins 1965.

# John Scott Lidgett
## (1854–1953)

John Scott Lidgett was one of the century's great Free Church leaders and held high office in the Methodist Church during the early years of the century when the Free Churches exerted considerable political influence. Eventually he became a distinguished Free Church 'establishment' figure and was rewarded with several honorary doctorates and made a Companion of Honour (1933), but throughout his life he fought strongly for social justice and worked ceaselessly for church unity.

The depth of his commitment was reflected in the fact that, having founded the Bermondsey Settlement in 1891 to minister to some of London's poorest poor, he continued to live there until 1949, by which time he was aged ninety-five. The idea came to him while serving as a young Methodist circuit minister in Cambridge. During this time he became specially conscious of the wide gulf between rich and poor in Britain and of the great evils of unemployment, poverty and bad housing.

In the heart of London's dockland he established a centre for evangelical and social work, with himself as Warden and a group of permanent residents – laymen who worked in London during the day. An educational institute encouraged study of literature, science and art; boys' and girls' clubs were established; a working women's society was copied in many other areas of social deprivation; and the settlement became a mini-welfare state in itself. The headquarters of the South London Dockers' Union was located in the premises, and acts of worship, Sunday Schools and eventually the sustaining of two Methodist churches in nearby Rotherhithe testified to the Christian inspiration of the whole enterprise.

However, Lidgett, who had an acute mind and was a compelling preacher and speaker, saw clearly that social work was not enough, and members of the settlement were encouraged to enter local governments. He was himself an Alderman of London County Council from 1905 to 1910 and again from 1922 to 1928. Betweentimes he represented Rotherhithe on the LCC and from 1918 to 1928 was Leader of its Progressive Party.

# John Scott Lidgett (1854–1953)

Education was always one of his special concerns. He was elected to the London Schools' Board in 1897, and was a member of the LCC Education Committee from 1905 to 1928. The 1902 Education Bill won his support for its provisions for more and better higher education, but in company with other Free Church leaders he strongly opposed the proposal that church schools should be supported from the rates, provided that one-third of their management committees were nominated by Local Education Authorities. He saw this as unfair to the Free Churches, and also likely to impede the provision of religious education in non-church schools, but he parted company with those of his colleagues who set up a resistance movement which encouraged Free Church people to refuse to pay their rates. Later he became involved in the affairs of London University and was its Vice-Chancellor from 1930 to 1932.

Lidgett was born into a well-known Methodist family, in Lewisham, South London. He left school early to work as a clerk with a firm of insurance and shipping brokers, but after a short time at this went to University College, London, where he secured an MA in logic and philosophy. He was ordained into the Methodist ministry in 1876 and served in Tunstall, Southport, Cardiff and Wolverhampton before reaching Cambridge and reflecting on the social implications of his faith. Later he acknowledged his debt to F. D. Maurice, whom he regarded as the most significant religious thinker of the nineteenth century.

In 1908 he was President of the Methodist Conference, having earlier become Chairman of the London South District of his church. He also became President of the National Council of Evangelical Free Churches and urged that the Free Churches should unite, then seek to become united with the Church of England. Little progress was made in this direction, but Lidgett played an important part in the uniting of the Wesleyan, Primitive and United Methodist Churches in 1932. He was one of the earliest advocates of a Council of Churches in Great Britain and a founder member of the British Council of Churches in 1942.

He was a prolific writer: his most significant book was *The Spiritual Principle of the Atonement* (1897) and the most interesting *The Idea of God and Social Ideals* (1938), in which he explained the relationship between theology and social action. He was editor of the *Methodist Times* from 1907 to 1918 and succeeded his uncle as editor of *Contemporary Review* in 1911. Many of his contemporaries found him an austere, formidable character, and he had few intimate friends, but no one doubted the authenticity of his deep spirituality.

John Scott Lidgett, *My Guided Life*, Methuen 1936.

# Muriel Lester

## (1883–1968)

Muriel Lester, known in Japan as the 'Mother of World Peace', was a Christian pacifist who devoted the first half of her life to social work in London's East End and then, as an ambassador at large for the Fellowship of Reconciliation, travelled to virtually every part of the world pleading the cause of non-violence. She was one of the first to declare the inseparability of peace and justice, and much of her campaigning was concerned with the alleviation of hunger and poverty. Human rights, women's liberation, internationalism, ecumenism and inter-faith dialogue and action were also on her agenda long before they became matters of general concern, and during the 1939–45 war she was interned for three months, first in Trinidad, then in London's Holloway prison for an alleged 'breach of Colonial regulations'.

Born in Leytonstone, Essex, the daughter of a wealthy London businessman, Lester was educated in Scotland. Her family background was Baptist, but she usually attended the Congregationalist church in Leytonstone. On leaving school she began the kind of social round common to girls of her class, but in 1902 accepted an invitation to a Factory Girls' Dance in Bow, and this led to involvement in the weekly meetings of the girls' club. Familiarity with the poverty and squalor of the East End of London at that time, together with a personal conversion experience, resulted in a deep commitment to what she called a 'new radical Christian discipleship'. This eventually led her to renounce her wealth and to take a vow of poverty. She and her sister moved into Bow and, with the aid of their father's money, established, in 1915, Kingsley Hall in memory of their brother who had died young.

This substantial building, developed from a former Baptist church, became the base for a variety of social work activities. The two sisters emphasized that it was not concerned with the dispensing of charity but rather with the securing of justice for the poor. Regular Sunday evening services, conducted by Muriel, were also held, and on the outbreak of war in 1914 she announced, 'There is no moratorium on the Sermon on the Mount.' She demonstrated this in the following year by joining the newly formed Fellowship of Reconciliation, and was soon put on its committee. Before long, however, she became ill and attributed this to her neglect of prayer. Throughout her life she emphasized the importance of linking prayer and action and wrote a book on worship.

Next she entered local government as an alderman of Poplar Council, serving as chairman of its Maternity and Child Welfare committee and as a member of its Public Health and Housing committees. Concern for children was always important to her and this led to the building of East End Children's Home – the first in London. In 1926 she went to India to meet Mahatma Gandhi and during the course of a four-week stay in his ashram established what was to become a life-long friendship with India's spiritual leader. When he attended a Round Table Conference in London in 1931 to discuss the future of India he stayed at Kingsley Hall for three months. Later she came to know Pandit Jawahalal Nehru and described one discussion with him on prayer as 'perhaps my greatest day'.

From 1933 onwards international travel in the cause of world peace occupied the greater part of her life. She was in the USA when war broke out in 1939 and after much agonized thought decided that as she was employed by the International FOR as its Travelling Secretary, she ought to maximize her freedom by remaining in America and using this country as her base for future work for peace. A broadcast advocating US neutrality in the war was well received by its largely isolationist American audience but news of it caused outrage in Britain, and after a successful visit to Latin America the ship on which she was returning to New York called in at Trinidad, whereupon she was taken ashore and put in a detention camp.

A London campaign to secure her freedom eventually led to her being returned to Britain, but on arrival she was despatched to Holloway prison in North London. Strong representations by friends and other influential contacts secured her speedy release and her incarceration was said by Home Office officials to have been the consequences of 'a mistake'. Her passport was restored in 1945 and for the rest of her life she travelled, from her old base at Kingsley Hall, to all parts of the world, speaking, preaching and conducting prayer schools in the cause of reconciliation and peace.

Jill Wallis, *Mother of World Peace*, Hisarlik Press 1993.

# Roland Allen

## (1868–1947)

Roland Allen was a missionary in China for ten years and a parish priest in England for five, then spent forty years without an official appointment but fully occupied in a one-man campaign to get the church to change radically its missionary strategy both in Britain and overseas. His experience in China led him to a close study of the Acts of the Apostles and the Pauline epistles and to the belief that the church must return to the basic principles of mission and ministry discernible in these writings.

Missionaries must not be paid professionals, maintained by distant, foreign societies, but members of local Spirit-filled Christian communities. Equally the clergy, for the most part, must not be paid professionals dispatched to parishes from distant universities and theological colleges but leaders chosen by and from within local churches and continuing in their secular occupations. Local churches must be responsible for their own finances – raising whatever money might be needed for their work and deciding how it should be spent. All of which, he insisted, was not a matter of expediency in the face of a declining church life but rather of obedience to the will of God as revealed in Christ. Much of the church's organizational life was, he believed, plain sinful. These views, expressed in a multitude of books and pamphlets, were regarded as revolutionary and were strongly criticized, not least by missionary societies.

Allen was born in Bristol. He attended the local grammar school, became a scholar of St John's College, Oxford, where he studied classics and modern history, and prepared for holy orders at Leeds Clergy Training School. During this time he felt drawn to overseas missionary work and, after serving as a curate in Darlington for three years, went in 1895 to the Society for the Propagation of the Gospel's North China Mission. He spent two years as chaplain of the British Legation in Peking while learning Chinese, and for a short time lectured at a training school for Chinese clergy, but this ended abruptly with the Boxer Rising and the siege of the Legation in 1900. He then became the bishop's chaplain for a couple of years before going as a missionary to a country station at Yungching. Within a year his health had broken down and it was necessary for him to return to England, but in a report to the SPG from

Yungching he said that foreign missionaries were stifling the development of the church's mission and that the church should become indigenous.

From 1903 to 1907 Allen was Vicar of Chalfont St Peter in Buckinghamshire, where he was a much-loved parish priest, but he resigned because he felt unable to officiate at the baptisms, marriages and funerals of non-practising Christians. Thereafter, with the help of friends and later the Survey Application Trust, he wrote and lectured about mission strategy, with a brief interruption during the 1914–18 war when he was chaplain to a hospital ship that was sunk in the North Sea. He travelled extensively, visiting bishops in Kenya, Southern Rhodesia, Canada and Assam, and moved to East Africa in 1933, dying there in 1947.

Although his books tend to be repetitious and sometimes tedious, they contain some striking passages and forthright criticisms of the church's hierarchy and its missionary societies. The first, *Missionary Methods: St Paul's or Our Own?* (1912), consisted mainly of an exposition of New Testament material and concluded with some recommendations: 'The test of all teaching is practice. Nothing should be taught which cannot be so grasped and used.' 'All organization in like manner must be of such a character that it can be understood and maintained . . . It must not be so elaborate or so costly that small and infant communities cannot supply the funds necessary for its maintenance.'

A short volume *Voluntary Clergy* (1923) was expanded to more than 300 pages on *The Case for Voluntary Clergy* (1940). In it he asserted that forbidding men to earn their own livelihood in secular occupations made void the word of Christ. He went on to say that the stipendiary system 'binds the church in chains and compels us to adopt practices which contradict the very idea of the church'. The moral and leadership qualities of the clergy were, he believed, more important than their educational attainments, and he could see no point in lay readers who were authorized to perform the more difficult task of preaching, but denied the simpler task of administering the sacraments. Allen was not opposed to the church employing a number of stipendiary clergy for service in large parishes and as scholars, but his vision was of close-knit, dynamic local churches in which the distinction between clergy and laity was simply the distinction between one form of service and another.

*The Ministry of the Spirit: Selected Writings of Roland Allen*, edited by David M. Paton, World Dominion Press 1960.

# Geoffrey Studdert Kennedy

## (1883–1929)

Geoffrey Studdert Kennedy was a legendary army chaplain in the First World War who became known nationally as 'Woodbine Willie'. The name was given to him by soldiers serving in the trenches of France and Flanders because he handed out Woodbine cigarettes to relieve the stress of their appalling situation. But their affection for him owed more to his deep love of humanity, of which the gift of cigarettes was a simple expression. He also had a unique ability to get alongside ordinary soldiers and express their feelings in vivid speech, and often dialect poetry:

> Yes, I used to believe i' Jesus Christ,
>> And I used to go to Church.
> But sin' I left home and came to France
>> I've been clean knocked off my perch.
>
> It ain't the same out 'ere, ye know,
>> It's different as chalk fro' cheese
> For 'arf on it's blood and t'other 'arf's mud,
>> And I'm damned if I really sees
> 'Ow the God, who 'as made such a cruel world,
>> Can 'ave Love in 'Is 'eart for men,
> And be deaf to the cries of the men as dies
>> And never comes 'ome again.

This apparent conflict between faith in a loving God and the suffering of the soldiers in the trenches was a subject to which Kennedy often returned, and he was driven by his experience of war to conclude that God shares in the suffering of his people.

> How can it be that God can reign in glory,
>> Calmly content with what His Love has done,
> Reading unmoved the piteous shameful story,
>> All the vile deeds men do beneath the sun?
>
> Are there no tears in the heart of the Eternal?
>> Is there no pain to pierce the soul of God?

Then must He be a friend of Hell infernal,
    Beating the earth to pieces with His rod.

Father, if He, the Christ, were Thy Revealer,
    Truly the First Begotten of the Lord,
Then must Thou be a Sufferer and a Healer
    Pierced to the heart by the sorrow of the sword.

Kennedy was born in Leeds. He read Classics and Divinity at Trinity College, Dublin, then taught in a Liverpool school before preparing for ordination. Curacies in Liverpool and Leeds were followed by appointment in 1914 as Vicar of St Paul's Church, Worcester. But soon after the outbreak of war he enlisted as an army chaplain. For part of this time he was based at Rouen railway station, where soldiers assembled in order to be transported to the front line. In the coffee shop he played the piano, talked to the men, prayed with them, wrote letters home for them and as they got into the trains gave them copies of the New Testament and packets of cigarettes. It was a ministry of pure compassion.

But he was not always behind the lines. He served for long periods in the trenches under fire and was awarded the Military Cross in 1917 for tending wounded soldiers. He had no doubt about the validity of the Allied cause and the duty of men to fight for their country, but he was often highly critical of politicians and also of church leaders for their calls to patriotism made from safe positions far removed from the horrors of the front line. When called to preach before King George V, Kennedy dispensed with the text and began his sermon 'I have come to you from the bloody slime of the trenches'. On leaving the army in 1919 he was made a royal chaplain and returned for a time to his parish in Worcester. But he needed a wider sphere of work and, having served for a time on the staff of St Martin-in-the-Fields in London's Trafalgar Square, he was appointed in 1924 Rector of St Edmund's Church in the City of London.

The duties of this post were light and enabled him to take on the additional responsibility of Chief Missioner of the Industrial Christian Fellowship – a national organization that was concerned to strengthen, and in most cases establish, links between the church and the world of industry. Kennedy travelled all over England conducting services in factory canteens and addressing meetings in town halls. But the human burdens he shouldered were too heavy and he died while conducting an ICF crusade in Liverpool in 1929. At his funeral a packet of Woodbines was placed on the coffin. Archbishop William Temple said that he was the finest priest he ever knew.

# John R. Mott

## (1865–1955)

John Raleigh Mott, the 'Father of the Modern Ecumenical Movement', was an American Methodist layman whose fervent missionary spirit led him to believe that a divided church could never be an effective instrument of the gospel. He worked tirelessly, and during his lifetime travelled more than two million miles, to encourage the different churches to collaborate in mission. He played a crucial part in the foundation of the World Council of Churches. During the first half of his long life he had a particular concern for the Christian mission to students and through his ability to inspire and challenge exercised an enormous influence. He was largely responsible for the formation of the World Student Christian Federation in 1895 and served for many years as its General Secretary, then as Chairman. Although he believed passionately in the vocation of the Christian layman to witness to his faith through involvement in the secular world, Mott declined President Woodrow Wilson's request that he should become the US Ambassador to China, out of a conviction that his vocation was to help change the church and further its work of evangelism. In 1946 he shared the Nobel Peace Prize.

Mott was born in New York State, but brought up in Iowa. He attended Upper Iowa and Cornell universities and planned to enter public life, until challenged by an English evangelist from Cambridge to make 'a life investment' decision. This took him to a month-long Mount Hermon Student Conference where Dwight L. Moody, the leading American evangelist of the time, proposed a Student Volunteers Movement for Foreign Missions. Of the 251 students present, 100 offered for service, Mott among them, and he served as its chairman from 1888–1920. In 1888 he also became Student Secretary of the International Committee of the YMCA and began an association with the movement that lasted for sixty years, including a spell as its Assistant General Secretary.

It was now becoming apparent that Mott was likely to serve the church as a missionary thinker and strategist, rather than as someone engaged in evangelism overseas. His first book, *The Evangelization of the World in This Generation* (1900), attracted a great deal of interest and the title became a catch-phrase among the many missionary enthusiasts of those days. He drew a distinction, however, between preaching and conversion, and said that the Christian mission should 'give all men an equal opportunity of knowing Jesus Christ as their Saviour and becoming his real disciples'. In 1908 he became chairman of a committee which convened the first World Missionary Conference. This was held in Edinburgh in 1910. It also marked the beginning of a long and fruitful partnership between Mott and J. H. Oldham, a Scot, who was organizing secretary of the conference and shared his vision.

The success of the Edinburgh conference owed much to them, and this was acknowledged by their appointments as chairman and secretary of the continuation committee. Mott's next book, *The Decisive Hour of Christian Missions,* again emphasized the urgency of the missionary task, and a permanent International Missionary Council was seen as the next step after the Edinburgh conference, but the 1914–18 war intervened and it was not until 1921 that this Council was able to meet – with Mott in the chair. Before the war came, however, he had undertaken a remarkable journey to the Far East. Between 11 November 1912 and 11 April 1913 he presided over twenty-one conferences and formed National Christian Councils of Japan, Korea, China and India. These facilitated collaboration between the main missionary agencies and started the ecumenical movement in Asia. In 1913 he was also secretary of a committee concerned with missionary co-operation in Latin America and during 1918 was director of a campaign which raised $200 million to assist American servicemen returning home from the war.

Between February and April 1924 Mott conducted a series of 'Moslem Conferences' in Algeria, Egypt, Lebanon and Iraq which led eventually to the setting up of a Near East Christian Council. The presence for the first time of Orthodox leaders at a second World Missionary Conference which he chaired in Jerusalem in 1928 was due to his influence. The 1930s found him chairing the business committee of the Oxford Conference on Church, Community and State, and another world missionary conference at Tambaram. He also wrote *The Present Day Summons to the World Mission of Christianty* and *Liberating the Lay Forces of Christianity*, and was pushing the churches towards the formation of a World Council. When this came into being in 1948 he was made its Honorary President. Mott was often consulted by church leaders and Heads of State and President Woodrow Wilson once said: 'Mr Mott occupies a certain spiritual presidency in the spiritual university of the world.'

C. H. Hopkins, *John R. Mott*, Eerdmans 1979.

# Vincent Lebbe

## 1877–1940

Vincent Lebbe was a Belgian priest who devoted his life to missionary work in China and fought a long and successful battle for the creation of an indigenous Chinese church. The missionary must, he argued, be totally identified in love with those whom he desires to win for Christ. He became a Chinese citizen in 1927 and following his death was proclaimed a national hero. His name is in the annals of China.

Born in Ghent, Lebbe entered the Lazarist Order at Paris where he embraced the modern ideas of biblical criticism and strongly supported the infant liturgical movement. In 1902 he was sent to China, where the signs of the Boxer uprising, in which 225 missionaries and 30,000 Chinese Christians had been killed, were still evident. He was also shocked by what he found at the Catholic seminary in Peking – where European and Chinese priests sat at different tables for meals, and the courses of study for Chinese students were set at a much lower level than those of their European counterparts. It was alleged that higher standards of education might encourage pride and ultimately revolt.

From 1906 to 1916 Lebbe was at Tientsin, engaged in mission work and trying to make links between Christian faith and the renewal taking place in Chinese national life. He believed that the church should be set free from its cultural and political ties with the West, but when he spoke about the possibility of there being Chinese bishops he was told firmly by the heads of missions that the white races could produce an uninterrupted supply of bishops, whereas the Chinese and other races were incapable of exercising leadership in the church. This conflict led to his being removed from Tientsin and sent to South China. Lebbe then began sending to Rome critical reports of the church's policy in China and in 1917 addressed a letter to a French bishop in the Vatican in which he proposed: (i) Chinese Christians needed to be patriotic; (ii) the church should be freed from its attachment to colonial powers; (iii) an indigenous clergy should be created; (iv) such clergy to be eligible for any office in the church, including the episcopate.

The Vatican, which had for some time been trying to establish direct contact with the Chinese government and to wrest control of Catholic missions from the French colonizers, responded by sending a bishop on a fact-finding tour of China. A year later Pope Benedict XV issued an encyclical which has been described as 'the Magna Carta of modern (Catholic) missions'. In it he deplored the attitude of the European clergy to the Chinese and urged the missionary bishops to ordain more Chinese clergy. Preparations should be made for the transferring of the church's administration to them. The church should also show greater concern for the physical as well as the spiritual welfare of the Chinese people. The encyclical annoyed Lebbe's opponents and in 1920 he was sent back to Europe to be a chaplain to Chinese students. In 1922, however, the Vatican appointed a new Apostolic Delegate to China with instructions to pursue the new Roman policy vigorously, and early in 1926 Lebbe was summoned to Rome for a consultation with Cardinal Van Rossven. He was also received by the Pope, now Pius XI, who shared his predecessor's enthusiasm for missionary work and invited him to submit the names of Chinese priests who would make suitable bishops. Three of these were among the six Chinese bishops consecrated by the Pope himself in St Peter's later that year.

One of these bishops asked Lebbe to return to China in 1927, and on his arrival he took out Chinese citizenship, assumed a Chinese name – Lei Ming-yuan – and placed himself under the jurisdiction of the Chinese bishop. A number of other European priests were inspired to do the same and this led to the foundation of Mission Auxiliaries, which encouraged European and American priests to work alongside indigenous clergy and under their leadership. Lebbe also founded at An-kwo the Little Brothers of St John the Baptist and the Little Sisters of Teresa, which attracted both Europeans and Chinese who felt called to combine the monastic life with social work.

On the outbreak of the Sino-Japanese war in 1937, Lebbe and the Little Brothers organized a corps of stretcher-bearers to serve with the Chinese army, and in the following year, by which time the Japanese were occupying part of China, he was asked by the Chinese government to initiate a patriotic movement for the remainder of the country. All these tasks he undertook with enthusiasm and skill, but the burden of them eventually proved to be too heavy and, worn out, he died at Chungking in June 1940.

J. Leclercq, *Thunder in the Distance*, Sheed and Ward 1958.

# Nicolai Berdyaev
## (1874–1948)

Nicolai Alexandrovich Berdyaev was one of the century's foremost philosophers of religion. Although much of his life was spent in exile in Paris and he drew heavily on Western thought, his fundamental understanding of life's meaning and purpose was firmly rooted in the ancient Russian tradition. His high estimate of man was derived from the belief that in every human being there is a divine element. 'The very idea of revelation is made meaningless,' he argued, 'if he to whom God reveals is a creature of worthless insignificance who in no respect corresponds to the One who reveals himself.' Another of his major concerns was with human freedom, which – he said – is a consequence of life in the spirit, and distinguishes human beings from the rest of creation whose ways are pre-determined.

This concern with freedom led Berdyaev at an early age to rebel against his aristocratic family background and, under the influence of Marxism, engage in revolutionary activity. But when the Bolsheviks seized power in Russia he opposed the totalitarian element in the new regime and was dismissed from his post as Professor of Philosophy at Moscow University. Equally, after he had joined the Russian Orthodox Church in 1907 he was soon in difficulties with the Holy Synod for alleged non-conformity, and was always regarded as heretical by some Russian church leaders.

Berdyaev was born in Kiev. His father had a distinguished military career and his mother was a French princess. It was intended that he should follow his father into the army, but after attending a military school for some years he went to Kiev University to read natural science, then law. From his earliest years, however, he wanted to be a philosopher and this brought him to the study of Karl Marx. He became a leading figure in the Social Democratic Party in Kiev and following his arrest, along with 150 other students, for offences against the state he was sentenced to two years' imprisonment followed by three years' exile in Northern Russia.

This period of exile was by no means disagreeable and left him free to write his first book, *Subjectivism and Individualism in Social Philosophy*, which indicated some deviation from orthodox Marxism. On his return to Kiev he was much influenced by Professor Sergius Bulgakov, who was himself moving from Marxism to Christianity, and even more by the reading of Dostoevsky's story of the Grand Inquisitor. Of his conversion in 1907 Berdyaev later wrote: 'I never pretended that my religious thought had a churchly character. I sought the truth and experienced as truth that which was revealed to me.' And although he attended the liturgy, he sought always to distinguish between committed Christians and those whose church attendance was only formal – a distinction which the Russian Orthodox Church never accepts.

In 1912 he spent some time in Italy, and while staying on the island of Capri wrote *The Meaning of the Creative Act*, which expressed his religious vision – a vision which he spent the rest of his life developing. Back in Russia in 1913 he was in trouble with the Holy Synod over an article about the church's leadership which appeared under the title 'Quenchers of the Spirit'. He was arrested and charged with blasphemy, but the outbreak of war in 1914 delayed the trial and the Revolution in 1917 ensured that it would never take place.

After the October Revolution he denounced the materialism of its leaders in a book *Philosophy of Inequality*, which could not be published in Russia. He and his wife were subsequently compelled to join a labour battalion employed on keeping rail tracks clear of snow during the winter, but he was also allowed to lecture and to organize a Free Academy of Spiritual Culture which survived for three years. From 1920 to 1921 he even lectured at Moscow University and, though he had no degree, became Professor of Philosophy. During this period he wrote a number of important books – *Worthiness of Christianity and Unworthiness of Christians*, based on a series of lectures given to unbelievers, *The Meaning of History*, and a classic study of Dostoevsky.

The change in Russia's leadership in 1922 created a different climate, however, and Berdyaev was imprisoned, then exiled for life. He settled first in Berlin, but after a time moved to Paris, where he remained until the end of his life. There he lectured, edited many Russian periodicals and wrote many more books. His relations with the large Russian emigré community in Paris tended to be uneasy. He regarded himself as an exile rather than an emigré and accepted the Revolution as a necessity, as a judgment on 'bourgeois Christianity', even though he disapproved of the philosophy and methods of the Communist Party. And his religious views were often suspect.

Donald A. Lowrie, *Rebellious Prophet: A Life of Nicolai Berdyaev*, Gollancz 1960.

# George Lansbury
## (1859–1940)

George Lansbury, a Christian Socialist and a leading figure in local and national government for most of the first half of the century, was described by the historian A. J. P. Taylor as 'the most loveable figure in modern politics'. In London's East End, where all his political life was spent, he was a hero and at Westminster he is generally credited with having ensured the survival of the Labour Party following its crushing defeat at a General Election in 1931.

In 1913, at an Albert Hall rally in support of votes for women, he said, or at least implied, that the destruction of property by militants was acceptable provided there was no danger to life. He was charged in court with seditious speech and ordered to keep the peace for the next twelve months, but he refused to comply and was sent to Pentonville prison for three months. He immediately went on hunger strike and widely expressed public concern led to the government ordering his release. Eight years later he was in Brixton prison for six weeks when he and his fellow councillors on Labour-controlled Poplar Borough Council refused to pay a precept levied by the London County Council. They believed that the money was most needed for the relief of acute poverty in their own neighbourhood.

Among other causes strongly supported by Lansbury during the early years of the century were independence for India, Home Rule for Ireland, the abolition of hereditary peers in the House of Lords, special benefits for the poor and holidays with pay for all workers. He also played a leading part in the founding in 1912 of the *Daily Herald* – the first mass-circulation Labour supporting newspaper – and was for a time its editor, emphasizing always the Christian element in socialism. Although he was MP for Bromley and Bow for a short time between 1910 and 1912, it was not until 1922 that he was returned to Parliament with a large enough majority to ensure him a secure place in the House of Commons and the opportunity to become a major left-wing figure. He advocated separate parliaments for England, Scotland and Wales, with a joint committee to deal with matters of common concern, and supported a General Strike in 1926. From 1929 to 1931 he held office in a minority

Labour government as First Commissioner of Works.

Lansbury was born in Suffolk, but his parents soon afterwards moved to London and settled in Whitechapel. He left school when only eleven to work in a coal merchant's office, but after a year of this returned to school and remained there until he was fourteen. For the next eleven years he was involved in the family business of unloading coal from barges and trains in Dockland, and during this time became much involved in the life of the local churches. In 1884 he and the other members of his family emigrated to Australia, but it proved difficult to find work there and he returned to the East End of London and a life of poverty. His first political work was with the local Liberal Party, which invited him to stand for Parliament in the Liberal interest, but he declined, as by this time he had become a socialist. He joined the Socialist Democratic Federation, on whose behalf he travelled the country to address meetings.

Lansbury stopped attending the Church of England in 1890 because he was disillusioned with many of its clergy, who tolerated poverty, condemned strikes and generally had little concern for the poor. Instead he went to the Ethical Sunday School in Bow, and it was not until 1900 that, as a result of a chance encounter with the Bishop of Stepney, Cosmo Gordon Lang, he returned. Of the connection between his political and religious convictions, he wrote:

> I am a socialist pure and simple . . . I have come to believe that the motive power which should and which *will*, if men allow it, work our social salvation, is the power that comes from a belief in Christ and his message to man.

A lifelong pacifist, Lansbury opposed the 1899–1901 Boer War and throughout the 1914–18 World War often spoke against the human slaughter it involved. At meetings he was sometimes assaulted, and there were 'To the Tower with Lansbury' posters. Shortly before the outbreak of war in 1939 he urged Hitler and Mussolini to take part in a peace conference proposed by President Roosevelt of the USA, and in an article in the *Daily Sketch* wrote:

> I write not as a censorious judge of others, but as one who has discovered through long experience that Jesus truly has the words of eternal life. We must learn the path to peace through him.

Bob Holman, *Good Old George*, Lion Publishing 1990.

# Joseph-Léon Cardijn

## (1882–1967)

Joseph-Léon Cardijn was a Belgian priest who promised his dying coal-merchant father: 'You killed yourself for me; I shall kill myself to save the working class of the world.' He went on to found and devote his life to a movement of Young Christian Workers, *Jeunesse Ouvrière Chrétienne*, which by the time of his death had two million members in forty-two countries. Pope Paul VI recognized the importance of his work by making him a cardinal.

Cardijn, who had exceptional powers of imagination, organization and oratory, offered young Catholics an inspiring vision, expressed powerfully in a speech at the movement's silver jubilee celebrations:

> It is not your business to imitate priests and religious. The worker's tool stands in his hand as the chalice and paten in the hands of the priest. Just as the priest offers the Body and Blood of Christ on the paten and in the chalice, so the worker-apostle must learn to offer to Christ with his tools.

He was born in Brussels, but the family soon moved to Hal, ten miles south of the capital, where great sacrifices were made to enable young Joseph to attend the junior seminary at Malines. During school holidays he became conscious of a growing gulf between himself and other local boys, who regarded him as having gone over to the enemy. In 1906 he was ordained priest by the Archbishop of Malines, Cardinal Mercier, who sent him to Louvain to study in the Faculty of Philosophy and the School of Political and Social Sciences. He then became a teacher and used school holidays to study the conditions of workers abroad.

This was followed in 1912 by his appointment as curate of Laeken, in Brussels – a parish which included the royal palace, but where ninety per cent of its population were overworked and ill-paid workers. When the parish priest put him in charge of a girls' club for thirteen- to sixteen-year-old workers, he turned this into a Women's Christian Workers' League, which within a year had 1,000 members and its own paper. Opposition in the parish led to the curate being branded an agitator and revolutionary, but following the outbreak of war in 1914 and the occupation of Brussels by the Germans, Cardinal Mercier asked Cardijn to take charge of all the church's social work in the capital and to be chaplain of the Christian trade unions. When, however, he denounced the deportation of Belgians to Germany for work in munitions factories he was imprisoned for six months. On his release he was immediately re-arrested and given a further year in prison for alleged spying.

After the war he and three young laymen founded *Jeunesse Syndicaliste* – a youth trade union – which soon spread from Brussels to the main towns of Belgium. Study days and days of recollection were part of the programme, but Cardijn was accused of fostering left-wing activity and weakening the parishes' ministry to their young people. In the end Cardinal Mercier condemned the new organization, whereupon Cardijn took himself to Rome, and by persistence and force of personality secured an audience with an astonished Pope Pius XI. The Pope heard his story and responded, 'Not only do we bless your movement, we want it. We make it ours. I will have your Cardinal informed of all this.' In 1925 Mercier formally approved the Young Christian Workers in Belgium and Cardijn compiled a manual for the training of the Jocists, as they came to be called. See, Judge, Act was their method, with equal emphasis on each word.

The movement next spread to France, where it was immediately successful, and the first members of the priest-worker movement were nearly all YCW chaplains. In Spain, where only three per cent of the workers were in touch with the church, many thousands of young workers were recruited, and in Canada there was also a huge response.

The 1939–45 war drove the movement underground in occupied Europe, and 600 secret sections were formed among workers deported to Germany and Austria. In 1942 Cardijn was again imprisoned for a time, and in the following year two of the three young men who had been his fellow-pioneers died in Dachau concentration camp. Others were shot or sent to concentration camps, but after the war 300,000 young Belgians attended the movement's twentieth-anniversary celebrations in Brussels, and within a few years it was flourishing throughout Western Europe, in both North and South America, and in India, Ceylon and Japan. Cardijn was a consultant at the Second Vatican Council and played a large part in the drafting of its pronouncement on the laity.

Michael de la Bedoyere, *The Cardijn Story*, Longmans 1958.

# Toyohiko Kagawa

## (1888–1960)

Toyohiko Kagawa was a world-famous Japanese Christian who was both a powerful evangelist and a social reformer and exercised considerable influence in the life of his nation. He lived through the period when Japan was emerging from its mediaeval imperial past to become a modern industrial society, and when it lacked the social and political structures necessary for the development of democracy and justice. Much of his life was spent sharing the appalling conditions prevailing in the slums of Kobe and Shinkawa, where he lived in poverty in a small hut and gave himself to the pastoral care of communities, in which as many as half of the children did not reach their tenth birthday. At the same time he campaigned ceaselessly for social change, led a number of strikes, and on several occasions was arrested and imprisoned. For many years his was a lone voice in Japan, but he had a huge following among the poor, which made it difficult for the authorities to silence him. He was a prolific writer, and his novel *Before the Dawn* (1925) had a massive readership.

Kagawa was born in Kobe – the result of a liaison between his wealthy politician father and a geisha. Although adopted by his father, he was left an orphan when only four and then brought up by a foster grandmother. He was sent to the local Buddhist temple for religious training, then to a boarding school on the island of Shikoku. There he was welcomed into the homes of two Christian couples who lived nearby and, through their influence, was baptized in 1903. This led to complete rejection by his family, and he went to live in the slums before entering the Presbyterian College in Tokyo.

By this time he was committed to the service of the poor and shared his college room with a beggar. He also gave away his money and clothing to beggars, went about in rags and began to advocate socialism as the answer to poverty. About this time, however, he contracted tuberculosis – the first of many physical ailments which dogged his entire life. When he was sufficiently recovered, he went to the Kobe Theological Seminary to train for the Presbyterian ministry, and while still a student went to live and work in the slums of Shinkawa. He remained there for fifteen years, preaching at a street meeting at 6.00 a. m. and spending the rest of the day engaged in pastoral and social work. He also began writing, and gradually brought the sufferings of slum-dwellers to the attention of the nation.

From 1915 to 1917 Kagawa was at Princeton University studying social service institutions in America, and on his return faced increasing opposition from the conservative and military elements in Japanese society. In 1921 he led a strike of 30,000 dockyard workers who were seeking recognition of their trade union, and as a result was arrested and imprisoned for thirteen days. In the same year he also organized the first peasant union, arising from severe social problems in the agricultural sphere, and his hut in the slums became its headquarters. Later he helped to found a Federation of Labour, and became head of the Osaka Spinners' Union and adviser to the All-Japan Peasant Union. In 1925 he secured the amendment of a law against trade unions.

Meanwhile, following a disastrous earthquake in 1923, he was recruited to an Imperial Economic Commission to formulate a recovery policy, and joined another Commission on Unemployment and Immigration. The government could not manage without him. In 1929 he turned to the organizing of a three-year crusade which he called the Kingdom of God Movement. He firmly believed that, while Christian witness certainly required social action, if social action was to be effective it required Christian insights and motivation. And he also believed that the churches needed to be at least one million strong before they could make an impact on Japanese society. But the Japanese people were not responsive to Christian crusades, even when led by Kagawa.

His pacifist convictions frequently landed him in trouble with the authorities. In 1940 he was arrested and charged with engaging in peace propaganda, and following Pearl Harbour was twice arrested for failing to support Japan's war effort. When the war ended, however, he was invited to join the Cabinet to assist with the reconstruction programme. This he declined, choosing instead to be adviser to the Department of Public Welfare, though later he became a member of the House of Peers. Although ceaselessly active in the cause of social justice, he was essentially a mystic who spent long hours in contemplation and once said, 'Jesus set up no definitions about God, but taught the actual practical practice of love'. This was Kagawa's creed.

C. J. Davey, *Kagawa of Japan,* SCM Press 1960.

# Dick Sheppard
## (1880–1937)

Hugh Richard Lawrie Sheppard was the Church of England's most notable twentieth-century parish priest and one of its most powerful prophets. Although in his later years he held, briefly, the posts of Dean of Canterbury and Canon of St Paul's, his greatest work was accomplished during his time (1914–26) as Vicar of St Martin-in-the-Fields in London's Trafalgar Square. When at the age of thirty-four he was appointed to this large church, its average Sunday congregations were six in the morning and seven in the evening. Eleven people attended his Institution as Vicar, but on St Martin's Day three years later 4,000 shared in the patronal festival celebrations, and following his death in 1937 over 100,000 people filed past his coffin in the church where his remarkable ministry had been exercised.

Sheppard's influence over individuals owed much to the simplicity and intensity of his personal faith. But there were other factors. He had a remarkable facility with words and made telling use of epigrams; he had many of the gifts of the actor; and he was also a competent organizer. The advent of broadcasting in 1924 provided an ideal medium for the extension of his influence throughout Britain and eventually to other parts of the English-speaking world. Yet there was nothing glib about his preaching and he employed none of the techniques of the mass evangelist. Although for Sheppard faith was an intensely personal matter, he was not unaware of its social and political implications. Thus the crypt of St Martin's became a centre of social work serving thousands of London's social and economic casualties, and in his closing years he was a co-founder and the chief activist of the Peace Pledge Union – formed in the hope of halting the 1930's movement towards world war.

Sheppard was born in Windsor, where his father was a royal chaplain. Although he left Marlborough College early and had no intellectual ambitions, he went to Trinity Hall, Cambridge, and on completion of his degree did social work at Oxford House, Bethnal Green, in East London. In 1907 he was ordained as chaplain of Oxford House, and two years later became its head, but was soon obliged to resign because of ill health caused by overwork – a recurring pattern in his ministry. By 1911 he was

35

sufficiently recovered to be able to accept responsibility for St Mary's – a small church in London's Mayfair – and in 1913 he moved to the Grosvenor Chapel in the same area. In both places he made a considerable impact, and this led to his appointment to St Martin-in-the-Fields.

Three months elapsed between the announcement of his appointment and his institution as vicar, and these he spent serving as chaplain to a military hospital in France soon after the outbreak of the 1914–18 war. This experience had a profound effect on him, and he told the handful of people who greeted his arrival at St Martin's of a vision he had experienced while visiting soldiers in the trenches:

> I saw a great church standing in the greatest square in the greatest city of the world. And I stood on the west steps and I saw what this church would be to the life of the people. There passed me into its warm inside hundreds and hundreds of all sorts of people, going up to the temple of their Lord, with all their difficulties, trials and sorrows. I saw it full of people, dropping in at all hours of the day and night. It was never dark, it was lighted all night and day, and often and often tired bits of humanity swept in. And I said to them as they passed, 'Where are you going?' And they said only one thing: 'This is our home. This is where we are going to learn of the love of Jesus Christ. This is the altar of our Lord, where all our peace lies. This is St Martin's.'

The next twelve years were spent turning this vision into reality. The church was immediately opened all night for the benefit of soldiers passing through London to and from the front line in France. Private pews were abolished, and soon queues of people formed before crowded services. The poor, the unemployed and the drop-outs came to the crypt for practical help. The parish magazine was transformed into the *St Martin's Review*, to which leading writers contributed.

Although Sheppard had little time for church structures, he was, with William Temple and others, a founder of the Life and Liberty Movement which sought to make the Church of England more democratic and give it greater freedom from the state. On his resignation on health grounds from St Martin's in 1926 he was appointed a Companion of Honour. His 'Plea for the Recovery of Vital Christianity', published as *The Impatience of a Parson* (1927), sold 100,000 copies and caused great offence to the church leaders of the time.

Carolyn Scott, *Dick Sheppard – A Biography*, Hodder and Stoughton 1977.

# J. H. Oldham

## (1871–1969)

Joseph Houldsworth Oldham was one of the most influential laymen in the church of his time, combining vision with an acute intelligence and outstanding administrative ability. His direct missionary experience was very limited, but nonetheless he acquired immense knowledge of missionary work and had prophetic insights into the development of the churches' missionary strategy. He was also a pioneer leader of the ecumenical movement and deeply involved in the formation of the World Council of Churches. As a lay theologian, he sought to awaken the church to the importance of the laity's ministry in the world, and of the need to equip them for this ministry. Much of his influence was exercised through private meetings with either individuals or small groups, but he was not afraid to speak out if he believed the occasion demanded this and in his classic *Christianity and the Race Problem*, published in 1924, he declared: 'Racialism is the deadliest enemy of humane civilization'.

He was born of Scottish parents in Bombay and sent to Britain to be educated at the Edinburgh Academy, then at Trinity College, Oxford. He originally intended to join the Indian Civil Service, but having experienced a religious conversion, he returned to India in 1897 to work with the YMCA among government employees and students at Lahore. After two years, however, he was invalided home and studied theology at New College, Edinburgh, followed by research into missionary theory and practice at Halle University in Germany. He was initially a Presbyterian and, although never ordained, served for a time as ministerial assistant at Free St George's Church in Edinburgh. He became an Anglican in mid-life. In 1906 he was appointed Study Secretary of the Student Christian Movement, but after two years was allowed leave in order to become organizing secretary of a World Missionary Conference attended by 1,600 delegates in Edinburgh in 1910. The success of this conference, which marked the beginning of the modern ecumenical movement, owed a great deal to Oldham.

He stayed on as secretary of a continuation committee and became the first editor of a new quarterly, *International Review of Missions,* a post he held until 1927 and in which he attracted brilliant contributions. His first book, *The World and the Gospel* (1916), sold 20,000 copies, and when the war ended in 1918 he negotiated with various governments to ensure that German missionaries might return to Africa and India and that none of their missionary property was confiscated for reparations.

After the war Oldham also turned his attention to the plight of forced labourers in Kenya and organized a massive and successful protest which was supported by academics and politicians as well as by church leaders. In 1921 he was appointed secretary of the newly formed International Missionary Council, and throughout the 1920s was involved in negotiations between rival interests in East Africa. From 1931 to 1938 he was administrative director of the International Institute of African Language and Culture. A second great missionary conference held in Jerusalem in 1928 alerted Oldham to the fact that 'the chief threat to Christian faith is not rival religions but secularism, expressed in totalitarianism and in scientific humanism'. He shared this with his friend William Temple and, in 1934, as chairman of the research committee of the Universal Christian Council for Life and Work, began preparation for a major world conference on Church, Community and State. By the time the world conference came to be held in Oxford in 1937 the confrontation between the totalitarian state and the church and its gospel was the chief item on the agenda and it was also decided to try to bring the existing ecumenical movements into a single World Council of Churches. Oldham had spoken of the desirability of this in 1921.

He was not, however, primarily concerned with ecclesiastical organization, but rather with the role of the laity, seeking to live their faith in the secular world. A small and distinguished commission on which he served produced a 450-page report on unemployment, *Men Without Work,* and this led to his founding, soon after the outbreak of war in 1939, the *Christian Newsletter.* Paper rationing dictated a modest format, but the quality of the content was consistently high and Oldham formed the Christian Frontier Council – a thirty–forty strong think-tank for the consideration of public affairs in a Christian context. 'Our main concern,' he wrote in the first number, 'is big news, rather than hot news.' The big news at the end of the war was the arrival of *The Era of Atomic Power* – the subject of a British Council of Churches report which a committee chaired by Oldham completed in 1947 in less than a year. There was still time for one more personal book: *New Hope in Africa* (1958).

# Conrad Noel

## (1869–1942)

Conrad le Dispenser Roden Noel was a colourful priest of aristocratic background who became a leader of the Christian Socialist Movement and from the tower of his beautiful fourteenth-century church at Thaxted, in Essex, where he was vicar for thirty-two years, flew not only the flag of St George but also the Red Flag and that of Sinn Fein. He believed the Kingdom of God to be something achievable in the world's social order – an expression of God's plan from the beginning of creation, reinforced by the teaching of Jesus. 'In the age-long warfare between rich and poor,' he said, 'God has always taken sides.' He believed, too, that the church's liturgy should be a reflection of life in the Kingdom and the worship at Thaxted was singularly beautiful in its ordering.

Noel was born at Kew, Surrey, where his father, being Groom of the Privy Chamber, occupied a royal grace-and-favour residence. His grandmother was a lady-in-waiting to Queen Victoria. Young Conrad was unhappy at school and was sent down from Corpus Christi College, Cambridge, for drunkenness, but not before he had been converted to socialism. He then decided to seek ordination and secured a place at Chichester Theological College. But a problem arose over his ordination and he was refused by the Bishop of Exeter on the grounds that his beliefs were pantheistic and his religious practices extremely High Church. He was eventually ordained to a curacy at St Philip's Church, Salford, Manchester, and also served at St Mary's, Primrose Hill, in North London before becoming a curate of C. N. Moll at St Philip's, Newcastle-upon-Tyne.

Moll was a leading Christian Socialist, and Noel was very much at home in the parish, but when he preached a sermon against the Boer War many of the local people, who worked in munitions factories, threatened to blow up the church unless the curate was forbidden to preach. In 1909 he and Moll and some others founded the Church Socialist League, which was more radical than the other Christian socialist groups and established links with Labour Members of Parliament. It aimed at 'the political, economic and social emancipation of the whole people, men

39

and women, by the establishment of a democratic commonwealth in which the community shall own the land and capital collectively and use them for the good of all'. Twelve months after its foundation the League had about 1,200 members and Noel was its General Secretary, but he left Newcastle without a church appointment and worked for short periods in Paddington, London and in the French port of Boulogne while writing *Socialism and Church History* (1910). He was rescued by Lady Warwick, who had been converted to socialism and used her patronage to appoint him as Vicar of Thaxted.

There he re-ordered the interior of the cathedral-like building, installed shrines to Archbishop Thomas à Becket and John Ball, who was executed as one of the leaders of the Peasants' Revolt in 1381, filled it with colourful banners, and introduced a dignified High Church ceremonial. A daily eucharist was started and processions in the village marked the festivals of Corpus Christi and Thomas à Becket. Gustav Holst, who lived in the parish, contributed to the fine music and his daughter, Imogen, conducted the church orchestra. Morris dancing also became a feature of the great days in the church's year, and from time to time prayers were offered for the conversion of the evangelical Bishop of Chelmsford to 'the true faith'. For Noel the sacraments were pointers to heaven, but at the same time he saw the whole of the created order as sacramental and on the basis of this criticized many aspects of industrialization. He looked back to the days of the skilled craftsman and Guild Socialism and strongly supported Irish unity as well as supporting the coal miners during the 1926 General Strike.

Earlier, in 1918, he and some radical members left the Church Socialist League to found the Catholic Crusade of the Servants of the Precious Blood to transform the Kingdom of this World into the Commonwealth of God. This was intended to emphasize more strongly the relationship between sacramental theology and political action, and it was never envisaged that it would become a mass movement – which it did not – but Noel and his friends felt bold enough to announce that the role of the Catholic Crusade was 'to become the first socialist organization to welcome the Russian Revolution'.

Noel wrote many books, including a *Life of Jesus* (1937) and *Jesus the Heretic* (1939), but towards the end of his life he became blind. He learned the liturgy by heart so that he could continue to preside at the eucharist.

R. Groves, *Conrad Noel and the Thaxted Movement,* Merlin Press 1967.

# John Flynn
## (1880–1951)

John Flynn was a Presbyterian minister who devoted his life to the service of Aborigines and settlers in the Australian outback – a vast region covering over two million square miles. He was one of the first to perceive the need for isolated people to be provided with the means for their own community development and care, and this led to the creation of a 'Flying Doctor' service to enable skilled medical help to reach remote places quickly. Although he faced much resistance in the early years of his projects, he eventually won the support of the Australian government and became a national folk-hero.

The son of a schoolteacher, Flynn was born in Moliagul, Victoria. There was no money available to finance further education after he left the local state school, so he became a pupil-teacher, then joined an extra-mural course for student lay pastors until the Presbyterian Church accepted him for ministerial training. On his ordination in 1911 he volunteered for mission in the Northern Flinders Ranges of South Australia where, at the furthest point of the railhead, the church had placed a nursing sister to begin medical work. With Flynn's assistance a nursing hostel was opened at the end of that year and he was then commissioned to survey the medical and mission needs of the whole of the Northern Territories.

He accomplished this within twelve months and produced two long and detailed reports on the needs of Aborigines and another on the needs of the white settlers. The church responded by setting up an Australian Inland Mission and making him its first superintendent – a task he carried out until his death thirty-nine years later. Starting with one nursing sister, a nursing hostel, a minister and five camels, he built an extensive 'canopy of safety' in the outback, available to all irrespective of race, nationality or creed. The first issue of the *Inlander* magazine, published in 1915, was devoted to photographs and stories about the plight of Aborigines: 'A blot on Australia is shown on our frontispiece . . . there is no call for sensation. Sensation is too cheap. We need action.' After pointing out that the Aborigines were competent and capable, and cared well for their own elderly people, he went on: 'We who so cheerfully sent a cheque for £100,000 to Belgium to help a people pushed out of their own inheritance by foreigners – surely we must just as cheerfully do something for those whom we clean-handed people have dispossessed.' This was a revolutionary proposal in the Australia of that time.

In 1917 Flynn received a letter from a lieutenant in the Australian Flying Corps which inspired his vision of a medical service using aircraft. There was no possibility of developing such a service at the time, partly because of the war and lack of money, but chiefly because of the need to develop a means of radio transmission that would provide a link between patient and doctor. When the war ended he sought technical information and finance, and secured the assistance of George Towns, an ex-service radio technician, who in 1925 helped him carry out an experiment in radio transmission, using the jacked-up back wheel of a lorry to generate electricity. In the following year he secured the assistance of Alfred Traeger, the pedal-radio pioneer, and in May 1928 his vision became a reality when the newly established Australian Inland Mission Aerial Medical Service responded to its first call by despatching a doctor in a De Havilland 50 aircraft.

Flynn also recognized the importance of two-way radio for the development of community in remote areas and encouraged Adelaide Miethke to use the 'Flying Doctor' network for a 'school of the air' which provided both education and a means of communication about matters of common concern. But once the viability of the 'Flying Doctor' service was established it became apparent that the Presbyterian Church could never hope to organize and finance it on a national scale. Two-thirds of the whole of Australia needed to be covered, and during the early 1930s Flynn pressed for a national service to be run in partnership with the State and Federal governments. Resistance from the church was overcome when he challenged its assembly: 'We must either shrink back into a mere preaching agency or become a dynamic partner in a national enterprise to help the frontier people. If the Assembly baulks at the hurdle I believe the Australia Inland Mission will shrivel into a selfish little runt.' The National Aerial Medical Service of Australia was inaugurated soon afterwards, and Flynn played a leading part in the settling of its constitution and organization. Later he became one of the founders of the United Church in North Australia.

W. S. McPheat, *John Flynn: Apostle to the Inland*, Hodder 1963.

# Basil Jellicoe

## (1899–1935)

John Basil Lee Jellicoe was a young Church of England priest who devoted virtually the whole of his short ministry to schemes for improving the housing of the poor. His chief contribution was made in Somers Town, a particularly bad slum area of North London between Euston and St Pancras railway stations, but he also assisted in the starting of similar housing projects in other parts of England, and as far away as Canada.

Jellicoe was motivated by the sacramental principle which lay at the heart of his deep Anglo-Catholic faith. The transformation of bread and wine at the eucharist was, for him, a model, requiring the transformation of the whole of life, so that every aspect of human existence might be sanctified and become a channel of divine grace. His passion for social justice was sustained by daily presence at the altar and intense personal prayer.

He was born at Chailey, Sussex, his father being a cousin of Earl Jellicoe, the famous World War I naval commander. From his earliest years he felt called to the priesthood and as a schoolboy gave a talk on Christian Socialism to a group of men in the village inn. His studies at Magdalen College, Oxford were interrupted by a brief period in the wartime Royal Navy and when he completed his degree in 1921 he was, as a layman, appointed Head of the College Mission in Somers Town. This was in poor shape – badly organized and heavily in debt – and no longer in close touch with the parish church, St Mary's. It did not take Jellicoe long to discover that a programme of clubs and camps hardly improved the lives of the 22,000 people who were living in the overcrowded slums, two or three people to every room. The need was for better housing.

In 1922 Jellicoe was ordained and joined the staff of St Mary's Church, which soon became the spiritual power-house of his work for the rehousing of the poor. He was a spontaneous, open, dynamic, joyous man who walked about the parish in an old cassock and was generally surrounded by crowds of children. On one occasion, when returning from a visit to Chichester Theological College, he bought on impulse a pet monkey. Every year he went to a fair at Bude in Cornwall and, in the same old cassock, had a ride on all the roundabouts.

But there was a darker, melancholy side of his personality which made him especially sensitive to the presence of evil and led to periods of ill health related to emotional breakdown. 'The slums of Somers Town,' he said, 'produce something much more terrible than mere discomfort and discontent. They produce a kind of horrible excommunication; a fiendish plan on the part of the Powers of Evil to keep people from the happiness for which God made them, and from seeing the beauties of his world. It is not more policemen who are wanted in Somers Town and Battersea: it is God Incarnate in the hearts of loving human beings.'

In 1925 Jellicoe and five other people formed the St Pancras House Improvement Society. With the aid of £7,000 raised by subscription, seven slum dwellings occupied by twenty-one families were bought and reconditioned as self-contained flats, each with its own bathroom. In the following year sixty-nine houses and an open space of 10,000 square yards were acquired, even though the purchase money was not immediately available, and by 1929 a block of new flats had been erected to provide fifty-two families with good housing. The dynamiting of a particularly squalid block of housing was celebrated with a huge bonfire on which were placed models of a bug, a flea, a rat and a louse – all stuffed with fireworks.

Ill-health had driven Jellicoe to resign from the chairmanship of the Magdalen College Mission in 1927, by which time it was in a flourishing condition and free of debt, but he remained chairman of the Improvement Society and continued to raise money for the rehousing of the poor. By 1933 it had built 170 new flats and created others in existing houses. Many more were to follow. This inspired other Christians to tackle similar problems in the East End of London, Bristol, Tyneside and Penzance, and Jellicoe, who was a powerful orator, was always on hand to encourage and advise.

The physical and emotional strain of all this was, however, too great for him to carry and he died in a Sussex nursing home in 1935. Learning of his death, Archbishop William Temple wrote: 'There are some with whom it seems to be a necessary quality that they die young – Mozart among musicians, Keats and Shelley among poets; and among saints, with many another, Basil Jellicoe.'

Kenneth Ingram, *Basil Jellicoe*, Geoffrey Bles 1936.

# R. H. Tawney

## (1880–1962)

Richard Henry ('Harry') Tawney was an economic historian whose studies and Christian faith led him to embrace socialism and become a powerful influence on the British Labour Party. At a time of deep social and political division in Britain, his primary concern was with the moral basis of socialism, though he did not hesitate to make proposals for change and saw education as a means of social emancipation. This took him into the Workers' Educational Association in its earliest days and his involvement in its work, as a teacher and committee member, extended over forty-two years.

In his *Religion and the Rise of Capitalism,* published in 1926 and re-printed many times in paperback, he examined religious thought on social issues from the later Middle Ages to the early eighteenth century and concluded that unrestrained capitalism developed from the belief of the later Puritans that man's self-love is God's providence. Demonstrating the degree of social and economic control exercised up to that point by Christian thinking, he said that the idea of the church's concern for these matters being a modern innovation did not stand up to historical examination. In his final book, *The Radical Tradition*, published post-humously, he said that capitalism should be condemned outright by the church since it corrupted human relations.

Tawney was born in Calcutta but came to England to be educated at Rugby School and Balliol College, Oxford. At both institutions he had as a contemporary William Temple, the future Archbishop of Canterbury, and they struck up a close life-long friendship in which each exercised a considerable influence on the other. After Oxford, Tawney spent two years engaged in social work at Toynbee Hall in East London, where he established another influential friendship with William Beveridge, whose report laid the foundations of the post-1945 welfare state.

In 1906 Tawney joined the Fabian Society and in the same year moved to Scotland to teach political economy at Glasgow University, but in 1908, having helped to write a report on Oxford and Working-Class Education, he returned to England to pioneer WEA classes in Rochdale and Longton (in the Potteries). When the outbreak of war in 1914 robbed him of his pupils, he moved to the London School of Economics as director of a foundation concerned with the study of poverty. In 1915, however, he enlisted in the Manchester Regiment, refused the offer of a commission, and, as a sergeant, was seriously wounded in the Battle of the Somme. This led to his being invalided out of the army, and he became a Fellow of his old Oxford college as well as a Lecturer in Economic History at the LSE. He also found time to do some work for the Ministry of Reconstruction and to help draft a Church of England report on Christians and Industrial Problems.

Tawney joined the Independent Labour Party in 1909 and was an unsuccessful candidate in the 1918 General Election, as he was destined to be in three subsequent General Elections. But during the 1920s his political influence increased considerably. In *The Acquisitive Society* (1921), which was reprinted fourteen times, he contrasted acquisitive societies which were subject to no moral criteria with functional societies in which rights and privileges depended on service performed. He concluded that the Christian tradition of private property was inappropriate for an industrial society. 'Give me neither riches, nor poverty, but enough for my sustenance' was his personal motto, and he believed this to be valid for communities, too.

As a member of the 1919 Sankey Coal Commission, Tawney was harsh on the coal owners for their attitude to the welfare of the miners – a long-standing concern – and it was noticeable that the report on Industry and Property from the 1924 Conference on Politics, Economics and Citizenship, in which he was involved, reflected the thinking of *The Acquisitive Society*. He was a member of a committee which proposed, some twenty years ahead of its time, the raising of the school leaving age from fourteen to fifteen. Later he was one of the first to advocate all-ability comprehensive schools – a development which he thought should be accompanied by the abolition of fee-paying schools.

The Labour Party's 1928 General Election manifesto was written largely by Tawney, and in his book *Equality* (1931) he argued that the key positions of the economic system should be taken out of private hands, since capitalism treats men as less than men and makes riches a god. Offers of a peerage were declined, and his main concern was always his teaching work at the LSE where he was Professor of Economic History from 1931 to 1949. He was a humble, courteous man, who took endless trouble over his students, and Beatrice Webb described him as 'the saint of socialism'.

# Pierre Teilhard de Chardin
## (1881–1955)

Pierre Teilhard de Chardin was a French Jesuit priest-scientist who reinterpreted the Christian faith in terms of his discoveries in the realms of geology and palaeontology and whose religious books, of which he wrote a large number, could not be published in his own lifetime because they were deemed to contain heresy. When the books were published, two years after his death, they aroused considerable interest and were translated into all the main languages of the world. Before long he had become almost a cult figure, though Rome issued a warning about what were perceived to be 'dangers inherent in his writings'.

Most of his writing is intensely personal, and his quest for the truth took place in the field of human origins and development, where he had an expertise that was acknowledged world-wide. He was concerned to give his fellow Christians an enlarged vision of God through a better understanding of the creative energy at work in the universe. And he tried to give his fellow scientists a statement of religious insights that would enlarge their vision of reality and enable them to discover the divinity that lay within the subjects of their research and gave meaning and purpose to life itself.

Not everyone finds his thinking easy to understand, for he grappled with the most profound religious questions of the twentieth century and invented a new terminology in which to express his answers. His starting point is evolution and he points out that the evolutionary process displays a tendency towards greater complexity of organization. As matter becomes more complex and more highly organized, there is a rise in consciousness – ending with human beings, who have the unique ability to reflect on the meaning and purpose of life itself. This consciousness is not imported into matter from outside: it is one of matter's fundamental properties, and Teilhard calls it radial energy.

Teilhard believed the process to be purposeful and saw the Incarnation as a sign of God's evolutionary purpose, culminating in the perfect union of God and man. What is more, in Jesus the human race is shown how every man and women may come to the same unity with the divine. This movement towards God – 'Christogenesis' – is still in its early stages and because the universe is a dynamic structure life is full of the most exciting possibilities. 'We must dare all,' declared Teilhard, 'and assist in the process of ending the violent conflicts between the nations: within the nations racial, social and economic divisions must give way to a deeper human unity; the age of pure individualism is now past and individual talents must be developed for the benefit of others; because we are a part of the natural order, an order infused with divinity, we must treat the environment with the most profound reverence.'

Teilhard de Chardin was born in Central France where his father, a local historian, inculcated in him a passion for stones, rocks and fossils. At the age of seventeen he joined the Society of Jesus and was sent to a seminary in Jersey where he was able to continue his studies in geology. This led to his going to teach science in a Jesuit school in Cairo, followed by a period of theological study in England, after which he returned to France to continue his scientific work in the fields of geology and palaeontology.

During the 1914–18 war he chose to serve as a stretcher-bearer, rather than as a chaplain, in the French army and was decorated three times for bravery. He also managed to write down in rough notebooks his reflections on the unity between the earth, man and God, and after further research at the Sorbonne, when the war was over, he came to be recognized intellectually as an authority on the development of primitive human life. He continued, however, to say Mass every day, to preach and to conduct retreats.

After a visit to China in 1923 conducting field work there he returned to Paris and wrote a book, *Le Milieu Divin*, which the authorities in Rome would not allow to be published and which did not appear until 1957. His lectures aroused considerable excitement in the student world, so he was sent back to China where he was obliged to remain for eighteen years – until 1945.

During this time he wrote many essays on the development of religious thought, including an important book, *The Phenomenon of Man*, which, again, could not be published until after his death. When he returned to Paris in 1945 he was forbidden to teach or to publish anything on religious subjects, and in 1951 the Jesuit Order sent him to America, where he spent the rest of his life as a research fellow at an institute in New York. He died on Easter Day 1955.

C. E. Raven, *Teilhard de Chardin: Scientist and Seer*, Collins 1962.

# Eric Gill

## (1882–1940)

Eric Gill was the leading English artist-craftsman of the century who combined high skill as a sculptor, letterer, typographer and engraver – to which must be added aspirations as a writer and social reformer. Converted to Roman Catholicism when he was just over thirty, his outlook on life was in many respects mediaeval. He sought the integration of the sacred and the secular and shortly before his death wrote: 'What I hope above all is that I shall have done something towards reintegrating bed and board, the small farm and the workshop, the home and the school, earth and heaven.' To assist this process he established communities of craftsmen which had a religious dimension reflecting his own commitment as a tertiary of the Dominican Order. He usually wore a belted smock of hand-woven material, with knee socks.

His output was prolific and of his 100 sculpted figures and reliefs the best known are the *Stations of the Cross* (1918) in Westminster Cathedral, *Prospero and Ariel* (1932) over the entrance to Broadcasting House, London, and *Creation of Adam* (1938) in the League of Nations Council Hall, Geneva. The finest is a torso of Christ in black marble, *Deposition* (1924), now in King's School, Canterbury. Over 1,000 wood engravings of striking simplicity and directness illustrate many books, more than 750 examples of his lettering, mainly on monuments and tombstones, remain, and of his six typefaces, Perpetua and Gill Sans-serif seem likely to enjoy abiding admiration.

Although Gill's work was in no sense *avant garde,* it frequently caused controversy. His engravings were often highly erotic, and when the governors of the BBC first saw the nude figures to be placed on their headquarters they asked for modifications in the interests of modesty. A war memorial for Leeds University, portraying Christ turning the money-changers out of the Temple, provoked a hostile reaction which was not allayed by his explanation that Christ's action was courageous and warlike and that modern war had a lot to do with money. Further controversy arose half a century after his death, when a biography revealed previously concealed details of his sexual proclivities, which included adultery, incest and bestiality, and led some to wonder if

49

*Stations of the Cross* by such an artist was appropriate for Westminster Cathedral.

Gill, the son of a Free Church minister, was born in Brighton. He attended the Chichester Art School and was then articled to a London architect, but he rebelled against the current architectural fashions and became a part-time student at the Central School of Arts and Crafts, where he learned masonry and lettering. He soon found there was a demand for his lettering and left the architect in 1903 in order to concentrate on letter cutting. In 1907 he returned to Sussex, and at Ditchling broadened his work to include painted signs, tombstones, sculpture and engraved titles for books. While on his way to Brussels in 1913 to an exhibition which included some of his work he stayed in the abbey at Mont César, and was so impressed by the plainchant that on his return to England he became a Roman Catholic.

He then invited a number of other artist-craftsmen and their families to join him and his wife at Ditchling to form a community based on mediaeval beliefs and values, and sharing creative insights and skills. In 1921 the Guild of Saints Joseph and Dominic was formed. Its members were solemnly professed as brothers of the Guild and aimed, for the love of God, to produce work that was good in itself; and for the love of neighbour, work that was good for use. By the following year forty-one people were living and working in the community.

Sadly, the vows and Christian spirit did not prevent serious disagreements and financial problems, and in 1924 Gill and his family loaded their belongings and livestock onto a lorry and set off for a disused monastery at Capel-y-ffin in the Welsh mountains. There they, and some others who helped form a new community, remained for four creative years, but Gill was not a mountain man and in 1928 they moved once more to a farm with several outbuildings, named Pygotts, near High Wycombe, in Buckinghamshire.

Two visits to the Holy Land in the mid-1930s and the threat of European war combined to persuade Gill to oppose the basis of twentieth-century civilization, and he received a warning from the Archbishop of Westminster for associating with the left-wing British Artists' Congress. This did not worry him overmuch, and until the end of his life he lived by the belief that 'in normal society the artist is not a special kind of man, but every man is a special kind of artist'.

Fiona MacCarthy, *Eric Gill*, Faber 1989.

# Karl Barth

## (1886–1968)

Karl Barth, a Swiss Protestant theologian, was described by Pope Pius XII as the greatest theologian since St Thomas Aquinas. Certainly he was the most influential in the twentieth century, and the publication of his commentary on St Paul's Letter to the Romans, in 1918, changed the course of theological thinking in the Western world. His subsequent thirteen-volume, incomplete *Church Dogmatics*, which was his life's work, bears comparison with St Thomas's *Summa Theologica* though its insights and conclusions could hardly have been more different.

Barth's exposition of the Christian Gospel represented a fierce rebellion against a liberal understanding of the faith which had become influential in nineteenth-century Germany and promoted an alliance between religion and culture. This tended to encourage a critical view of the Bible and traditional doctrine and an uncritical view of much that was happening in the secular sphere. Barth set against this the great themes of the sixteenth-century Reformers, who were re-stating the gospel according to St Paul which declared the absolute sovereignty of the ineffable, infinite God and the finite sinfulness of man. Human reason was incapable of attaining any knowledge of God – everything depended on God's revelation of himself in Jesus Christ, conveyed through his Word in the Bible. The Word was always one of judgment on individuals and on all human institutions and cultures, and this was a comtemporary expression of God's final judgment at the end of history.

The Christian believer therefore lived in a situation of perpetual spiritual crisis in which he must decide whether or not to respond by faith to God's grace. Although Barth was at the time only a young pastor, ministering in a Swiss village, the publication of his *Romans* commentary was a bombshell in theological circles and the leading liberal scholars described him as a heretic. But in the political crisis, caused by the rise of Nazism in the 1930s, it was Barth's 'theology of crisis' which provided the basis of the Confessing Church's opposition to Hitler.

Barth was born in Bern and studied initially at the local university, but then went to German universities in Berlin, Tübingen and Marburg. There he managed to secure only second class honours in theology and was unable to proceed to a doctorate. He was ordained in 1909, and after two years as assistant minister in a German-speaking Reformed church in Geneva became minister of Safenwil, in north-east Switzerland.

He was a diligent pastor and a powerful preacher, but spent much time in his study and during the 1914–18 war increasingly questioned liberal values. The first edition of *Romans* sold only 300 copies, but after he had spoken on its main theme at a conference in 1919 he became famous overnight and spent the next year revising it for an edition that went world-wide.

In 1921, somewhat to his surprise, he was appointed a professor of theology at Göttingen; four years later he moved to the chair of dogmatics and New Testament at Münster, and in 1930 he became a professor at Bonn. By this time he was exercising a considerable influence, through his public utterances and writings, and after joining the Social Democrat Party in 1931 he published a pamphlet *Theological Existence Today*, in which he exposed the fundamental errors of the German Christian movement which supported Hitler's bid for power. 37,000 copies were sold.

Under Hitler, as a Swiss he had greater freedom than his German colleagues and he lost no opportunity to speak and preach about the demands of the transcendent God on the allegiance of his people. The historic Barmen Declaration of 1934, which provided the foundations of the Confessing Church, was largely Barth's work, and after he had refused to take an oath of unconditional allegiance to Hitler he was deprived of his chair at Bonn.

Back in Switzerland in 1935, he was immediately appointed Professor of Theology at Basel, where he continued to work on his *Church Dogmatics*, and to keep in touch with his friends in Germany.

On his seventieth birthday Barth was presented with a list of all his publications – 406 items – and in one of his sermons preached in the chapel of Basel prison after his retirement he told the prisoners:

> You have perhaps heard it said that I have written a great many books, and that some of them are fat ones. Let me, however, frankly and openly and even gladly confess that the four words 'My grace is enough' say more and say it better than the whole pile of books with which I have surrounded myself. When my books have long since been superseded and forgotten, then these words will still shine on in all their eternal richness.

John Bowden, *Karl Barth*, SCM Press 1983.

# C. F. Andrews

## (1871– 1940)

Charles Freer Andrews was in his time the best known and most influential Christian in India. He went there as a conventional Anglican missionary, but after ten years he abandoned his teaching post and the priesthood in order to promote the cause of Indian independence and to fight for justice for the poor and oppressed more widely. He enjoyed close friendships with Mahatma Gandhi and the poet Rabindranath Tagore and not only shared fully in their sacrificial protest work but sought to explain them to the West.

His commitment to justice and freedom was undergirded by a deep spirituality which was rooted in Christian faith but embraced Hindu insights and devotional practices. Towards the end of his time as a missionary he said in a pamphlet *India in Transition:* 'If Christianity is to succeed it must come as a helper and fulfiller, a peacemaker and friend. It must be able to gather up all that is great and noble in a higher synthesis. There must no longer be the desire to capture converts from Hinduism.' He concluded: 'The great principle of racial equality has to be fought out once more.'

It was in South Africa in 1914 that Andrews first met Gandhi. Both had gone there to plead the cause of Indian labourers who were being grossly exploited by their white employers. The two men were immediately attracted to each other and Gandhi was one of the last people to visit Andrews when he lay on his deathbed more than a quarter of a century later. On his return from South Africa Andrews lived in Tagore's ashram, but in the following year went at the request of Congress to investigate the conditions of the indentured Indian labourers on the sugar estates in Fiji. His report told of appalling degradation and inhumanity and this, combined with a further report in 1918 and persistent pressure by Andrews and Indian politicians, led to the abolition of indenture throughout the British Empire.

In 1921 he went to Kenya to support the Indian demand for political equality and a common electoral roll for Europeans and Indians in Kenya. Having earlier accused the white settlers of 'racial prejudice camouflaged as patriotic duty' he was not well received and on two occasions was physically assaulted. Two years of campaigning concluded with a visit to London to secure action by the British government, but this failed, and in a sermon preached in the Danish Church in Madras on his return he repudiated the claim of Europeans that the colour bar was needed 'in order to save Kenya for Christian civilization'. This was, he said, 'a travesty of the Christian faith and I repudiate it in Christ's name'. In spite of his extensive travels Andrews spent most of his time in India, where he identified himself closely with the aspirations of the Indian people. He was in touch with Viceroys, politicians and religious leaders, insisting that independence must include freedom for the oppressed classes and that religion was 'the one foundation of all true political action'.

Andrews was born in Newcastle-upon-Tyne, where his father was a minister of the Catholic Apostolic Church. At Pembroke College, Cambridge, he took a double First in classics, was much influenced by the thought and action of Bishop Westcott of Durham, and became an Anglican. He then became the Pembroke College missioner in Walworth, a poverty-stricken area of South London, and in 1897 was ordained priest. Two years later, however, his health broke down, as it frequently did throughout his life, and he returned to Cambridge where, after recuperation, he was made Fellow and Chaplain of Pembroke College and also appointed Vice-Principal of the Clergy Training School (later Westcott House). In 1904 he became a lecturer, then Vice-Principal, at St Stephen's College, Delhi and soon caused concern because he wanted the college to become ecumenical and also because he made so many Indian friends.

His work on behalf of the Indian people involved journalism, and the writing of many pamphlets, mainly on political and social matters. His autobiographical *What I Owe to Christ* (1932) was a best-seller. In 1930, with the agreement of Gandhi, he returned to England, believing that he would be more effective there. Ramsay MacDonald, the then Prime Minister, admired and supported him, but when Stanley Baldwin took over the premiership in 1935 his influence waned. Andrews went back to India in 1937 and during the remaining years of his life wrote and spoke about Hitler's persecution of the Jews. Gandhi said of him: 'Andrews is a humanitarian, pure and simple, and therefore he trusts everybody. The whole world is free to deceive him, and he would still say "Humanity! With all thy faults I love thee still".'

Hugh Tinker, *The Ordeal of Love: C. F. Andrews and India*, Oxford University Press 1979.

# Maude Royden

## (1876–1956)

Agnes Maude Royden was one of the outstanding preachers of the century who, because of her sex, was unable to exercise a ministry in the Church of England. Instead, she served for a time as 'pulpit assistant' at the City Temple – the leading Congregationalist church in London – and from 1920 to 1936 at the Guildhouse, an interdenominational meeting place in Westminster. Earlier she was deeply involved in the women's suffrage movement, serving on the executive council of its National Union and editing its journal, *The Common Cause*. She was also the first chairman of the Church League for Women's Suffrage, and when this battle was won she directed her considerable energy to the fight for women to have an equal place with men in the life of the church – including ordination to the priesthood. She declared women's ordination to be 'the most profoundly moral movement since the foundation of the church'.

From 1914 onwards Royden was a leading figure in the peace movement. An avowed pacifist, she became Travelling Secretary of the Fellowship of Reconciliation in 1915 and also Vice-Chairman of the Women's International League. Following the outbreak of the Sino-Japanese war in 1931, she and Dick Sheppard, Vicar at St Martin-in-the-Fields, sought to create a 'Peace Army', the members of which volunteered to place themselves between combatants. A few hundred joined, but it proved impossible for them to go into action. In 1938 she resigned from the League of National Union over its policy on sanctions and joined the Peace Pledge Union. But, to widespread astonishment, she renounced pacifism in 1940 and supported Britain's involvement in the Second World War.

Royden was the daughter of a prosperous Liverpool ship owner and went from Cheltenham Ladies' College to Lady Margaret Hall, Oxford, where she read history. She then returned to Liverpool to spend three years working in the Victoria Women's Settlement, though her efforts were curtailed by a nervous breakdown. On recovering from this she became a parish worker at South Luffenham, in Rutland, where she came under the influence of its remarkable vicar, Hudson Shaw, with whom she also established in 1908 a deep loving relationship which

55

culminated in their marriage in 1944, just two months before his death.

Shaw, a liberal churchman of considerable courage as well as intellectual power, combined his parish work with that of an Oxford University extension lecturer and it was on his recommendation that Royden, after considerable hesitation on the part of the university authorities because of her sex, also became an extension lecturer. It was in the course of travelling the country lecturing on English literature that she discovered her speaking gift. This soon came to be employed in the causes of women's suffrage and peace, but there was no opportunity for her to preach in church until the invitation came from the City Temple. Her first sermons, preached there on 18 March 1917, attracted huge congregations, and police were needed to control the long queues of people seeking admission. The *Daily Express* announced 'Woman Crank's Sermon' and the *Daily Sketch* reported 'Girl Preacher in Parker's Pulpit'. A fortnight later she was in the Albert Hall speaking to thousands of people celebrating the Russian Revolution.

In September 1918 Shaw, by this time Rector of St Botolph's, Bishopsgate, invited his friend to occupy the pulpit of his City church. This was against the wishes of the Bishop of London, but she went ahead and the church was packed. In the following year, when she was billed to conduct the Good Friday Three-hour Devotion in St Botolph's, the Bishop of London wrote on Maundy Thursday expressly forbidding her participation, so the service was transferred to the parish room. Wherever Royden went large crowds assembled to hear her speak and in 1920 she, together with Percy Dearmer, a maverick Anglican priest, started Fellowship Services – first in Kensington Town Hall, then in a refurbished former Congregationalist church in Westminster which was renamed the Guildhouse.

Preaching tours in India, China, Australia, New Zealand, and the United States met with equal success and she became the first woman to occupy Calvin's pulpit in Geneva. In 1930, however, not long after she had been appointed a Companion of Honour, she became exhausted and was required to rest for twelve months. This inevitably affected the life of the Guildhouse, and although she returned to its pulpit when her health improved, the centre never recovered its early support and dynamism. In 1936 she resigned in order to devote herself to peace work.

The war years restricted her travelling and the combination of long-standing lameness and rheumatism added to her difficulties, though in the 1950s she developed a new ministry as a popular broadcaster.

Sheila Fletcher, *Maude Royden,* Blackwell 1989.

# John Groser

## (1890–1966)

Beverley St John Groser was one of the greatest East End of London priests during the inter-war years. He belonged to the Church of England's Anglo-Catholic tradition and saw commitment to socialism, as expressed by the Labour Party, as inseparable from the church's sacramental life. His entire ministry was devoted to the service of the poor and he became a legend in his own life-time in the East End. He also enjoyed fame of a wider and different kind when, in 1949, he played the part of Thomas Becket in a film of T. S. Eliot's *Murder in the Cathedral*.

Father Groser, as he was always known, was born in the Australian outback and sent to England to be educated. After training at Mirfield's monastic theological college he became a curate at All Saints' Church, Newcastle-upon-Tyne, in 1914. This was a docklands parish of slums and dosshouses, and it was his experience there which set Groser on the path towards social justice and deep concern for the underprivileged.

After only twelve months, however, he responded to a call for army chaplains and was sent immediately to an infantry regiment serving in the front line in France. He never ceased to be a priest and when, after the sustaining of heavy casualties, the Commanding Officer asked him to take charge of a group of soldiers who had been left without an officer, he refused on the grounds that, as a chaplain, he could not take part in killing. However, the conversation was interrupted by a heavy barrage of gunfire and when this ended Groser agreed to take over the leadership of the men provided that he did not have to carry arms. The CO agreed. On another occasion, having encountered a group of German prisoners-of-war, he set up a temporary altar and gave them holy communion. This led to a severe rebuke from the Chaplain General. In 1918 he was wounded and sent home, by which time he had won a Military Cross and been mentioned in despatches.

He then became a curate at St Winnow in Cornwall in order to read and pray about the social and political problems he had encountered in the trenches and the slums. During his time there he met Conrad Noel and joined his Catholic Crusade – a High Church movement with an extreme Left-wing political agenda – and in 1922 he and his brother-in-law, Jack Bucknell, went as curates to All Saints' Church, Poplar, in London's East End. The area was beset by chronic unemployment, poor housing and deep poverty, and Groser organized processions of protest led by the Cross and the Red Flag, and sometimes by a statue of Thomas Becket. During the 1926 General Strike he attended strike meetings and helped to maintain the peace, though this sometimes involved him in trouble with the police.

In the end this led to problems with the Vicar of the parish and in 1927 they parted company. This left him without a church job, so he took secular employment, first as a clerk, then as a weaver. In 1929, however, he offered to be responsible for another East End parish – Christ Church, Watney Street – which was in a run-down condition; a commission was considering the closure of the church. This commission never in fact reported and Groser stayed there until the building was bombed during the 1939–45 war. He made it a centre of colourful, sacramental worship and spent long hours in pastoral and social work in the homes of the people.

In 1931 Groser broke with Conrad Noel. The occasion was a Parliamentary bye-election when he supported the Labour Party candidate in preference to Harry Pollitt, a Communist, who had Noel's backing. As a result he left the Catholic Crusade and joined the Society of Socialist Christians, in which he urged his idealist friends to take account of the reality of sin and of the need for both individuals and communities to be redeemed in Christ. Later he formed the League of Redemption to emphasize this point more strongly.

From 1937 to 1939 he was much involved in battles to improve housing conditions in the East End, and although throughout the 1930s he had spoken openly against war, he stayed put when war came and worked heroically to make provision for parishioners who lost their homes in the blitz. When his church and vicarage were bombed he moved to the nearby parish of St George's-in-the-East, and soon after the end of the war he was appointed Master of the Royal Foundation of St Catherine at Stepney, from where he continued to work for 'the suffering victims of the class system' in the context of Christian redemption.

Kenneth Brill (ed.), *John Groser: East London Priest*, Mowbray 1971.

# Barbara Hepworth

## (1903–1975)

Jocelyn Barbara Hepworth is widely regarded as the world's greatest woman sculptor. Her work is represented in over 100 public collections throughout the world, as well as on many outdoor sites, and the style is unmistakable. Abstract in form, it owes more to the character of the material used than to what it actually represents, and invariably conveys a sense of harmony and serenity. Another common feature is the use of the 'abstract hole' which brings light and air to heavy, solid pieces and is the result of a technique which involved burrowing into the material, rather than cutting out on its surface. Hepworth's first use of this technique in 1931 in the alabaster *Pierced Form* (also known as *Abstraction*) was regarded as a breakthrough in sculpture, though Archipenko and Gaudier-Breska experimented with it some twenty years earlier.

Although her personal life was sometimes unconventional, she made no secret of her Christian convictions, which in the end owed more to Christian Science than to traditional orthodoxy. She was baptized and confirmed in Wakefield Cathedral, but later found in Christian Science something much closer to her artistic insights and feelings. In a letter to Ben Nicholson, the painter, to whom she was married for thirteen years, she described this faith as belonging to 'the very core of my being – the lovely Genesis of perfect Creation and the unfolding of spiritual ideas'. In another letter she wrote: 'Identity is the reflection of the spirit, the reflection of the multifarious forms of the living principle – love. One has to hold the clear thought so that it destroys the evil.' Sculpture, for her, simply involved the removal of that which stood in the way of her vision.

She was born and brought up in Wakefield, Yorkshire, where her father was a civil engineer. At the age of sixteen she went to the Leeds School of Art and within a year had won a scholarship to the Royal College of Art in London. At both institutions one of her fellow students was Henry Moore, also destined to be among the world's greatest sculptors, with whom she established a life-long friendship. Each greatly influenced the other's work and, together with Herbert Read, who also came from Yorkshire, created a distinctive British style which proved to be important in the history of modern art. In 1924 Hepworth secured a scholarship to enable her to study in Florence and Rome, and while she was in Italy she met and married John Skeaping, who was also a sculptor. In Italy she learned how to carve stone, which was unusual for a trainee sculptor at that time, since modelling in clay was considered better. She returned to England in 1928 to live in Hampstead where, in the same year, she held her first solo exhibition of stone carvings of figures and animals.

In 1933 her marriage was dissolved and she began an association with Ben Nicholson, which led to the birth of triplets in the following year. By this time her sculpture was entirely abstract; visits to Paris put her in touch with the avant-garde, including Picasso, Braque and Mondrian, and during the mid-1930s her Hampstead studio became the centre of the abstract art movement in Britain. She married Nicholson in 1938, and in August 1939, with war imminent, they moved to St Ives, in Cornwall, which became home for the rest of her life. She produced little sculpture during the war years, for the first three of which she ran a nursery school and a market garden, but the Cornish landscape and light were influencing her and when she started working again in 1944 the results were no longer completely abstract, but related to landscape forms and the patterns of nature. The ancient standing stones of West Cornwall were specially important to her, and her bronze *The Family of Man*, with its nine standing figures, was the equivalent of an ancient stone circle.

Hepworth's marriage to Ben Nicholson ended in 1951, but he remained in St Ives for another seven years and they continued to influence each other's work. She also produced drawings, paintings and lithographs, and during the 1950s her international reputation became firmly established, with major exhibitions of her sculpture throughout Europe, and in America, Australia and Japan. Her most important commission *Single Form* (bronze, 1964) stands outside the United Nations building in New York as a memorial to Dag Hammarskjöld, who was a personal friend.

In May 1975 she died in a fire in her studio, and her home and studio, Trewyn, were presented to the nation with a collection of her work. Small of stature and of intense appearance, she was awarded many honours, including appointment as a Dame in 1965.

Barbara Hepworth, *A Pictorial Autobiography*, Adams 1970.

# E. W. Barnes

## (1874–1953)

Ernest William Barnes was a highly controversial Bishop of Birmingham from 1924 until a few months before his death. Before entering into the full-time service of the church in 1915 he was a brilliant Cambridge mathematician and this led him to apply to traditional expressions of the Christian faith the criticisms of early twentieth-century science. Thus he rejected the miraculous elements in the Bible and was strongly opposed to any contemporary religious practices that might encourage what he regarded as superstition.

His own faith, which ran deep, and which he earnestly and consistently commended to others, was of a simple evangelical kind. Jesus, the Son of God, was the supreme teacher and exemplar of the way of life that every human being was designed to live. Unfortunately, the revelation had been cluttered up with material from inferior pagan religions, such as miracles, magical elements and doctrinal statements influenced by philosophy.

He often spoke out on behalf of the poor, the homeless and the unemployed. As early as 1933, not long after the Nazis had come to power, he deplored the treatment of the Jews in Germany and helped to organize a protest meeting in Birmingham. But his life-long pacifist stance landed him in much public controversy after the outbreak of war in 1939, when he protested against the bombing of Germany. Towards the end of his life he became interested in eugenics. He said that Britain was not only becoming over-populated, but was inhabited by too many bad stocks. This required sterilization of the unfit and euthanasia for children born defective. 'I foresee a time coming when the great geneticist will be accepted as one of the leading agents of Christian progress.' He also advocated the limitation of immigration, but spoke at his Diocesan Conference of the Christian duty of caring for immigrants and encouraged the Birmingham churches to set up a joint committee for the welfare of overseas nationals.

Barnes was born in Altrincham, Cheshire, but the family moved to Birmingham in 1876; he went from King Edward VI Grammar School to Trinity College, Cambridge as a scholar. After taking a First in mathematics, he was elected to a fellowship, and by the age of thirty-five was both a DSc and a Fellow of the Royal Society. In 1902 he was ordained by the Bishop of London, but remained at Trinity College as a Fellow until 1914, when he was virtually forced to resign because of his preaching of pacifism following the outbreak of war. From 1915–20 he was Master of the Temple, where he exercised a much valued preaching and pastoral ministry among London's leading lawyers.

He then became a Canon of Westminster, where controversy arose from a sermon in Westminster Abbey on evolution and Christianity in which he said that the doctrine of the Fall must be abandoned. He also created a stir by writing to the Press after a royal wedding, complaining about the use of archaic language in the service. In 1924 Barnes became the first English bishop to be appointed by a Labour Prime Minister – Ramsay Macdonald. His nomination to Birmingham occasioned some hostile comment, and many, including most of his fellow bishops, came to believe that his liberal beliefs – described at the time as Modernism – were incompatible with his position as a church leader.

Refusal to institute to an Anglo-Catholic parish a priest who was unwilling to abide by the requirements of the Book of Common Prayer in worship and also desist from reservation of the sacrament led to a High Court hearing at which Barnes was ordered to institute. When he refused to do so, another court ordered the Archbishop of Canterbury to carry out the ceremony. Among the many other controversies in which Barnes was involved, the most notable arose from his publication in 1945 of *The Rise of Christianity*. This questioned the reliability of the Gospels and asserted that more could be known about the teaching of Jesus than about his life. Once again he repudiated any miraculous element in the origin of Christianity, and he accused St Paul of disturbing the faith by introducing non-Christian concepts.

The book, which was a great publishing success, caused a huge rumpus. The Archbishop of Canterbury, Geoffrey Fisher, denounced it in the Convocation of Canterbury and concluded: 'If his (Barnes) views were mine, I should not feel that I could still hold episcopal office in the church.' Nonetheless, Barnes continued to hold office for almost another eight years. The people of Birmingham enjoyed having a bishop of outspoken views and many lay people appreciated his advocacy of a 'simple' form of Christianity, of the sort that they themselves embraced.

John Barnes, *Ahead of His Time*, Collins 1979.

# Georges Rouault
## (1871–1958)

Georges-Henri Rouault, a French Expressionist painter, is generally regarded as the greatest religious painter of the century. He was also a notable ceramicist, printmaker and stained-glass maker, and his early training in a stained-glass studio had a marked effect on his painting, which was characterized by rich colour, especially red and blue, and harsh black outlines. His particular contribution to French art was to re-unite the religious and secular traditions which had been divorced since the Renaissance, and in this he was inspired by the mediaeval masters, not least those of Chartres, whose glass he helped to restore.

He was a prolific artist, but could sometimes take as long as twenty years to complete a painting, and in 1947 he publicly burned 315 of his canvases which he regarded as not representative of his best work. He became a devout Roman Catholic in 1895, largely through the influence of the French writer Léon Bloy. To another friend in intellectual circles, who was a lawyer, he owed the opportunity to attend Paris law courts to study some of those who appeared there – prostitutes, pimps, thieves and pitiless judges. These provided subjects for his earliest paintings, which have crude force in their illustration of what Rouault believed to be corruption at the root of modern life, expressed in vice, hypocrisy and cruelty. A contemporary critic descibed him as wishing 'to thrust at God the insistent cry of dereliction and anxiety for the orphaned multitude'. Another of his early subjects was the tragic clown, whom he saw as representing the artist and prophet, separated from his fellows and often regarded as a figure of fun.

Rouault was born in a Paris cellar during a bombardment of the city by the opponents of the Commune. His father was a cabinet-maker, and his grandfather, who was interested in art, owned a collection of lithographs by Honoré Daumier. These attracted him to the life of an artist and in 1885 he was apprenticed to a glazier who specialized in the restoration of mediaeval glass. At the same time he enrolled as an evening student at the Paris School for Decorative Arts. In 1891 he went to the School of Fine Arts to study under the Symbolist painter Gustave Moreau and, following this artist's death in 1898, he became curator of a small museum devoted to his pictures. Soon afterwards, however, he went through a psychological crisis, during the course of which he came under the influence of Van Gogh, Gauguin and Cézanne. Gradually he evolved a style which had certain affinities with that of the Fauves (Wild Beasts) who made arbitrary use of strong colour, but his paintings – in water colour and oil on paper – while making use of dominant blues and dramatic lighting displayed a certain moral earnestness lacking in the Fauves. His Expressionism was never extreme.

From 1914 onwards Rouault turned more to oil and began to use thick and rich layers of paint on simplified forms. He also embarked on a series of etchings *Misère et Guerre,* which were not completed until 1927 and had to wait until 1948 for publication. During the inter-war period he devoted a good deal of his time to engravings, for the illustration of books, and in this he was encouraged by a Paris art dealer, Ambroise Vollard, who provided him with a room in his premises. This had important repercussions when Vollard died in 1947 and left a large number of engravings to his heirs. Rouault sued for the recovery of his own and established the legal right of artists to their unsold works in such circumstances.

In 1929 Rouault designed the set and costumes for Diaghilev's ballet *The Prodigal Son* with music by Prokofiev, and during the 1930s painted a striking series on the Passion of Christ, with portrayals of Christ mocked by the soldiers, the holy face, and Christ and the high priest. After 1940 he devoted himself almost exclusively to religious art; among his many paintings was a series of New Testament events and parables in the setting of the industrial suburbs of Paris. He was never a church artist in the sense of producing work for church buildings or on traditional Christian subjects, but he had a deep concern with sin and redemption and brought to their representation an introspective vision which not everyone could share.

During the last ten years of his life Rouault renewed his palette by adding yellows and greens, and he used these colours in a series of almost mystical landscapes. Examples of his paintings are to be found in the major art galleries of Europe and America and a rare example of his designs for stained-glass can be seen in the church at Plateau d'Assy in the French Alps.

Pierre Courthion, *Georges Rouault*, Thames and Hudson 1962.

# Gilbert Shaw
## (1886–1967)

Gilbert Shieldham Shaw, a Church of England priest, was not ordained until he was almost forty, but during the next half century he exercised notable ministries, first as a politically conscious priest in London's East End, then as a teacher and writer on prayer. His work in the East End occupied only eight years in the 1930s, but when in 1984 the Greater London Council staged an exhibition on London's modern history a stand was devoted to Shaw's social and political activity in pre-war Poplar. His movement from the realm of social action to that of prayer and contemplation was no less influential, and he was at one time hearing the confessions of as many as two thousand penitents.

Shaw was born in Dublin, but brought up in London, where his father was a wealthy lawyer. At Eton he was deeply shocked by a visit to the college mission in Hackney where, for the first time, he experienced the plight of the poor, and at Trinity College, Cambridge, where he studied history and economics, visits to the college mission in Camberwell increased his awareness of Britain's pre-1914 social problems.

On leaving Cambridge he was invited to enter politics in the Conservative interest, but this he declined, and in 1913 he was called to the Bar. In the same year he embarked on what proved to be an unhappy marriage. He was commissioned in the army on the outbreak of war in 1914, but shortly before embarking for France fell from his horse, and the consequent injuries led to his being discharged. His father then set him up as a farmer, with no success, and he went to live in Glasshampton, Worcestershire where a monk, William Sirr, was trying to establish a new religious community. Shaw stayed – helping to select and train leaders of parish and university missions – until in 1922 he had a psychological breakdown.

A year later, when he had recovered, he entered Westcott House, Cambridge, to prepare for Holy Orders, but before he had completed the course he accepted an invitation to become Vice-Principal of St Paul's Missionary College at Burgh, Lincolnshire. Soon afterwards he was ordained. His four years at this college were remembered for his teaching on St John of the Cross and for the tough spiritual discipline he imposed on the students. In 1928 he left to become secretary of the Association for Promoting Retreats and travelled widely, conducting retreats, hearing confessions and offering spiritual counsel. After four years, however, he came to dislike what he called the 'drawing room' mentality of most of those to whom he ministered. He perceived that their spirituality included no awareness of social and political issues, so he resigned from the Association with no other job in prospect.

At this point he decided to move to London's East End and, with enough personal money to be able to live simply, he became loosely attached to All Saints Church, Poplar, where he soon established the Poplar Deanery Unemployment Centre. With Father John Groser he then formed a Tenants' Defence Association, and in 1939 led a success-ful rent strike. Twelve months earlier he had been given charge of St Nicholas Church, Blackwall Steps, but this was destroyed by wartime bombing. Since conscription had temporarily solved the unemployment problem, he left the East End in order to resume his work as a spiritual director.

In 1942 he became Warden of St Anne's Centre, Soho – a project which aimed to relate the Christian faith to contemporary culture and attracted the support of T. S. Eliot, Dorothy Sayers and other intel-lectuals. Unfortunately a conflict soon arose over the relationship between the intellectual and the spiritual in the Christian life and Shaw left to establish a new personal base in a room in the vicarage of St. Alphege's Church, Southwark. He remained there for the next seven-teen years and in 1947, to the surprise of many, became chairman of the company responsible for publishing the *Church Times*. This did not last long, and the 1940s and 1950s were for him a time of loneliness and despair as he grappled with apparent failure and rejection.

During this time he continued to exercise a wide-ranging personal ministry, became deeply involved in pioneer work in the realm of psychic phenomena and exorcism, and enjoyed the support of Orthodox theolo-gians in Britain and France who appreciated his approach to spirituality. A meeting on Waterloo railway station in 1957 with the Mother General of the Sisters of the Love of God at Fairacres, Oxford, led to a close friendship and his appointment as Warden of this community. The Russian Metropolitan Anthony Bloom described him as 'the greatest priest I have ever known in any tradition – Orthodox, Catholic or Anglican'.

R. D. Hacking, *Such a Long Journey – A Biography*, Mowbray 1988.

# Reinhold Niebuhr

## (1892–1971)

Karl Paul Reinhold Niebuhr was the most significant American theologian in the twentieth century; his influence extended far beyond his homeland and sphere of work as a pastor and teacher. Christian social ethics was his chief interest and he sometimes disclaimed the title 'theologian', but his insights were derived from a prophetic understanding of man's relationship with God, and his two-volume *The Nature and Destiny of Man* (1941–43) is a classic apologia for the Christian faith. Niebuhr's distinctive contribution to theology and ethics came initially as a reaction to the prevailing liberalism of American Protestantism in the 1920s and 1930s. The 'Social Gospel' proclaimed at that time was, he believed, altogether too optimistic about human nature and the possibility of human progress. Furthermore it ran contrary to biblical revelation and observable facts and it oversimplified the problems of living in community.

Niebuhr set against this a dialectical theology centred on God as loving Father, yet exacting Judge, and on Man, born in God's image and likeness, yet subject to universal sin, especially pride, and therefore in need of redemption through sacrificial love. Armed with this doctrine, and aided by an encyclopaedic knowledge of the Bible and history, allied to compelling power as a speaker and writer, he analysed the great social and political issues of his day in ways that won the respect of leading politicians as well as other students of theology. *Moral Man and Immoral Society* (1932) startled many with its forthright distinction between the ethical potential of individuals and that of organized groups. Ten years earlier he had declared that the church 'must be able to apprehend sin in the respectable conventions and traditions of society no less than in individual wrongdoing'. Having pointed out that the ethic of Jesus does not deal with the immediate moral problems of everyday life – 'for it transcends the possibilities of human life, as God transcends the world' – he argued for what he called 'Christian realism'. Justice, being the expression of love in a fallen world, invariably involves an element of compromise and Christians, living under the judgment of God, must work for responsible compromise. When there is no clear choice between right and wrong, they must choose the lesser evil: 'The whole art of politics consists in directing rationally the irrationalities of men.'

Although Niebuhr in his early years acknowledged the validity of Karl Barth's rejection of liberalism and the 'Social Gospel', he came to recognize the flaw in Barth's extreme view of God's otherness, which he described as 'transcendental irresponsibility'. He also had little time for philosophy, asserting that the proper response to the biblical revelation was action rather than argument. His emphasis on the Bible did not, however, make him unsympathetic to other religious faiths since, he said, 'There is always the possibility that those who do not know the historical revelation may achieve a more genuine repentance and humility than those who do.'

Niebuhr was born in Wright City, Missouri, where his father was the pastor of a German immigrant Evangelical and Reformed Church. He was educated at Elmhurst College, Eden Theological Seminary and Yale University before in 1915 becoming pastor at the Bethel Evangelical Church, Detroit. He remained at this church until 1929, during which time the congregation grew from 100 to 600 and a new church was erected on a prime site in the town. His preaching attracted large crowds, and many were captivated by his dialectical message of hope and repentance: 'Man is at once a saint and a sinner.' He was himself much influenced by the conditions under which the employees of the motor industry were living and working, especially during the years of economic depression, and he became a founder and the leading voice of the Fellowship of Socialist Christians.

By this time he was becoming a national figure, and in 1928 was appointed Professor of Applied Christianity at the Union Theological Seminary, New York – a post he held until his retirement in 1965 and where he exerted enormous influence. During the 1930s he abandoned his pacifist stance, was strongly opposed to Hitler and said that military intervention against Nazi Germany was necessary. He also became increasingly critical of the Protestant Church in Germany for its failure to stand up to Hitler. In 1937 he made a considerable impact at the Oxford Conference on Church, Community and State and became deeply involved in the ecumenical movement. At the first assembly of the newly-formed World Council of Churches at Amsterdam in 1948 he clashed memorably with Karl Barth.

During the post-war years his socialism was modified somewhat and he supported the Cold War, believing that Soviet expansion must be checked. However, he was strongly opposed to the Vietnam war. He wrote more than twenty books and innumerable articles.

# Charles Raven

## (1885–1964)

Charles Earle Raven was a leading liberal theologian and churchman between the two world wars. He combined brilliant scholarship with passionate concern for the truth and for social justice, and he was one of the most compelling orators of his time. The reconciliation of religion and science was a burning issue for him, as also was pacifism, and it fell to him to carry the flag of liberal Christianity during a period when it had gone out of favour and the biblical theology movement was in the ascendancy.

Raven was born in the Paddington district of London. He went from Uppingham School to Cambridge where he took Firsts in classics and theology. He then spent a short time with Liverpool City Council's education department before his ordination in 1910 and return to Cambridge as Fellow and Dean of Emmanuel College and Lecturer in Divinity. He taught at Tonbridge School from 1915–17 and during this time made several attempts to join the wartime army as a combatant. Every time, however, he was rejected on medical grounds, so he entered as a chaplain and was soon at the front line in France. His wartime experience affected him greatly. Amid the suffering and death in the trenches, he became vividly aware of the presence of Christ and saw the war in terms of the cosmic struggle between good and evil spoken of by St Paul in Romans 8, a theme which attracted him in the 1960s to the mysticism of the Jesuit priest-scientist Pierre Teilhard de Chardin.

Proximity to so much suffering also led him to question the orthodox doctrines of God's omnipotence and inability to feel pain; and what he discerned as the humanizing influence of women in military hospitals and canteens turned him into a strong advocate of the admission of women to all areas of life – including the priesthood. The end of the war found him optimistic about the future of liberal Christianity, for in the trenches he had encountered widespread rejection of the authority of the Bible and of the church. He believed that a simple gospel which concentrated on God's love and his call to men and women to respond in the way that Jesus had responded would attract many of those who wished to make a new start after the horror of war. This was the message he preached with considerable power at Bletchingley, Surrey, where he was Rector from 1920 to 1924. By this time, however, he was on the way to beoming a national figure – a chaplain to the king, and, with William Temple, involved in the organization of a major conference on Politics, Economics and Citizenship held in Birmingham in 1924.

After this conference he was appointed a Canon Residentiary of Liverpool Cathedral. This new cathedral was the flagship of the liberal movement in the Church of England and Raven attracted large congregations to Sunday evening services which consisted mainly of an address by him. It was during this time that he became a pacifist and wrote *Jesus and the Gospel of Love* (1931). In 1932 he went back to Cambridge as Regius Professor of Divinity – a post combined with a canonry of Ely Cathedral. This was a strange appointment in some ways, for the influence of neo-orthodoxy was growing rapidly. Nonetheless his lectures attracted large audiences. He spoke extempore on the great Christian doctrines, which he interpreted in the context of scientific thought and current social need. He also worked for the widening of the Cambridge Divinity syllabus, but this was not achieved until after his retirement.

Among his other concerns was the chairmanship of the pacifist Fellowship of Reconciliation, and the sponsorship of the more militant Peace Pledge Union. He had a great love of wild flowers, insects and birds, which he painted with great skill, and he wrote *In Praise of Birds* – a charming book containing deep religious insights. A later book, *Science, Religion and the Future* (1943), and his Gifford Lectures (1951–52), on *Natural Religion and Christian Theology,* both expressed the breadth of his thinking, but during the 1930s he, in common with other Cambridge scholars, failed to grasp the danger of Communism and went so far as to suggest that 'the hope of the future' might lie in a synthesis of Communism and Christianity.

In 1939 he became Master of Christ's College, Cambridge, where his pacifism created problems and reduced his influence during the war years. He would have liked a bishopric and when the war ended in 1945 put himself at the disposal of the Archbishop of Canterbury, Geoffrey Fisher. However, his offer was flatly rejected. Instead, he became a very successful Vice-Chancellor of Cambridge and presided over the admission of women to full membership of the university.

F. W. Dillistone, *Charles Raven*, Hodder and Stoughton 1975.

# Dorothy Day
## (1897–1980)

Dorothy Day was the most significant woman in the history of American Roman Catholicism. Daniel Berrigan described her as 'a people's saint' but her response to this was, 'Don't call me a saint. I don't want to be dismissed so easily.' Her chief concerns were with justice for the poor and peace between the nations. Under the influence of a remarkable French itinerant personalist philosopher, Peter Maurin, who had once been a Christian Brother, she also founded the Christian Workers' Movement which established farm communities and 'houses of hospitality' for people adversely affected by the economic depression of the 1930s. There are now 150 of these 'houses' throughout the world and the voluntary helpers live in the community with the poor. On May Day 1933 she co-founded, with Peter Maurin, and began to edit, the *Catholic Worker*, which sold at one cent a copy and within a year had achieved a circulation of 100,000. This became an important organ in the cause of social justice in the English-speaking world.

Although Dorothy Day was radical in social and political matters, she was traditional in theology and, while often outspokenly critical of the Catholic hierarchy, attended Mass daily, read Vespers, went to confession weekly and attended regular retreats. She was passionate in her convictions and determined in pursuing what she believed to be right, and this made her impatient with many of the post-Vatican II Catholic liberals, who seemed to her to be indefinite in their beliefs and too ready to compromise with the world's standards. A literal understanding of the Sermon on the Mount was the basis of her Christian life.

The daughter of a sportswriter, Day was born in Brooklyn, New York. The family then moved to Chicago, but Dorothy, having dropped out of college, returned to New York, where she worked for a time as a nurse in the slums. By now she was an atheist and secularist, and led a Bohemian life with writers, artists and radicals. She became a reporter on various Marxist papers and had an affair with another journalist which led to her having an abortion. When this affair ended in 1919, on the rebound she married an unstable man, and this relationship lasted less than a year. A happy common law-marriage to Forster Batterham

71

followed. Gratitude for the birth of a daughter in 1927 and the influence of a nun, Sister Aloysis, led to her conversion to Catholicism, and she committed herself to a lifetime of voluntary poverty and service of the poor. This led to her separation from Batterham, who was an atheist and an anarchist, and had no sympathy for any form of religion.

A difficult period followed in which she sought to work out the relationship between her new faith and her concern for the poor, but in December 1932 she chanced to be visited in her New York apartment by Peter Maurin. He introduced her to the thought of Nicolai Berdyaev and Jacques Maritain, and to the ideas of English Distributists such as G. K. Chesterton, Hilaire Belloc and Eric Gill. Thomas Aquinas's doctrine of 'the common good' also profoundly influenced her.

The *Catholic Worker*, deliberately named as a challenge to the Communist *Daily Worker*, crossed swords seriously with the American bishops in 1936 because they supported Franco in the Spanish Civil War. On the outbreak of World War II in 1939 the paper adopted a pacifist stance, as a result of which its circulation dropped, and many of the Houses of Hospitality were closed down. Again, in the 1950s, the paper protested against what it called 'the war mentality' of the time and its editor was often arrested, and sometimes gaoled, for her involvement in demonstrations. During the 1960s, however, she broke with the anti-war movement in America because of its violence and because, as she put it, 'People are losing sight of the primacy of the spiritual.'

Although she fought for justice for all the poor, she had a particular concern for the victims of injustice in the realm of agriculture. During the 1960s she strongly supported a movement for the unionization of farm workers and in 1973 went to California to join in the organizing of migrant farm workers. Now aged seventy-five, she was obliged to sit on a stool at some of the meetings and demonstrations and on one occasion, having read the Sermon on the Mount to two policemen, she was arrested for civil disobedience and sent to prison for ten days. In 1998 the official process was started for her to be canonized as a saint. The *Catholic Worker* is still published – seven times a year – and its price remains one cent.

Dorothy Day, *On Pilgrimage*, Catholic Worker Books 1948; *The Long Loneliness*, Harper and Row 1972.

# Donald Soper

## (1903–1998)

Donald Oliver Soper was the best known and most widely respected Methodist churchman in Britain during the second half of the century. Liberal in his religious beliefs and emphatically socialist in his political convictions, he attracted much attention and admiration by his combination of eloquence and ability to simplify (some said over-simplify) major moral issues. He was an uncompromising pacifist who courageously aired his beliefs in public throughout the 1939–45 war, and in 1950, when the Korean War was at its height, shocked the Methodist Conference by declaring that Communism was preferable to war. He was also a founder member of the Campaign for Nuclear Disarmament and a prominent figure in its Easter protest marches to the nuclear research establishment at Aldermaston.

Soper's pacifism was inseparable from his socialism, which went back to his experience as a circuit minister in a deprived area of South London and which he regarded as the political means for helping to establish the Kingdom of God. He was an active member of the Labour Party, serving as an Alderman on the Greater London Council and in 1965 becoming the first Methodist minister to enter the House of Lords as a Life Peer. Towards the end of his life, however, he often complained that the Labour Party had abandoned its radical aims. At various times he denounced capital punishment, boxing and hunting, and during his year as President of the Methodist Conference in 1953 criticized the recently crowned Queen for going to the races and her consort, Prince Philip, for playing polo on Sunday. On the other hand he welcomed the liberalization of the laws on homosexuality and also said that in certain circumstances euthanasia might be permissible.

Soper was born, of middle-class Methodist parents, in Wandsworth, South London. At Cambridge he studied history and the philosophy of religion, in which he was awarded a First, and although he was for a short time an atheist, he recovered his faith and prepared for the Methodist ministry at Wesley House, Cambridge. Later he studied Gallicanism and Ultramontanism at the London School of Economics and gained a PhD. From 1926–29 he was a minister at the South London

Mission and, besides the leading of worship, was engaged in much social work among the poor and the unemployed. In 1927 he went to Tower Hill, where on Wednesday lunchtimes a number of outdoor speakers could be heard. He immediately decided to join their number and began a weekly act of witness that he repeated on Sunday afternoons in Hyde Park and continued for the remainder of his life. A short statement on some current issue, seen in a Christian context, was followed by questions from the often very large audiences, and his sharp mind and ready wit rarely left him without an answer. Long years of outdoor speaking did, however, ruin his voice.

In 1929 he moved to the Central London Mission where, until 1936, he was minister of Islington Central Hall. His preaching attracted large congregations and, as in South London, was accompanied by social action in the poor neighbourhood. On the strength of his success there he was appointed Superintendent of the West London Mission and remained there until his retirement in 1978. The largest of the Methodist Church's London Missions, it was based on Kingsway Hall – a seven-storied building which housed a lecture hall, a gymnasium, meeting rooms, and an auditorium where, in the 1930s and 1940s, as many as 2,000 people would assemble for worship and to hear Soper preach. Other social work, including a girls' hostel and a holiday home, was carried out elsewhere. This provided a base for Soper's ministry for more than forty years, during which he travelled extensively in Britain and in many other parts of the world, where he was in great demand as a preacher. His controversial views did not win the approval of all Methodists, and his election as President of the Conference created some unease. He was a high churchman inasmuch as he regarded the Holy Communion as the central act of worship and was for many years President of the Methodist Sacramental Fellowship. The League against Cruel Sports and the housing charity Shelter also benefitted from his dynamic leadership.

Christianity was for Soper a revolutionary movement and his outspoken views led to his being banned from broadcasting during World War II. Officers of the police Special Branch were sometimes observed among the audience at his Tower Hill meetings. But he believed with equal fervour in the importance of personal conversion and he began his maiden speech in the House of Lords with a quotation from John Wesley's Journal: 'What is a Lord but a sinner born to die?'

Brian Frost, *Goodwill on Fire: Donald Soper's Life and Mission*, Hodder 1996.

# Marc Chagall
## (1887–1985)

Marc Chagall was one of the century's most important painters and the first to apply seriously to religious art the avant garde style that emerged in Paris during the early years of his career. His distinctive contribution to modern painting lay in the realm of poetic symbolism and fantasy, and in the use of radiant colour to convey intensity of light. Many of his pictures portray a variety of animals, often in humorous, semi-human postures, while men and women float in the air, sometimes minus their heads. The circus was also one of his favourite themes, but his purpose was always the serious one of sharing with others his dreamlike insights into the nature of reality.

The Bible was Chagall's other main source of inspiration and led to the creation of what are arguably his finest works. The element of fantasy remains in these paintings but is subordinated to the reality of Old Testament prophets and the crucifixion. Although he was born a Jew and was steeped in the Scriptures and Jewish mysticism, he came to see the crucifixion of Jesus as a supreme act of sacrificial love and Jesus as the man with the most profound understanding of life, a figure central to the mystery of life. His masterpiece *Golgotha* or *Calvary*, painted as early as 1912, in brilliant greens and reds, was inspired by Russian icons, while *White Crucifixion* (1938) portrays Jesus on a cross surrounded by scenes of Jewish pogroms in Europe.

Chagall (originally Moyshe Segal) was born in 1887 in Vitebsk, Belorussia. His parents were Hassidic Jews. From an early age Moyshe wished to become a painter, but there seemed little possibility of his realising this dream until 1906, when a notable painter, Yehuda Pen, opened a studio in Vitebsk. Moyshe's parents were too poor to pay the required fees, but he attended the studio for two months, earning a little money by working for a photographer. Pen soon recognized that he had a student of unusual talent, and recommended him to the main art school in St Petersburg, where he was introduced to French art. The years 1910–14 were spent in Paris, where he was influenced by the Impressionists. He also discovered Cubism, but, although he owed much to these new movements, he was always true to his own vision.

In 1914 he returned to Russia, for what was intended to be a brief visit, but was trapped by war and the 1917 Revolution, and had to remain until 1922. Following the Revolution he was appointed Commissar of Fine Arts in the province of Vitebsk, and began to paint theatre sets, but his designs for the State Jewish Chamber Theatre in Moscow provoked such a violent reaction that he went into exile. From 1923 to 1941 he was in France, where his output on a great variety of subjects was prolific; in 1931 he began a series of over 100 illustrations for *The Bible*, a task that was not completed until 1956. Three of his paintings were burnt by the Nazis in 1933, others were removed from German art galleries.

The plight of European Jewry increasingly influenced his painting, and following the German occupation of France he fled to New York. There he began to design for the ballet – but from 1943 onwards his paintings became more sombre and he produced many crucifixions, symbolizing the martyrdom of Russia. His beloved wife Bella died tragically in 1944, and he did not paint for the next nine months. In 1948 he returned to France, remarried and spent the next thirty-seven years happily in Provence. He painted twenty-nine pictures as a tribute to Paris and later painted walls and ceilings at the Paris Opéra and the Metropolitan Opera in New York. His twelve paintings illustrating episodes in Genesis and Exodus, and five illustrating the Song of Solomon, for a disused chapel at Vence, were not accepted by the church authorities, so he gave them to the city of Nice, where a museum, Musée National Message Biblique, was opened in 1973.

When he was seventy, Chagall discovered the possibilities offered by stained glass, and his first work in this medium (1956) is to be seen in the church at Plateau d'Assy in the French Alps. Accompanying these windows in the baptistery is a large ceramic by Chagall which portrays The Crossing of the Red Sea and is dedicated 'In the name of freedom for all religions'. In the following year he embarked on a series of huge windows for Metz Cathedral, and before the end of his life he had completed thirteen other window commissions, including the savage red illustration of the Psalm 150 in Chichester Cathedral and a series of twelve windows in the village church at Tudeley in Kent.

Daniel Marchesseau, *Chagall: The Art of Dreams*, Thames and Hudson 1998.

# William Temple

## (1881–1944)

William Temple is believed by many to have been the greatest Archbishop of Canterbury of the century. Certainly he has so far been the most wide-ranging in his gifts, and during the twentieth century was unsurpassed in his influence. He occupied the Primatial See of Canterbury for only two years (1942–44), but this coincided with the dark days of World War II, when his frequent broadcasts and sermons and speeches in many parts of Britain provided spiritual leadership of the highest order. His early death was lamented by all sections of society and he was described in the Press as 'The People's Archbishop' and 'The Churchill of the Church'.

Temple's intellectual capacity was astonishing. He was essentially a philosopher rather than a theologian. His Gifford Lectures, published in 1934 as *Nature, Man and God*, would have been a notable achievement for a professor with ample leisure. That it should have come from the pen of someone who not only was Archbishop of York, with major national responsibilities, but also occupied a world stage as a leader of the rapidly developing ecumenical movement and as the most important Christian social thinker of the time, beggared belief. *Christianity and Social Order*, published as a paperback in 1942, sold 150,000 copies in a matter of months, and is still regarded as one of the most significant contributions to social thought in the twentieth century.

Temple was born in Exeter, where his father, Frederick (later to become Bishop of London, then Archbishop of Canterbury) was Bishop. He went from Rugby School to Balliol College, Oxford where he secured a double First in classics, became President of the Union and was then appointed a Fellow and Lecturer in Philosophy at the Queen's College, Oxford. In 1906 he began to explore the possibility of ordination but was turned down by the Bishop of Oxford because of his hesitations about the virgin birth and the physical resurrection of Jesus. Two years later, however, his doubts largely resolved, he was ordained by Archbishop Davidson in Canterbury Cathedral.

In 1910, to the surprise of many, including himself, he became Headmaster of Repton School. On his own admission he was not a born headmaster, but he made a considerable impact on the school before moving to London in 1914 as Rector of St James', Piccadilly. His arrival at this central London church coincided with the outbreak of the 1914–18 World War, and during the next three years his sermons attracted large congregations. Besides this he was editor of Challenge, a weekly newspaper which became an outlet for his own views, and in 1916 he had a leading role in a National Mission of Repentance and Hope which the Archbishops of Canterbury and York inflicted on a war-torn Britain. In 1917 he published his first major book *Mens Creatrix*, then resigned his rectory in order to lead a Life and Liberty movement – designed to give the laity a greater say in the affairs of the Church of England and at the same time secure for the church a measure of freedom from state control. It secured in 1919 the passing of an Enabling Act which led to the formation of the Church Assembly.

At this point Temple was appointed a Canon of Westminster in the belief that he needed a rest, but after less than two years he left to become Bishop of Manchester. In this large industrial diocese Temple gave dynamic pastoral and prophetic leadership. But he had many other irons in the fire. He was chairman of an Archbishops' Commission on Christian Doctrine and also of an international conference on Politics, Economics and Citizenship held in Birmingham in 1924. At Lausanne in 1927 he was deputy chairman of a section of an international Faith and Order Conference and, besides a number of smaller books, published *Christus Veritas* – a substantial essay in which he presented the Incarnation as the key to the world's unity and rationality.

He became Archbishop of York in 1929, and the next thirteen years saw him at the height of his powers – indefatigable in preaching and lecturing in different parts of the world, chairman of innumerable committees and conferences, most importantly the Lambeth Conference Committee on Church Unity (1930), the Edinburgh Conference on Faith and Order (1937) and the Malvern Conference on the Church and Social Issues (1941). He was deeply involved in the formation of the World Council of Churches and in 1939 became its provisional chairman. *Readings in St John's Gospel*, published in two volumes, 1939–40, became a classic. Although a giant in every way, including considerable physical girth, Temple was a kind and friendly man, given to explosive laughter. At the time of his death a Canon of York described him as 'the most generously and effectively tolerant person I have ever known'.

F. A. Iremonger, *William Temple*, Oxford University Press 1948.

# Simone Weil

## (1909–1943)

Simone Alphonse Weil was a French philosopher who, although she was never baptized a Christian, had deep religious insights and a faith which embraced most of the fundamental Christian beliefs. The teaching of Jesus attracted her; the crucifixion was central to her writing at one point; she recognized the importance of the church as a guardian of truth; but she had difficulties over the resurrection and believed that much of the church's institutional life was a denial of the gospel and a hindrance to its propagation. Her intensely personal faith and close identification with the sufferings of the victims of the 1939–45 war led to her death by self-imposed starvation.

Her wealthy parents were Jewish but agnostic in faith and she had no religious upbringing. At an early age, however, she developed a sympathy with the poor and during the 1914–18 war had some of her meagre rations sent to soldiers serving at the front. In her teens she began to experience the crippling headaches that were to dog the remainder of her life and also to display what T. S. Eliot later described as 'a difficult, violent, complex personality'. This included a brilliant intellect. She was one of the first women to be admitted to the École Normal Supérieure, where she read philosophy and was greatly influenced by the study of Marx. This led to her organizing her fellow students in support of striking railwaymen and unemployed coal miners, but in spite of these distractions she had a brilliant academic career and hoped to become involved in workers' education.

In the event, she was sent to a school in the picturesque, tourist town of Le Puy in the Auvergne, but soon made contact with the trade unions in St Etienne. There, at weekends and during the school holidays, she advised the coal miners on the presentation of their case for improved wages and working conditions, spoke on their behalf, and waved the Red Flag in their processions. When they demonstrated outside her school, she joined them, and this so angered the rest of the teaching staff and the parents that she was obliged to resign. She secured another teaching post at Auxerre, but this was no more successful, and desiring to experience industrial life at first hand, she returned to Paris and took jobs in three different factories. In 1936 she was active in the metal-workers' strike – one of a series of strikes which paralysed France – and wrote about her experience in *Révolution Prolétarienne*. The same year found her also in Spain, fighting against Franco, but an accident with hot cooking oil brought this to an end after three months.

It was about this time that she became more interested in religion, and spent Holy Week and Easter 1938 at the Benedictine monastery at Solesmes, where she was specially moved by the Gregorian chanting. Just before the fall of Paris in 1940 Weil moved with her parents first to Vichy, then later to Marseilles. There she wrote for clandestine newspapers and also sought guidance from a blind Dominican monk, Père Perrin, with whom she established a close friendship. She attended Mass and began to see identification with the poor as a participation in Christ's sufferings. This was the period of her most brilliant writing, and her *Cahiers* has been likened to Pascal's *Pensées*.

When she was dismissed from her minor teaching post at the university because she was Jewish, she became an agricultural worker in the Ardèche, so that she could experience the poverty of the peasant. Her chief wish, however, was to join the Free French Forces in England. She achieved this when her family were given permission to sail to America – she then travelling from New York to London. By this time she was in poor health and ate very little. The French authorities asked her to draw up a spiritual statement to be used as the basis for a constitution for the Fourth Republic when the war ended. This was published as *The Need for Roots*, but no one was really interested in it, and she became disenchanted with the Gaullist movement.

In 1943 she was suffering from tuberculosis and severe malnutrition, refusing to have more food than the rations of the French people. Her request to be taken to a place as near as possible to France was granted, and she was moved to a sanatorium near Ashford, in Kent. Refusing to co-operate with the doctors, she died on 24 August and was buried in a pauper's grave, with only a few people, and no priest present. She believed that she was called to live 'at the intersection of Christianity and all that was non-Christian'. Another French philosopher Gabriel Marcel called her 'a pilgrim of the absolute'.

David Anderson, *Simone Weil*, SCM Press 1971.

# Rudolf Bultmann
## (1884–1976)

Rudolf Karl Bultmann was one of the great theologians of the century – some say the greatest. Certainly he was the most radical in his approach to the New Testament. This may explain why, so far, he has been less influential than Karl Barth and Paul Tillich, who were his contemporaries. He was often accused of being reductionist in his presentation of the Christian faith, but this was a superficial judgment, since his theology and preaching were focussed in the heart of the gospel and offered the sharpest of challenges.

Another accusation was that he was an 'ivory tower' academic whose concern for the intersection of theology and philosophy was unrelated to life in the contemporary world. But again, this was wide of the mark, for the driving force of his work was a deep concern that the Christian faith should be presented in ways that were credible to the modern mind. Soon after the outbreak of the 1939–45 war he was distressed to hear from army chaplains how little response to their preaching they were getting from soldiers, and in 1941 he circulated to a small group of friends, on duplicated sheets, an essay 'New Testament and Mythology'. This was published later in a symposium *Kerygma and Myth* (English translation 1952) and included a warning to the church: 'It is impossible to use electric light and the wireless and to avail ourselves of modern medical and surgical discoveries and at the same time believe in the New Testament world of demons and spirits.'

Nothing less than a radical reinterpretation of the gospel was, he believed, required and this must involve what he called 'demythologizing' – the separation of the essential truth preached by Jesus from its mythological framework in the New Testament which presupposed a three-storied universe, with the angels above and Satan and his demons below. Such a demythologizing, unlike earlier attempts to discern a historical Jesus behind the Gospel narratives, must leave history on one side and, instead, concentrate on the message he preached, seeking to present it in a form intelligible today. The insights of the existentialist philosopher Martin Heidegger were, Bultmann thought, ideally suited to this purpose.

This was an original approach to the solution of a serious problem which, in spite of much criticism from other theologians and church leaders, made a permanent impact on New Testament studies and attracted significant support, particularly in Germany. In Britain it first came to public attention sensationally through its use by Bishop John Robinson in his *Honest to God* (1963).

Bultmann was born in Wielfestede, near Oldenburg in North Germany. He studied at the university of Marburg and also at the universities of Tübingen and Berlin. In 1912 he returned to Marburg as a lecturer, then became a Professor at Breslau and at Giessen. He went back to Marburg in 1921 as Professor of New Testament and remained there until his retirement thirty years later.

In his first book, *The History of the Synoptic Tradition* (1921), Bultmann applied the methods of form criticism to the Gospels of Matthew, Mark and Luke. He argued that they were compilations of material designed to meet the teaching and devotional needs of the earliest Christian communities and were, therefore, to be regarded as theological, rather than as historical or biographical documents. The same was, he believed, true of the Fourth Gospel, which also showed clear signs of Gnostic influence. In *Jesus and the Word* (1934) he stated emphatically: 'We can know almost nothing concerning the life and personality of Jesus.' Beyond the fact that he lived and was crucified, history provides no firm evidence.

For Bultmann this did not, however, destroy the validity of the Christian faith, since something can be known of what Jesus taught, and the decision for which Jesus called in the face of the end-time is the heart of Christianity. Beneath the mythological language and imagery of the New Testament are truths about the meaning of human existence, for Jesus called his followers to abandon their longing for self-achieved security in favour of a security offered by divine grace and appropriated by faith. The significance of the death of Jesus lies in our willingness 'to make the cross of Christ our own, to undergo crucifixion with him'.

Such a faith response would liberate believers from this world and enable his life to be centred on God's world. This would not free them from personal ethical responsibility; on the contrary the liberation was to a life of devotion to others in faith and love. But Bultmann believed strongly that the church should not become involved in social and political issues, which was a dangerous belief during the Nazi era and which not everyone regarded as a necessary conclusion from his fundamental insights.

# George Bell
## (1883–1958)

George Kennedy Allen Bell was Bishop of Chichester from 1929 to 1957 and was one of the outstanding church leaders of the first half of the century. A good pastoral bishop in the Anglican tradition, he was known world-wide for his pioneering work in the cause of church unity and also for his deep concern for German Christians who were suffering under Hitler in the 1930s and 1940s.

His wide international contacts made him one of the first public figures in Britain to become aware of the threat posed by Nazi Germany and to recognize that it would become the central issue facing the civilized world. He wrote many letters to the London *Times* calling attention to the German problem and, after chairing a meeting of the Life and Work section of what was to become the World Council of Churches, held in Novi Sad, Yugoslavia in 1933, he wrote to the leaders of the German Lutheran Church expressing the meeting's concern about the actions being taken against the Jews and the restrictions being placed on everyone's freedom of thought and expression.

In 1935 Bell visited Rudolf Hess, Hitler's deputy, upon whom he impressed the need for the churches to have a genuinely independent place in the life of the nation. But although Bell was implacably opposed to Nazism, his friendships made him aware of the other side of Germany and until the summer of 1939 he urged negotiation and compromise rather than war. In May 1942 he flew to neutral Sweden with Sir Kenneth Clark, the art historian, and T. S. Eliot, the poet, on a three-week official visit designed to maintain contact between Britain and Sweden. During the course of this visit his friend Dietrich Bonhoeffer also arrived in Sweden from Germany with news of the growth of the underground movement and a request that the British government should encourage its further development by declaring that when the war ended special consideration would be given to those who had opposed and helped to undermine Hitler.

Bell conveyed this request in great secrecy to the British Foreign Secretary, Anthony Eden, but the British government, at this critical stage of World War II, felt unable to take such action. Later, in February

1944, he spoke in the House of Lords against the policy of obliteration bombing then being pursued against German towns and cities. This aroused a great public furore. Yet Bell was not a pacifist: earlier he had said that the Allied armies must occupy Berlin. His outlook was, however, informed by a deep humanitarian concern which he believed should temper the conduct of war. When the war ended he was active in schemes for the rehabilitation of Germany and opposed the trials of war criminals.

Bell's early career gave few indications of what lay ahead. He was the oldest of nine children of a Hampshire clergyman, went to Westminster School and on to Christ Church, Oxford where he read Classics and won the Newdigate Poetry prize. On the completion of his training at Wells Theological College he spent three years as a curate at Leeds Parish Church, then returned to Christ Church as chaplain and tutor. Shortly after the outbreak of war in 1914, however, he was appointed Chaplain to the Archbishop of Canterbury, Randall Davidson, with whom he enjoyed a close working partnership. Later he wrote a two-volume biography of Davidson which became a classic. In 1924, and aged only forty-one, he became Dean of Canterbury, where he remained for only five years but accomplished a great deal. The cathedral was opened to the public more frequently and entrance fees were abolished. A life-long interest in the arts led to a Festival of Music and Drama and Bell commissioned John Masefield to write *The Coming of Christ* and T. S. Eliot *Murder in the Cathedral*.

He was a delegate to the Stockholm conference on Life and Work in 1925 and edited the English edition of its proceedings. Before long he had become a key figure in the Life and Work movement, and when the World Council of Churches was formed at Amsterdam in 1948 he was elected chairman of its Central Committee. But in spite of his national and international responsibilities Bell did not neglect the Diocese of Chichester. He worked long hours, and a retentive memory assisted his pastoral care of the clergy.

When William Temple died in 1944, many hoped that Bell would become Archbishop of Canterbury, but his attitude to Germany and opposition to saturation bombing were seen as an insuperable problem, and the Church of England was denied the courageous leadership it desperately needed in the post-war era. Geoffrey Fisher, who succeeded to Canterbury, described him as 'a volcanic bishop'.

R. C. D. Jasper, *George Bell*, Oxford University Press 1967.

# Leslie Hunter

## (1890–1983)

Leslie Stannard Hunter was Bishop of Sheffield from 1939 to 1962 and under his leadership this industrial diocese became the most forward looking in the Church of England. Specially conscious of the gulf between the church and the working class, he attracted gifted young clergy who would engage in experimental work – notably in industrial mission and team ministry – and established a conference house for training courses and consultations on Church and Society themes. A youth training centre provided courses for young industrial workers.

Hunter was also concerned that the church should be more efficient in its own structures. In *A Parson's Job* (1931) he argued for a team ministry approach to secularized urban communities, but another thirty years were to pass before the church took this seriously. He also led a Men, Money and Ministry group of clergy and laity which proposed that all the church's parochial, diocesan and cathedral endowments should be pooled and used to finance the most pressing mission needs. Later, in a pamphlet *Putting our House in Order* (1937), the group made ten proposals for church reform, including the modification of the parson's freehold and the equalization of clergy stipends.

Hunter was born in Scotland, the son of a famous liberal Congregationalist preacher, but Alpine holidays introduced him to Anglican worship in continental chaplaincies, and during his time at New College, Oxford, he became an Anglican. On coming down from Oxford he joined the staff of the Student Christian Movement as travelling secretary for theological colleges, though he was himself still a layman, and later he became the movement's Bible Study secretary. At one time he considered the possibility of becoming an artist and his first book was *The Artist and Religion* (1915), but he was ordained in 1916 and then spent several months in France with the YMCA, working among soldiers. On his return he continued to serve the SCM.

In 1921 he joined the staff of St Martin-in-the-Fields in London's Trafalgar Square, under the dynamic leadership of Dick Sheppard, though his main ministry was as chaplain of the nearby Charing Cross Hospital. He also became secretary of a group planning the revision of the Book of Common Prayer. In 1922, however, he was appointed a Canon Residentiary of Newcastle Cathedral and this introduced him to the problems of bad housing, poverty and ill-health in North East England. After only four years at Newcastle, he decided that he ought to be a parish priest and became Vicar of Barking, Essex. This one-time country town now had a population approaching 50,000, of whom only 1.6% were churchgoers, but although Hunter was there for a mere four years – his ministry was terminated by ill-health – he established the Parish Communion as the chief act of Sunday worship (an unusual innovation at that time), restored the parish church, and established a first-class parish magazine.

A year of recuperation was needed after Barking, and he then returned to the North East as Archdeacon of Northumberland. During the next eight years, 1931–39, he flourished. Besides the parishes and their clergy, he had a special concern for the 74,000 unemployed on Tyneside and raised a large sum of money to provide them with occupational and recreational centres. He was also a prominent member of the Northumberland Education Committee, and played an important part in the 1937 Oxford Conference on Church, Community and State.

In the previous year he declined the offer of the Bishopric of Woolwich, in South London, and in 1938 he refused the chance to become Director of Religious Broadcasting at the BBC. But in 1939, less than a month after the outbreak of war, he became Bishop of Sheffield. Throughout the war years he gave outstanding spiritual and moral leadership in a heavily bombed city. He was not a pacifist but spoke out against the indiscriminate bombing of German cities and looked ahead to the time when reconciliation and the rebuilding of European life would be necessary. When the war ended in 1945 he visited Germany, spoke in the House of Lords on behalf of German prisoners-of-war in Britain, and took over from Bishop George Bell as chairman of Christian Reconstruction in Europe.

In the 1950s he helped to set up a Church of England Board of Social Responsibility and became the first chairman of its Industrial Committee, but in his later years he became anxious about the Church of England's preoccupation with structures, synodical government and liturgical reform, believing that those were unlikely to assist the Christian mission in a secular society. On the eve of his retirement he complained, 'The Church of England is not yet organized to be the church militant on English earth'.

Gordon Hewitt (ed.), *Strategist for the Spirit,* Becket Publications 1985.

# George MacLeod
## (1895–1991)

George Fielden MacLeod was a prophetic minister of the Church of Scotland who achieved international fame and exercised considerable influence through his foundation of the Iona Community, which is concerned to demonstrate the inseparability of the spiritual and the material and the relationship between faith and political and social action. He came from an aristocratic background, but the experience of working in Glasgow's slums in the 1930s changed the course of his life and ministry.

The Iona Community was formed to enable him to share his beliefs with others and to express them within a community that would be deeply involved in the service of the poor and in tackling the causes of poverty. The re-building of the ancient abbey on the island of Iona, developed from MacLeod's original vision, caught the imagination of thousands of young people in the 1950s and 1960s, and when he resigned from the leadership of the community in 1967 it had 143 full members, many more associates, and 625 youth associates – all committed to a disciplined devotional life and Christian service. Since then the membership has been enlarged by the admission of ministers and laity of other churches, and members and associates are to be found in twenty-seven countries.

MacLeod was born into an old Scottish clerical family, though his father was a Unionist Member of Parliament and eventually a Baronet. The young George was sent to Winchester College and went on to Oriel College, Oxford, to study law, but on the outbreak of war in 1914 he enlisted in the Argyll and Sutherland Highlanders and won a Military Cross and the Croix de Guerre. Afterwards he studied for the Church of Scotland ministry at Edinburgh University and the Union Theological Seminary, New York, where he met Tubby Clayton, the founder of Toc H. As a result of this encounter he became chaplain of Toc H in Glasgow before appointment in 1926 as associate minister of St Cuthbert's Church, Glasgow. This large and fashionable parish was one of the Church of Scotland's great preaching stations and MacLeod was immensely popular. In 1929 he was invited to become Minister of Govan Old Church, in the heart of Glasgow's dockland slums, but declined, recommending a friend for the post. Six months later the friend died of TB, and when the offer was renewed MacLeod accepted.

He was deeply affected by the level of unemployment and poverty he found in the parish, and disturbed that the church had no concern about the causes of these linked problems. Some kind of socialism was, he believed, the answer, and this required Christians to be involved in trade unions and political parties. But in 1933 he had a psychological breakdown, and while recovering from this in Jerusalem had the vision of a Christian community that would witness amid the poverty and squalor of Glasgow's worst slums. He was joined by a few young ministers and raised the money needed for the conversion of the parish institute into a community base. About this time he became a pacifist and played a leading part in the work of the Peace Pledge Union. Later he was one of the founders of the Campaign for Nuclear Disarmament.

In 1935 he conceived the idea of rebuilding the ancient abbey on the island of Iona in order that the community might have a second base in a place for ever associated with Celtic spirituality. He saw the two locations as providing the right environment for the training of ministers for special work in the toughest parishes. A large amount of money was raised for the rebuilding project, and in 1938 MacLeod resigned from his post at Govan in order to lead the community's work on Iona. The pace of rebuilding slowed during the war years, but study weeks and retreats were held and some preliminary training of future ministers undertaken. Inspired by MacLeod's book *We Shall Rebuild* (1944), the life of the community and the rebuilding advanced with great vigour after 1945. He had inherited his father's baronetcy in 1944 but never used the title, and during the 1950s became much involved in politics, joining the Co-op Party and playing a prominent part in the Christian Socialist Movement.

In 1957 he was elected, in the face of some opposition, as Moderator of the General Assembly of the Church of Scotland and in 1967 was made a Life Peer. At this point he resigned from the leadership of the Iona Community, which was timely, since he was frequently in conflict with a new generation of its members who wished to adopt new policies and became resentful of his somewhat autocratic style. Towards the end of his life he joined the Green Party and lost no opportunity to speak out in Parliament for justice and peace.

Ronald Ferguson, *George MacLeod: Founder of the Iona Community*, Collins 1990.

# Florence Tim Oi Li

## (1907–1992)

Florence Tim Oi Li was the first woman to be ordained to the priesthood in the Anglican Communion. Her ordination, which took place in the Portuguese colony of Macao in 1943 under the exigencies of war, caused considerable controversy, and the action of the Bishop of Hong Kong was condemned by the Archbishop of Canterbury and by the 1948 Lambeth Conference. But she was not herself a 'natural rebel', and the deep faith and courage she displayed in accepting her vocation also enabled her to witness heroically under Chinese Communist persecution.

She was born in Hong Kong, where her father was a schoolmaster. Although he was a Christian he had two wives; Florence (she adopted this name when she was a teenager in honour of Florence Nightingale) was a child of the second. Her education at her father's school was cut short when she was fourteen, as she was required to care for the rest of the large family. Seven years were to pass before she was able to resume her studies at another school and train as a teacher in the evenings, and it was not until she was twenty-seven that she became qualified to teach in a fishing village on an island near Hong Kong.

By this time she was a member of St Paul's Church in Hong Kong, and after a few years in teaching she went to the Union Theological College in Canton for training as a full-time lay worker in the church. In spite of frequent bombing of the college by the Japanese during her time there, she secured an honours degree and in 1938 joined the staff of All Saints' Church, Kowloon. Two years of work, mainly among refugees from China, was followed by a move to Macao where, after six months she was ordained deacon.

Following the Japanese occupation of Hong Kong in 1941, Macao was flooded with refugees travelling to what they mistakenly believed to be free China. Tim Oi Li was now leading the church's mission single-handed and in the absence of a priest was permitted to take baptisms, marriages and funerals. Anglican rules did not permit her to celebrate Holy Communion as a deacon, but when wartime conditions made it impossible for a priest to visit the colony she was given exceptional permission to do so in order that her church be not deprived of the sacrament. After two years, however, Bishop R. O. Hall of Hong Kong felt uneasy about this decision and, although not generally in favour of women priests, decided that it would be better for Tim Oi Li to be ordained priest, rather than continue to preside over the eucharist as a deacon. This solution was rejected by the Chinese House of Bishops and by the Archbishop of Canterbury when the war ended, and she was obliged to resign from the priesthood.

In 1947 she went to Hippo, near the Vietnamese border, where as a deacon she revitalized a weak church and after two years resumed work as a priest. When the church was closed by the new Communist government in 1951 she undertook further theological study in Peking and in 1953 joined the teaching staff of the Union Theological College in Canton. There she taught church history and English, and also the principles of a new 'Three-Self' movement which, it was hoped, would lead to the autonomy of every area of China's life, including the religious. The Communist authorities closed the college in 1957 and between 1958 and 1974 Tim Oi Li was forced to work, first on a chicken farm, then as a manual worker in various factories in Canton. For ten years she and some of her fellow Christians were allowed to meet early in the morning for Bible study and prayer, but after the 1968 Cultural Revolution all outward expressions of religious belief were forbidden in China. She now had to maintain her faith secretly, but relief came in 1979 when religious belief and worship were again permitted, and although she was by now long past retirement age she resumed her ministry in a re-opened Chinese church.

In 1981 she emigrated to Canada and for the next ten years ministered at an Anglican church in Toronto which was shared by English-speaking and Chinese congregations. On the fortieth anniversary of her ordination in 1984 she attended a service of thanksgiving in Westminster Abbey organized by the English Movement for the Ordination of Women. The appearance of this tiny, humble, down-to-earth woman in the Abbey made a considerable impact, and by the time of her death more than 1,000 women had been ordained to the priesthood of the Anglican Church worldwide.

Florence Tim Oi Li and Ted Harrison, *Much Beloved Daughter*, Darton, Longman and Todd 1985.

# Martin Niemöller

## (1892–1984)

Martin Niemöller was a submarine commander in the German navy during the 1914–18 war, then became a Lutheran pastor and, having for a brief period welcomed the advent of National Socialism, became one of its strongest opponents. During the post-1939–45 years he held high office in the German Evangelical Church and the World Council of Churches and became a controversial figure through his criticism of Allied treatment of defeated Germany, his embracing of pacifism, and his friendships with Russian church leaders.

Niemöller, the son of a Lutheran pastor, was born in Lippstadt in Westphalia. He was educated locally until he was eighteen, then he enlisted as an officer-cadet in the navy. He served in submarines throughout the war and was awarded the Iron Cross First Class for sinking Allied ships. When the war ended he displayed his intense patriotic spirit by refusing an order to tow two submarines to England, where they were to be surrendered under the terms of the armistice. This led to his resignation from the navy. He then decided to follow in his father's footsteps and went to study theology at the University of Münster. After serving as a trainee pastor in a Münster parish for a year in 1924 he was appointed Manager of the Westphalia Inner Mission – an organization concerned with youth and welfare work, and with the church's mission to non-believers. During his seven years in this post he voted for Hitler's National Socialist Party and was elected to his city council as leader of a group concerned with Protestant rights in a largely Catholic community.

In 1931 he was appointed one of the three pastors serving the large parish of Dahlem in one of Berlin's fashionable suburbs. Before long he had become senior pastor and told the congregation in 1933 of his great hopes of the Nazi movement. It seemed to have appealed to his patriotism, and he confessed later that he had been taken in by Hitler's use of religious language. Soon, however, he became anxious about the rise of the German Christian movement and joined a Young Reformation Movement which had been formed to uphold the priority of the Gospel over the claims of the State. He was among those who in 1933 opposed the Nazi demand that pastors of Jewish descent should be dismissed from office and in September of that year he circularized 2,000 pastors who were on the Young Reformation Movement's mailing list, inviting them to join a Pastors' Emergency League to deal with the growing church–state crisis. By the end of the month 2,300 pastors had joined. The leaders of the League met in Niemöller's home in October 1933 to set up the necessary organization, but in November he and two of the others were dismissed by the church authorities.

In January Niemöller and some other church leaders met Hitler in the hope of obtaining a relaxation of the pressure on dissenting Christians, but this got nowhere. During that year the Young Reformation Movement became known as the Confessing Church, which soon had 800,000 members, and Niemöller was among those who signed the historic Barmen Declaration defining the theological basis of the new body and, with Karl Barth, was one of its six-member Council. In March 1935 he was arrested and, following his release two days later, resumed preaching against the Nazis and naming other pastors who had been arrested. In December the Confessing Church was declared illegal and Niemöller was forbidden to speak in public.

By 1937 he was the leader of the opposition to the state's domination of the church, his passport was confiscated and he was again arrested for reading the names of prisoners from the pulpit, the parish council having refused to accept his dismissal. The trial took place secretly in February 1938 and the judge said that he had acted honourably but illegally. He was therefore fined and sentenced to seven months in prison, but since he had already served eight months he was immediately released. On hearing this Hitler was so angry that he ordered Niemöller to be sent to a concentration camp as his 'personal prisoner'. For the first four years at Sachsenhausen camp he was kept in solitary confinement, and later he was transferred to Dachau.

Soon after his release in 1945 he was one of the twelve Protestant leaders who signed a declaration of guilt at Stuttgart, and thereafter was rarely out of the public eye in Germany and many other parts of the world. He became a pacifist in 1948 and thereafter campaigned ceaselessly against war and its causes. On his ninetieth birthday he said, 'I began my political responsibility as an ultra-conservative. I wanted the Kaiser to come back; and now I am a revolutionary.'

James Bentley, *Martin Niemoeller,* Hodder and Stoughton 1984.

# Dietrich Bonhoeffer
## (1906–1945)

Dietrich Bonhoeffer was a German theologian whose work, carried out largely during the Nazi era, took him from a position of strict Lutheran orthodoxy to a radical questioning of traditional expressions of the Christian faith which had considerable influence, partly because of the manner of his death but also, and perhaps chiefly, because his published thought coincided with the unspoken thoughts of many other mid-century Christians.

As Nazi oppression grew during the 1930s his main work, published as *The Cost of Discipleship* (1937) and *Life Together* (1938), was concerned to emphasize the autonomy of the community of faith under God and its independence of the state. A book on *Ethics* in which he discussed some of the moral problems facing Christians in the modern world was published posthumously in 1949, and his *Letters and Papers from Prison* appeared in Germany in 1951 (English translation 1953).

It was the fragmentary reflections of these letters and papers that made the greatest impact worldwide. He said that the world in which Christians were called to immerse themselves had 'come of age – we are proceeding to a time of no religion at all; men as they are now simply cannot be religious any more'. He argued that the gospel is for human beings in their strengths as well as in their weaknesses. God – 'the beyond in the midst' – is involved in every part of human life, and the question therefore arises: 'How do we speak of God in a secular age?'. A related question is: 'Who is Christ for us today?' Bonhoeffer did not live long enough to find answers to these questions, and it is far from certain that he would have agreed with all the answers suggested by the radical theologians who came after him. But for many he encouraged a much more open and personal interpretation of the gospel.

Bonhoeffer was born in Breslau in 1906, but was brought up in Berlin, where his father was Professor of Psychiatry at the university. Although his father had no religious beliefs and his mother was a lapsed Moravian, he studied for the ordained ministry of the Lutheran Church. He proved to be a brilliant scholar and after two years as assistant pastor of a German-speaking congregation in Barcelona returned to Berlin in 1930 to teach at the university. Three days before Hitler became Chancellor of Germany in 1933, Bonhoeffer expressed his concern about the Nazi movement in a broadcast and soon afterwards spoke out against the movement's treatment of the Jews. He also became a leader of the so-called Confessing Church – established in opposition to those elements in the Lutheran Church that co-operated with Hitler.

At the end of 1933 he was sent to England to be the pastor of two German-speaking congregations in South London. After eighteen months he was recalled to set up a college for the training of pastors for the Confessing Church at Finkelwalde. This was closed by the Nazis in 1937. Bonhoeffer then took up a teaching post in the USA, but on the eve of war in 1939 he returned to Germany, having told his American friends: 'I will have no right to participate in the reconstruction of Christian life in Germany after the war if I do not share in this time with my people.' This sharing took him into the resistance movement against Hitler, but he also managed to become an honorary member of Army Intelligence which enabled him to travel widely on political and espionage missions.

These missions were used to maintain contact with church leaders in German-occupied territories and, most notably, in 1942 an attempted political negotiation in Stockholm with Bishop George Bell of Chichester who was a close friend. In May of the following year, however, he was arrested and spent the next eighteen months in a military prison in Berlin. It was there that his most original reflections took place and were conveyed to his friends in letters and smuggled papers. His concern for the reinterpretation of the gospel to meet the needs of the modern world inevitably led to a critique of the contemporary church, which, he said, must become 'the church for others' after the example of its servant Lord. This required it to give away its property to those in need; the clergy should live off the freewill offerings of their congregations or possibly engage in secular occupations; training for the ordained ministry must be reformed and the creeds revised.

Following a failed attempt on Hitler's life in 1944 Bonhoeffer's freedom was greatly restricted, and on 9 April 1945 he was hanged at Flossenburg, shortly before the American army occupied that part of Germany. His final words were: 'This is the end; for me the beginning of life'.

Eberhard Bethge, *Dietrich Bonhoeffer*, Collins 1970.

# Roger Schutz
## (1915–  )

Roger Schutz founded an ecumenical community at Taizé in Eastern France in 1949 which became internationally famous as a contemporary form of monasticism with a particular concern for reconciliation and a special attraction for young adults. It now has about eighty professed members in twenty countries in every continent, though Taizé remains the chief centre of its life, to which many thousands of visitors are drawn every year. Away from Taizé the brothers live in small communities, or fraternities, some of which are located in the poorest areas of Latin America, Asia and Africa. At the end of every year a European Meeting is held for several days in one of Europe's large cities and these attract huge numbers – as many as 42,000 at Wroclaw, in Poland, in 1989. A feature of the community's life is a balance between informal spontaneity and ordered discipline, displayed powerfully in its worship. Taizé songs and chants are widely used in all Christian traditions and in many cultures.

Schutz was born in a village in the high Swiss Jura, where his father was the Reformed Church pastor. As a child he heard a good deal about the seventeenth-century community life of the nuns of the severe Jansenist movement and in 1936 he went to study theology at Lausanne. Towards the end of his time there, to his great surprise he was elected President of the Student Christian Federation, and initiated a course of teaching on prayer. He also had the vision of a house with a small community living the essentials of the gospel. On completion of his degree he went to Vichy-ruled wartime France to search for a house, and discovered one in Taizé – at that time a half-ruined hilltop village near Cluny and a few miles south of the frontier of German-occupied France. He moved in and lived alone, receiving refugees from the North, including some Jews, and in 1941 produced a booklet on his community ideas. But in November 1942, while he was on a visit to Switzerland, the Gestapo occupied the house and the Germans closed the French-Swiss border. He was therefore unable to return to Taizé, so he found a flat in Geneva where he was joined by Max Thurian, who later became the theologian of the community, and two other students.

The four men lived a common life, and when France was liberated in 1944, Schutz returned to Taizé with his friends and they adopted a simple rule of life. Four years later they were joined by their first recruit, followed by two others – one of whom became the village doctor – and on Easter Day 1949 the seven brothers entered into a life commitment to Christ in community. By this time they had been given the use of the village Catholic church which was used only infrequently for Mass. They restored its interior and gathered for common prayer three times a day and for holy communion on Sundays. In 1951 the number of brothers rose to twelve, and two of them went to live and work in a coal-mining area north of Taizé. This was the beginning of the 'fraternities' aspect of the community's life. Meanwhile Schutz was spending the winter of 1952-53 in retreat, writing the Rule of Taizé – designed to create what he called 'a parable of community', with emphasis on the reconciliation of Christians as a means to furthering the reconciliation of the world's conflicting elements.

The 1960s saw major developments in the community's life. During the early part of the decade two Anglicans joined, and in 1969 a young Belgian doctor became the first Roman Catholic member. 1962 saw the founding of a milk co-operative with a number of farmers in the region and the building of the Church of the Reconciliation – designed in concrete by two of the brothers and including a crypt for Catholic masses. Pope John XXIII invited Schutz and Thurian to attend the Second Vatican Council as official observers, and during their time in Rome they made contacts with Latin American bishops. This led to Schutz attending important assemblies of bishops in Colombia (1968) and Mexico (1979).

As the community developed, some opposition came from the Reformed Church in France on the grounds that it was moving too quickly and away from the classical Reformed tradition. But this was not sustained for long, as the reputation of Taizé spread worldwide and attracted to the Burgundian village three successive Archbishops of Canterbury, Mother Teresa of Calcutta, who made two visits, and in 1986 Pope John Paul II. The Pope had made two previous visits when he was Archbishop of Cracow and on this occasion he opened his address to the brothers with a quotation from Pope John XXIII, who once greeted Roger Schutz: 'Ah, Taizé, that little springtime.'

J. L. Gonzalez Balado, *The Story of Taizé*, Mowbray 1981.

# Stafford Cripps

## (1889–1952)

Richard Stafford Cripps, one of the foremost Christian socialists of the century and of markedly left-wing views in the 1930s, held high office in Winston Churchill's wartime coalition government and was Chancellor of the Exchequer in the first post-war Labour government. He is remembered chiefly as a politician with a brilliant mind and high principles who, during a period of economic crisis, called for austerity from all sections of the nation's life and preached a doctrine of fair shares. Although this was at first unpopular with the electorate, he eventually won widespread support. Unfortunately the benefits of this were lost when, for other reasons, the pound had to be devalued and ill-health forced his resignation from the Chancellorship and from Parliament. He died in a Swiss sanatorium.

Cripps belonged to the Anglo-Catholic wing of the Church of England, was a regular communicant and believed that socialism was the natural expression of Christian social doctrine. Among those he convinced of the truth of this were Mervyn Stockwood, who was to become a notable Bishop of Southwark, and John Collins, who became a Canon of St Paul's and, with the encouragement of Cripps, founded Christian Action.

Cripps was born in London, where his father, who later became Lord Parmoor, was a prominent Conservative politician. He went to Winchester College as a scholar and his chemistry papers for a scholarship to New College, Oxford, were so brilliant that he was advised to go instead to Sir William Ramsey's laboratory at University College, London. At the age of twenty-two he was the part-author of a paper read to the Royal Society. On the outbreak of war in 1914 he enlisted as a lorry driver with the Red Cross, but was severely injured in France and returned to England to become assistant superintendent of what became the most efficient munitions factory in the country.

When the war ended he decided to study law and also became Treasurer of the World Alliance, which was concerned to promote international friendship through the churches. He represented Oxford in the newly created Church Assembly and in 1927 became the youngest KC in the country. This led to his earning very large fees in compensation and patent cases, and, after joining the Labour Party, he was made Solicitor General in the second Labour government in 1930, and knighted. In the following year he became MP for Bristol East.

He declined to serve in Ramsey MacDonald's 'National' government formed in 1931 and spent the rest of the 1930s involved in various left-wing organizations, including the Socialist League. This was formed as a ginger group in the Labour Party, and its lasting achievement was the *Tribune* newspaper. Concerned by the increasing Nazi threat, Cripps attempted in 1938 to establish a Popular Front to oust the Chamberlain government and reverse the policy of appeasement. This failed and led to his expulsion from the Labour Party, but the fact that he was now an Independent MP enabled Churchill to make good use of him during the war.

From 1940 to 1942 he was British Ambassador in Moscow and involved in the creation of an alliance following Hitler's invasion of Russia in 1941. He also reported that Stalin had betrayed socialism and established a tyranny every bit as bad as Hitler's regime. On his return to London he was made Lord Privy Seal and Leader of the House of Commons, with a seat in the War Cabinet, and he went to India with the offer of Dominion status for a united India. However, his negotiatons with Gandhi and Jinnah, the Hindu and Muslim leaders, were unsuccessful – largely, he said, because of Gandhi's intransigence.

Later that year, when doubts were being expressed in some quarters about the quality of Churchill's leadership, there was a minor plot to replace him with Cripps, but this came to nothing and Churchill removed him from the War Cabinet by making him Minister of Aircraft Production – a post he held until the end of the war. He also collaborated with the Archbishop of Canterbury, William Temple, in a campaign designed to arouse Christian concern for social and political matters.

When Labour returned to power in 1945 he was re-admitted to the Party and became President of the Board of Trade. By 1947, however, he was again involved in a plot – this time that he should replace Attlee as Prime Minister. Attlee headed this off by making him Minister of Economic Affairs, and a few weeks later he succeeded Hugh Dalton, who had been driven to resignation by indiscretion over the Budget, as Chancellor of the Exchequer. He soon became known as the 'Iron Chancellor' – a reflection of his temperament as well as of his policies.

Christopher Bryant, *Stafford Cripps*, Hodder 1997.

# Olivier Messiaen

## (1908–1992)

Olivier Eugène Prosper Charles Messiaen was one of the most idiosyncratic and influential composers of the century. His music is unmistakable for its rhythmic irregularity and intense colour, but, although some of it is abstract and atonal, his commitment to the supremacy of melody makes it accessible to those who cannot cope with avant-garde composers such as Karlheinz Stockhausen, Iannis Xenakis and Pierre Boulez – all of whom were his pupils. Most of Messiaen's compositions were religious and inspired by a deep Catholic faith, a love of nature and strong experience of human love. He was organist of Trinity Church in Paris for over forty years, this coinciding more or less with his time as a professor at the Paris Conservatoire, and he was essentially a mystic for whom music was the chief expression of his vision of God.

Messiaen, whose father was a poet, was born in Avignon, but brought up in Grenoble and Nantes. Largely self-taught, his musical gifts were noticed early, and he was only eleven when he went to the Paris Conservatoire. There he remained for the next eleven years. Greek and folk music and plainchant were his chief interests at that stage, and he also studied the French birds – notating their song and classifying them by regions. All of which were to become a powerful influence on his own compositions.

Two pieces, *Le Banquet eucharistique* (orchestra) and *Le Banquet céleste* (organ), written in 1928, were of a meditative character, but his first published work, *Eight Preludes for Piano* (1929), made use of a new and distinctive modal system which indicated a highly original musical mind. Two orchestral items, *Hymne au Saint Sacrement* (1932) and *L'Ascension* (1933), were followed by an organ cycle, *La nativité du Seigneur* (1935), which aroused considerable interest and is now recognized as one of the great organ pieces of the twentieth century.

In 1936 he began to teach at the École Normale de Musique and the Schola Cantorum and also formed La Jeune France – a small group of composers who were exploring new areas of music and met for mutual support and the promotion of their ideas. Messiaen published another organ cycle, *Le Corps glorieux,* in 1939, but following the German occupation of Paris in 1940 he was sent to a prison camp in Silesia. There he relieved hunger and the intense cold by composing and performing. *Quatuor pour le fin du temps* was composed for a broken piano, cello, violin and clarinet and he prefaced the score with a text from the Revelation of St John (10. 6): 'There shall be time no longer'.

He was released in 1942, and on his return to Paris became Professor of Harmony at the Conservatoire, where he remained until 1978. During the final years of the war he attracted a group of highly talented young composers who were to become leaders of the avant garde, and also a brilliant pianist, Yvonne Loriod, who became his second wife and exercised a great influence on him. He composed a number of pieces for her, including a two-and-a-half-hour work *Vingt regards sur l'enfant Jésus* (1944), which brought international acclaim.

In 1944 he also composed *3 Petites Liturgies de la présence divine*, with a women's chorus, and then embarked on a novel use of rhythm and irregular metres, which he explained in his two-volume *Technique de mon language musical* (1947). In his *Turangalîla Symphonie* (1948) he used Indian themes and rhythms and required the orchestra to include an Ondes Martenot – a newly created electrophonic instrument which made a swooping sound. During the 1950s, however, much of his work was based on adaptations of the birdsong which he had studied so assiduously during the early part of his life. This was not an original concept, since other composers had done the same with varying degrees of success, but Messiaen's work was enhanced by the introduction of the natural sound, most effectively in *Catalogue d'oiseaux* for piano (1956–58). He had in fact a considerable affinity with the birds and later wrote the libretto as well as the music for a four-hour opera *St François d'Assise* (1983).

After a decade of birdsong influence he returned to religious subjects which brought together all the aspects of his work, not least the passionate and dramatic elements. A small-scale piano concerto *Couleurs de la cité céleste* (1963) was followed by the large-scale *Et exspecto resurrectionem mortuorum* (1964), and in 1969 by a choral-orchestral work *La Transfiguration* and, for the organ, *Méditations sur le mystère de la Sainte Trinité*. Not long before his death he composed *Éclairs sur L'Au-Delà* (1991) – Illumination of the Beyond, vision of the divine spirit in all creation, and this summed up the whole of his life and work.

# Henri Perrin

## (1914–1954)

Henri Perrin was a French priest who left the Jesuit Order in order to become a priest-worker. He spent three years as a manual worker on the Isère-Arc Dam and Tunnel – a major construction project in South East France where he became secretary of a strike committee which led to successful industrial action on two occasions – one of forty-two days, the other of twenty-one days. The closure of the site on the completion of the project in 1954 came just a month after the French bishops, acting on instructions from Rome, formally ended the priest-worker movement, which by this time had seventy-eight members.

He was born in a village in the Vosges mountains, and at the age of twelve entered a junior seminary where he became involved in the Young Christian Workers movement. His training for the priesthood was, however, interrupted by two years' military service and he was ordained in 1938. The outbreak of war in 1939 took him back into the army, where he served with an Algerian regiment for eight months before being captured by the Germans at Sedan. On his release in October 1940 he entered the Jesuit novitiate and spent 1941–42 studying at Lyons before volunteering to join French workers who were being deported to work in German factories. A number of priests exercised a clandestine ministry in this way, and Perrin was discovered, arrested and imprisoned for a time in Leipzig.

After his release from prison early in the summer of 1944, Perrin continued his studies. In 1947, with the backing of the Archbishop of Paris, he became a priest-worker, joining two other priests living in an old house on waste land behind a Paris factory. During the next twelve months he had several jobs, which increased his concern about working conditions and wages in the factories, and about the alienation of the workers from any Christian belief or practice. In 1950–51 Perrin withdrew from this work in order to complete the final stage of his Jesuit formation, at the end of which it was decided that he should leave the Order. He regarded his priest-worker vocation as a life-commitment, whereas his Jesuit superiors saw it as only a temporary arrangement.

He now moved south and early in 1952 began work at the Isère-Arc project. Over 3,000 men – Spanish, Italian and North African, as well as French – were involved in this and many worked waist-deep in water and sometimes in intense heat. Pay was low and the men lived in dormitory huts on the site. Perrin shared this life, working as a mechanic for ten to twelve hours a day, including Sundays. Soon after Perrin's arrival on the site the workers staged a strike which lasted for six weeks and aroused national interest. He was elected to the strike committee, becoming its secretary, and was involved in the negotiations with a stubborn management. In the end the workers won their main demands over pay and conditions and Perrin became well-known and respected by the workers and managers. Whenever a worker was killed in an accident – thirteen were during the project's life – he conducted the funeral; he got union representatives and collectors appointed, ensured that the union was better organized, and became a member of a Joint Production Committee. However, he remained the only Christian in the section of 700 workers where he was employed.

In June 1953 Perrin was among a small group who were sacked, and it was generally believed that he was being victimized by the management. The rest of the workers contributed 40,000 francs to keep him going, and he continued as a permanent workers' representative during another strike over dismissals and employment rights. After twenty-one days of bitter negotiations, he and the other dismissed workers were reinstated, but in August of that year there was a massive national strike which paralysed much of French life. This ended when the Christian and Socialist trade unions negotiated an agreement with the managers, but the terms greatly upset the priest-workers and the Communist unions.

On 23 September the Papal Nuncio handed to the French Bishops and Superiors of religious orders instructions from Rome which ended the priest-worker experiment and allowed only for parish clergy to spend a limited amount of time in their local factories. Fifty of the French priests decided to continue their ministries and risk excommunication, but this was not open to Perrin, as his work-site closed. During the leave that followed he considered the possibility of applying for laicization in order to be able to return to a Christian witness among the workers. However, his life was cut short by a motor-cycle accident, the cause of which remains a mystery.

Henri Perrin, *Priest and Worker: Autobiography*, Macmillan 1964.

# Paul Tillich

## (1886–1965)

Paul Johannes Oskar Tillich was one of the most original and influential philosophers and theologians of the century. He combined theology, philosophy, history and literature remarkably in a lifelong attempt to relate the Christian faith to the culture of the modern world, seeing himself as a theologian of the boundaries and expounding what he called 'the method of correlation' as a means of matching divine revelation and human need. And he believed that myths and symbols provided the best language for interpreting and expressing Christianity.

This makes much of his writing, as he himself readily conceded, far from easy to understand; his monumental *Systematic Theology,* published in three volumes (1951–64), is for specialists. But even for those who cannot follow his arguments he offers flashes of profound illumination and has sometimes been likened to a surrealist painter. His theology is most accessible in three volumes of sermons widely circulated in paperback – *The Shaking of the Foundations* (1948), *The New Being* (1955) and *The Eternal Now* (1963). He also wrote essays for a wide variety of periodicals, including some devoted to art, dance, architecture and psychotherapy.

Tillich's understanding of God was expressed in the phrase 'The ground of all being', and he put it like this in one of his sermons:

The name of the infinite and inexhaustible depth and ground of all being is *God*. That depth is what the word *God* means. And if that word has not much meaning for you, translate it, and speak of the depths of your life, of the source of your being, of your ultimate concern, of what you take seriously without any reservation. Perhaps, in order to do so, you must forget everything traditional that you have learned about God, perhaps even that word itself. For if you know that God means depth, you know much about him. You cannot then call yourself an atheist or unbeliever . . . He who knows about depth knows about God.

Man, according to Tillich, is estranged from the ground of his being, and the way to his reunion with God is demonstrated by Jesus Christ, the 'New Being', who heals the estrangement and creates a spiritual community which exercises a prophetic witness in society.

Tillich, the son of a Lutheran pastor, was born in Starzeddel, in the province of Brandenburg, now in Poland. He studied at the universities of Berlin, Tübingen, Halle and Breslau. After ordination in 1912 he served in a Berlin parish before enlisting as an army chaplain on the outbreak of war in 1914. His experience of suffering and death at the front line (he was awarded the Iron Cross) was a major turning point in his life and greatly influenced his future work as a philosopher and theologian. During the war his wife, whom he had married in 1914, left him for an affair with a friend, and on leaving the army he had a somewhat Bohemian life-style until he remarried in 1924 and was appointed Professor of Theology at Marburg. After a year, however, he moved to Dresden and in 1929 became Professor of Theology at Frankfurt. About this time he became involved in the Religious Socialist movement in Germany, and in *The Socialist Decision* (1932) he emphasized what he believed to be a natural connection between Protestantism and socialism, at the same time recognizing the need for a Christian critique of socialism.

Before this could be much developed, however, the rise to power of National Socialism demanded greater attention, and as Dean at Frankfurt Tillich defended left-wing and Jewish students and demanded the expulsion of Nazi students who were creating violence in the campus. For this and open criticism of Hitler's government he was deprived of his professorial chair. This led to an invitation from Reinhold Niebuhr to join the teaching staff of the Union Theological Seminary in New York, where he became Professor of Philosophical Theology in 1932. He joined in Niebuhr's assault on the liberal theology then in vogue in America, though his own approach to the Bible, which was much influenced by the work of Rudolf Bultmann, was far more radical than that of Niebuhr.

Tillich became an American citizen in 1940, and his period of greatest influence was after the end of the 1939–45 war. In 1955 he became a Professor at Harvard Divinity School, where he was allowed to lecture on any subject he chose. At the age of seventy-six he became 'Distinguished Theologian in Residence' at Chicago University Divinity School and in his final lecture there shortly before his death he spoke of the presence of the Holy in all religions. He added: 'I would say, if religious experience is without the sacramental and the mystical element, it becomes moralistic and finally secular.'

# Kathleen Bliss

## (1908–1989)

Kathleen Mary Bliss was a Christian educationalist who had a special commitment to the church's mission on the frontier with the secular world and also to the ecumenical movement. She was involved in pioneering work in religious broadcasting during the 1950s and for many years was deeply involved in the work of the World Council of Churches. A book *The Service and Status of Women in the Church* (1951) was an early plea for the wider recognition of the part women might play in the ecclesiastical sphere. She was herself eminently equipped for high office in the church, but prejudice stood in her way.

The daughter of a Congregationalist deacon, Bliss took Firsts in history and theology at Girton College, Cambridge, where she was greatly influenced by the Student Christian Movement. After a brief teaching career she married Rupert Bliss, who later became an Anglican priest, and together they spent six years in India engaged in educational work. Returning to England in 1939 she became a regional director of Religion and Life Weeks – a wartime enterprise in which the main British churches came together to demonstrate to the public at large the way in which religion related to the world's major political and social issues. She also joined the staff of the *Christian Newsletter* – a modest publication which nonetheless enjoyed a wide circulation and had considerable influence under the editorship of J. H. Oldham.

Bliss succeeded to the editorship in 1945 and for the next four years continued the policy of making, and securing from others, acute assessments of the contemporary religious and social scenes, but amid all the multifarious developments of the postwar era the market for such a publication diminished. Aberdeen University recognized the importance of her work with an honorary DD in 1949. In 1951 she joined the staff of the BBC's religious broadcasting department in order to assist in thinking through the implications of a policy decision made by the Governors in 1947 about the content of religious broadcasting and the expression of a variety of religious and philosophical opinions. It turned out to be the final phase of radio's dominant position in broadcasting, for television was about to take over.

Bliss's 'frontier' outlook made her ideally suited to the task, though her intellectual approach proved to be something of a disadvantage when dealing with programme makers. She saw clearly that in an increasingly pluralistic and secularized society a public broadcasting authority could not continue to afford permanent protection for overtly Christian programmes. With equal clarity she recognized that if religious programmes were to engage the attention of people who were beyond the normal reach of the churches, they must be of a high quality and carry no hint of propaganda. After widespread consultation with most of the leading intellectuals in the country, she (in collaboration with J. H. Oldham, who remained a close colleague) devised an *Encounter of Belief* series of programmes in which space was allocated to proponents of mainly academic Humanism, Behaviourism, Marxism and Christianity. Some of the contributors let her down at the last moment, thus forcing the cancellation of programmes, and the series was not considered a success. Church leaders displayed little interest in the project. But it opened the way to a more liberal approach to religious broadcasting which flourished for a time until intense competition between radio and television and different broadcasting authorities led to the serious scaling-down of all forms of thoughtful programming.

Meanwhile Bliss had become an Anglican and been appointed General Secretary of the Church of England's Board of Occupation – a post which she occupied from 1958 to 1966. A major concern at this time was the church's ministry in the non-Oxbridge universities, the number of which was growing rapidly. The establishing of Anglican chaplaincies, served by a priest, was seen as the answer and under Bliss's energetic leadership many of these came into being. This guaranteed a Christian presence in the universities, but one unforeseen, perhaps inevitable, consequence of the development was the rapid decline of the lay-led and ecumenical Student Christian Movement.

In 1967 Bliss became a Lecturer in Religious Studies at Sussex University, where her open and widely cultured approach to religion was greatly appreciated, and in 1969 she contributed a volume *The Future of Religion* to the otherwise secular New Thinkers' Library. From 1967 to 1970 she was a member of the government appointed Public Schools Commission. Her life-long ecumenical commitment took her to membership of the Central and Executive Committees of the World Council of Churches, then at the peak of its influence, and to the chairmanship of the board of the Ecumenical Institute at Bossey, near Geneva. Her long and happy marriage to Rupert Bliss, who held several educational and rural parish appointments, produced three daughters.

# Thomas Merton
## (1915–1968)

Thomas Merton was a Trappist monk who became world-famous in the 1950s through his books on Christian spirituality, and equally famous in the 1960s through his commitment to radical social and political action. His witness was particularly important for its emphasis on the unity of prayer and action and owed much to the quality of his writing and even more to his dramatic personal change from a largely traditional understanding of Catholic faith to a new understanding of the demands made on faith by the modern world. He said that he had undergone two conversions – the first to the transcendent, awesome God, with whom communion may be enjoyed through worship and contemplation, the second to the immanent, approachable God, who is present in his world and its people.

Merton was born in a small town in the French Pyrenees. His father was a New Zealand artist and his mother, who died when he was only six, was American. His father also died a year after he entered Oakham School in England in 1929, and although he went to Cambridge to study modern languages, he left half-way through the course. At this time he was leading a somewhat dissolute life in the course of which he fathered an unwanted child. This child and its mother were later killed in London's wartime blitz. After Cambridge, Merton became a student at Columbia University, New York, where he continued in his dissolute ways but showed promise as a poet and writer. In 1939, when engaged on a postgraduate thesis on the aesthetic ideas of William Blake and Thomas Aquinas (as interpreted by Jacques Maritain), he attended Mass in Corpus Christi Church, in central New York, and, as a result of his experience of worship and a sermon about the love of God revealed in Jesus Christ, became a Christian and was baptized a Roman Catholic. He completed his thesis, wrote poetry and a novel, then sought to become a Franciscan friar, but was not accepted. In 1941, however, he went to stay at a Trappist monastery in Gethsemani, Kentucky, where he felt immediately at home and returned later for good. He was professed as a monk and ordained priest in 1949.

During his years as a novice monk he abandoned his ambition to be a writer but after a time the Abbot asked him to write a book about himself, showing how Prodigal Son-like he had 'come to the light'. This was published in America in 1948 with the title *The Seven-Storey Mountain* and in Britain in the following year as *Elected Silence*. It was an immediate publishing success and eventually 600,000 copies of the hardback edition alone were sold, together with translations into many other languages. The contents of the book expressed traditional Catholic piety, and after several other books on the spiritual life Merton became something of a cult figure. This proved to be a cause of stress in a monk who belonged to the most austere of religious communities, and he had periods of depression, exhaustion and general ill-health. In the early 1960s he went for consultation with a doctor in a nearby town, Louisville, and while he was in the centre of its shopping district he was 'suddenly overwhelmed with the realization that I loved all those people, that they were mine and I theirs, that we could not be alien to one another even though we were total strangers. It was like waking from a dream of separateness, of spurious self-isolation in a special world . . . Not that I question the reality of my vocation, or of my monastic life: but the conception of 'separation from the world' that we have in the monastery too easily presents itself as a complete illusion: the illusion that by making vows we become a different species of being'.

Thereafter, and within the constraints of his monastic life, Merton threw himself into campaigns for nuclear pacificism, the ending of the Vietnam war, and equal treatment of American blacks. He established contact with some of Latin American liberation theologians and developed a great interest in the spirituality of the Eastern religions. In 1968 his Abbot gave him permission to attend a major conference in Bangkok on monastic renewal and, having given a lecture of 'Marxism and Monastic Perspective', he retired to his room where he was later found dead – the victim apparently of a faulty electrical fan. At the requiem back in Kentucky the Abbot said: 'He was a young brother – because he was a man whose eyes and ears were always open, he was always listening to what was coming from the hearts of men and women the world over, and searching for light in that deeper intimacy with God through prayer and contemplation.'

Monica Furlong, *Merton*, Collins 1980.

# John Collins

## (1905–1982)

Lewis John Collins was a Canon of St Paul's Cathedral from 1948 to 1981 and for most of this time was Britain's chief Christian social reformer. He exercised this role through his leadership of Christian Action – an organization which came into being as a result of a meeting he convened in Oxford in December 1946 and which had the support of a number of prominent politicians and other public figures of that time. Such support was by no means universal. In many circles Collins came to be hated and was dismissed as a 'Red'. He was subjected to Special Branch investigation in Britain and banned from South Africa. The leadership of the Church of England regarded him with the deepest suspicion and there was never any possibility of his preferment beyond the canonry of St Paul's to which a Labour Prime Minister, Clement Attlee, had appointed him.

Two different influences converged to create the dynamism that inspired and sustained Collins' witness. After a conventional church-going upbringing in Kent he went to Sidney Sussex College, Cambridge to read mathematics and theology. He was ordained in 1928 but was a curate for only just over a year before embarking on an academic career in Cambridge, London and Oxford. During this time he developed a friendship with Albert Loisy, a French Roman Catholic scholar who had been excommunicated because of his liberal interpretation of the Bible. This caused Collins to question various elements in his own faith as well as his conservative approach to politics and the ordering of society. Service in the wartime Royal Air Force from 1940 to 1945 pressed on him the need for reform of society as well as of the church and his choice of socialist speakers to address educational meetings for RAF personnel and his frequent challenges to authority brought him into serious conflict with his senior officers. Although he resumed his post as Dean of Oriel College, Oxford when the war ended, he decided that prophetic witness in the cause of Christian social action was his true vocation.

Hence the public meeting in Oxford, attended by 3,000 people, and the foundation of Christian Action. Before long Collins was a national figure. He combined great energy and courage, and exploited the media with considerable skill, making good use of his position at St Paul's. A carefully orchestrated campaign, under the leadership of Collins and the Jewish publisher Victor Gollancz, led to the abolition of the death penalty, and he then turned his attention to the organizing of shelter and housing projects for the homeless. Soon, however, he was drawn to the leadership of two much larger enterprises.

After visiting South Africa in 1956 and being appalled by the sight of apartheid in action, he raised £20,000 for the legal defence and family support of 156 opponents of apartheid who had been arrested and imprisoned. Two years later a separate organization, the International Defence and Aid Fund, was set up with Collins as President and Director. Very large sums of money were raised and Defence and Aid became an important instrument of international opposition to apartheid. Collins's leadership was recognized in 1978 by the award of the gold medal of the United Nations' special committee against apartheid.

During the early part of 1958 he was also one of the sponsors of a national Campaign for Nuclear Disarmament, with the philosopher Bertrand Russell as its President and Collins as its Chairman. This attracted strong support, and a feature of its activities was an annual march at Easter to and from the nuclear research establishment at Aldermaston, Berkshire. The numbers taking part ranged from 7,000 to 20,000 and Collins, in a black cassock, and a number of prominent left-wing politicians always led the march. Before long, however, there were disagreements over tactics. A breakaway Committee of 100 was formed in 1960 to organize civil disobedience, and when indiscipline and violence spread to CND, Collins retired from the chairmanship, though his opposition to the making of nuclear weapons never wavered.

For thirty-six years he was a distinguished Canon of St Paul's, holding successively the offices of Chancellor, Precentor and Treasurer. Although his controversial sermons did not attract large congregations, they often received wide publicity through the media, and he invited to the cathedral pulpit many of the leading social reformers from all parts of the world. His colleagues on the Chapter did not, however, find him an easy companion, for he had his own distinctive vision of St Paul's as a national cathedral serving as a centre of culture and Christian faith and witness. It was a great disappointment to him that he was not appointed Dean when W. R. Matthews retired in 1967, but he remained at St Paul's until his seventy-sixth birthday and died after a brief retirement.

Diana Collins, *Partners in Protest,* Gollancz 1992.

# Norman Pittenger

## (1905–1997)

William Norman Pittenger, an Anglican theologian, was on the teaching staff of the General Theological Seminary, New York for thirty years and occupied its chair of Christian Apologetics from 1951 until his retirement in 1966. He was an authoritative and passionate exponent of process theology derived from the philosophies of A. N. Whitehead and Charles Hartshorne, and wrote ninety books in which a variety of subjects were examined from this angle. His influence on successive generations of young American theologians was considerable.

It was, however, for his views on homosexual relations that he became most widely known. Following his retirement from the General Theological Seminary he moved to England and lived at King's College, Cambridge, where he had no teaching role but was a valued member of the college community. At this time homosexual acts, even among consenting adults and in private, were illegal and generally condemned by the churches. In March 1967 Pittenger questioned this position in an article published in the radical fortnightly *New Christian*. He wrote:

> I cannot see that the fact that one loves a person of the same sex, and wishes to act upon that love, is in and of itself sinful; nor can I see that acting upon that desire, when there is the true intention of love with the mutuality, fidelity, respect and tenderness I urge, is in and of itself sinful.

He added that the separation of a loving couple, of whatever sex, was 'pretty close to spiritual homicide... just as it is death-dealing tactics to demand that they shall never in any way give physical expression to their love'.

Even in the liberal atmosphere of the 1960s this was sufficient to create an uproar. No professional theologian had ever gone so far. Pittenger was invited to expand his article to book length, and *A Time for Consent – A Christian Approach to Homosexuality* (1968) ran to several editions and sold over 10,000 copies. The way was now open for the subject to be widely studied and debated, and homosexuals had the assurance that their feelings and actions were not necessarily unacceptable in church circles. A number of the book's readers held a meeting in London and formed a vigorous movement which ensured that the issue was never for long off the church's agenda, though the end of the century found Christians still sharply divided in their response. Pittenger was himself homosexual and enjoyed a long-standing relationship with Carlo, an Italian, who, he wrote, 'has taught me what it means to love and to be loved'.

Pittenger was born in Bogata, New Jersey, and brought up in the traditional Catholic piety of the American Episcopal Church. During his preparation for holy orders, however, he came under the influence of Leonard Hodgson, an Oxford liberal theologian who had become a professor at the General Theological Seminary. This influence, together with that of the process philosophers and theologians, turned him in a new direction, and his own theological skill and teaching gifts led to his appointment to the seminary's teaching staff a year before his ordination.

Ninety books was probably too many, even for a scholar of Pittenger's longevity, and inevitably there was some repetition, but he had the gift for writing short paperbacks in which big theological subjects were explored and expressed in terms accessible to the ordinary reader. His most important book *The Word Incarnate* (1954) was, however, a substantial work of scholarship. Bishop John Robinson, who made considerable use of it in his own *The Human Face of God,* described it as one of the great books in the field of christology. Objecting to the classical statements about the nature of the incarnation, Pittenger wrote:

> Emergent humanity is itself the instrument for expressive Deity; the Word is made flesh in one of our own kind, our Brother, without overriding or denying the humanity which is ours, but rather crowning and completing all that is implicit in humanity from the beginning. The divine intention is 'enmanned' among us.

In another, smaller book *After Death: Life in God* (1980) he suggested that life after death is to be seen not in terms of mere survival but of all that was good in the life of an individual being taken into the eternal Mind, which is God, and used in his continuously creative activity.

During his long retirement Pittenger preached occasionally in King's College Chapel, and was in great demand as a counsellor, but he chose not to celebrate the eucharist and often complained that liturgical revision had attempted to return to ancient practice, rather than make use of newer theological understanding, and that biblical material had been used in a literalist fashion.

# Trevor Huddleston
## (1913–1998)

Ernest Urban Trevor Huddleston was Bishop of Mauritius and Arch-bishop of the Indian Ocean from 1978–83 and before that occupied the bishoprics of Masasi, in what is now Tanzania, and Stepney in East London. But he is best remembered as Father Trevor Huddleston, the monk of the Community of the Resurrection who exercised a remark-able ministry in the black township of Sophiatown, in South Africa, and became one of the most outspoken and courageous critics of apartheid. He was equally critical of those outside South Africa who advocated a gradualist approach to a great evil.

His book *Naught for Your Comfort* (1956) became an international best-seller and opened the eyes of the world to the dehumanizing, unjust effects of the white South African government's institutionalized racism. But, for some reason never satisfactorily explained, he was withdrawn from South Africa shortly before the book's publication in order to look after a handful of novices at his Community's mother house at Mirfield in West Yorkshire. This gave him freedom, however, to undertake speaking, preaching and further writing on apartheid, and when he became Bishop of Masasi in 1960 he and the President of Tanzania, Julius Nyerere, launched an Anti-Apartheid Movement. This had very considerable influence – encouraging opposition to apartheid, working with exiles from South Africa and preparing the most able of them for leadership in their home country when white rule ended.

Later, when he was Bishop of Mauritius and found himself in a situa-tion where Christians were heavily outnumbered by Muslims and Hindus, he came to appreciate the positive elements in non-Christian faiths and strongly advocated multi-faith collaboration, especially in the struggle against racism and poverty in all parts of the world. His support for the ordination of women to the priesthood was no less strong. Yet he did not on first meeting give the impression of being either a rebel or reformer. Quietly spoken and of a gentle disposition, he led the ordered life of a monk, spending many hours every day in prayer and deriving inspiration and strength from the sacramental life of the church.

His father, Captain Sir Ernest Huddleston, was Director of the Royal

Indian Marines and Trevor had a public-school education at Lancing College before reading history at Christ Church, Oxford. Involvement in hop-picking missions during vacations led to interest in the Christian Socialist Movement, especially in the work of Anglo-Catholic priests in slum parishes. Ordination followed, and after a curacy in a working-class parish in Swindon, Wiltshire he went to test his vocation as a member of the Community of the Resurrection. He was professed as a monk in 1941 and two years later was sent to be priest-in-charge of the Community's mission in Sophiatown and Orlando, near Johannesburg.

Thus began his heroic ministry, described in *Naught for Your Comfort*, leading to a lifelong witness against injustice. This included defiance of the Pass Laws, the Bantu Education Act and the Western Areas Removal Scheme. In 1953, when the Secretary-General of the Africa National Congress, Walter Sisula, and the Vice-President, Nelson Mandela, were about to be arrested, Huddleston threw himself in front of the police to prevent their action. Later he secured the release from prison of a prominent leader of the Indian Congress, and these experiences convinced him that he must do everything possible to acquaint the world with the repressive nature of South African society. Among the young people he influenced was Desmond Tutu, the future Archbishop of Cape Town.

Huddleston's eight years as Bishop of Masasi were spent helping both the church and the new nation to respond to the challenge of independence and to work for the eradication of deep poverty. He returned to England as soon as an African bishop was ready to succeed him. He spent the next decade as Suffragan Bishop of Stepney, where he was involved in trying to solve the problems of racism and poverty in London's East End. He was the first Bishop of Stepney to live in the East End, and his home became a place of welcome for exiled African leaders, representatives of local ethnic groups and others concerned with justice and peace issues.

Following his retirement from Mauritius and the Indian Ocean in 1983 he lived for some years in London, working ceaselessly to increase awareness of the deepening tragedy of the South Africa he loved. The ending of apartheid and the election of a multi-racial government under the leadership of Nelson Mandela in 1994 gave him unbounded joy, and in the following year he returned to live in South Africa. But he could not settle, so he came back to England where during his final years of increasing infirmity he lived with his community at Mirfield.

Robin Denniston, *Trevor Huddleston: A Life,* Macmillan 1999.

# Ernest Southcott
## (1914–1976)

Ernest William Southcott was Vicar of St Wilfred's, Halton, Leeds from 1944 to 1961. He was a man of vision and boundless energy, who for nearly two decades exerted a great influence on the life of many English parishes – partly by his writing and lecturing, but also by the example of Halton, which attracted the attention of a new generation of clergy.

Southcott was a striking figure. Standing several inches over six foot, his appearance was gaunt and the combination of jet-black hair, dark skin and hooked nose suggested Red Indian blood, for he was born and educated in British Columbia. Rarely was his body, or his mind, still, but his prophetic message was uncomplicated. Much influenced by the biblical theology and liturgical movements, he believed that 'the church must be the church' and that this required every parish to be a revolutionary community, demonstrating its engagement both with God and with the secular world. His training for holy orders at the College of the Resurrection, Mirfield, where for a time he was a novice monk, endowed him with a deep sacramental sense, and he was among the pioneers of the Parish Communion movement with its slogan 'The Lord's own people at the Lord's own service on the Lord's own day'. As a curate on Tyneside, however, he had become conscious of the wide gulf between the church and the working classes and of the need to link worship and mission.

At Halton the Parish Communion was a colourful, celebratory event with much lay participation, and followed by a breakfast. It was the occasion also for administering baptism. In a small book *Receive this Child* (1951), Southcott argued powerfully for the removal of baptism from the private to the public sphere and for the thorough preparation of the families, thus making the sacrament a focal point of evangelism. Equally important was the parish meeting. The church must meet not only for weekly worship but also, on a weekly basis, to work out the implications of the liturgy for its witness in the world. Southcott adopted this idea from Alan Ecclestone, who was holding weekly parish meetings in inner-city Sheffield.

More original, and the initiative for which Southcott is best remembered, was the house church. If the church is to be the church, and if the eucharist demonstrates and cements the church's identity as the body of Christ, it must meet outside church premises for the eucharist to experience and share with others its divine calling. This would also demonstrate the holiness of the secular. So the Halton parish was divided into six areas under lay leadership. Church members gathered regularly in living-rooms and kitchens for the eucharist and encouraged non-churchgoing neighbours to join them. They also undertook pastoral work in the locality. For a time this concept was controversial, but by the 1970s house churches had become commonplace, and later the name, but not the underlying theology, was adopted by sectarian evangelical groups.

Southcott's parish policy, which also included an intensive ministry to the sick, teaching programmes and support of the local United Nations Association, was carried out in five estates of mainly pre-1939 housing inhabited by the Leeds working classes. It added up to a hectic Christian life. Some of the house churches met at 6. 00 a. m. , while others, preferring an evening hour, found themselves talking beyond midnight. Between times there were few vacant spaces in the parish programme, and at the end of a twenty-four-hour pastoral visitation the Bishop of Ripon left confused and exhausted. Nonetheless he made the Vicar an Honorary Canon of Ripon Cathedral. Southcott survived on little sleep and found time for extensive lecture tours, teaching missions and the writing of a widely read book, *The Parish Comes Alive* (1956). In 1960, not long after Mervyn Stockwood had become Bishop of Southwark, the Prime Minister's Appointments Secretary suggested Southcott for the vacant suffragan Bishopric of Woolwich, but Stockwood said that he could not work with him ('he is too intense'), and opted for John (*Honest to God*) Robinson instead.

In the following year, however, Southcott became Provost of Southwark Cathedral. This was a mistake. He was already more or less burned out and had no aptitude for either cathedral politics or administration. Soon came a physical and psychological breakdown, and after a lengthy period of recuperation he became vicar of a small parish in Lancashire, where he tried valiantly to reproduce his Halton insights and was greatly loved. Denis (now Lord) Healey, who was MP for South East Leeds and became Defence Secretary and Chancellor of the Exchequer in successive Labour governments, acknowledged Southcott's powerful influence on him: 'Ernie's Christianity was numinous and he impressed me more than any priest I have met.'

John Mott

Mgr. Joseph Cardijn

Toyohiko Kagawa

Reinhold Niebuhr

Topical Press Agency

Donald Soper speaking in Manchester 1955

Margaret Webster

Florence Tim Oi Li

William Temple

Trevor Huddleston speaking in Mauritius

Beyers Naudé preaching in Johannesburg 1988

*Margaret Webster*

Una Kroll

*Roland R. Ropers*

Bede Griffiths

# John V. Taylor

## (1914- )

John Vernon Taylor was Bishop of Winchester from 1975 to 1985 and one of the most widely regarded churchmen of his time. His chief contribution to the life of the church was as a missionary statesman who had a key role in the devolution of authority to Africa's Anglican dioceses in the 1960s. He was first Africa, then General, Secretary of the Church Missionary Society and combined a deep love of the African people, gained during missionary service in Uganda, with a broad and exciting vision of how the Christian faith related to life in the turbulent twentieth century. The political as well as the religious leaders of the newly independent African states trusted him, and the transfer of authority in the church was effected smoothly.

Taylor was also equipped with a first-class theological mind, and the *CMS Newsletter,* which he inherited from his equally gifted predecessor, Max Warren, was essential reading for church leaders of every tradition and highly influential throughout the world church. *The Go-Between God* (1972), which won a major religious book prize and is now a classic, examined the evidence for the Holy Spirit's activity – everywhere – in the Christian mission. Its companion volume *The Christlike God* (1992) was a study of the ways in which Jesus reflects in a human life the being of God, and this too displayed its author's wide-ranging knowledge of the arts as well as of the Bible.

He was born in Cambridge where his father, who later became Bishop of Sodor and Man, was Vice-Principal of Ridley Hall theological college. Nurtured in the evangelical tradition of the Church of England, he was educated at St Lawrence College, Ramsgate and Trinity College, Cambridge, where he read English and history. During his preparation for Holy Orders at Wycliffe Hall, Oxford he took a degree in theology and from 1938 to 1940 was a curate at the famous evangelical church of All Souls, Langham Place, in London's West End. He then took charge of a church in St Helens, Lancashire, where he stayed until feeling drawn to overseas missionary work in 1943.

Wartime travel restrictions prevented him from going to Africa immediately, so he occupied the waiting time by obtaining a teaching qualification at London University. As soon as the war was over he became Warden of Bishop Tucker College at Mukona, Uganda, where during the next ten years he trained a new generation of African clergy for leadership in their church and started a love affair with Africa that lasted for the rest of his life. In 1955 he joined the staff of the International Missionary Council in Geneva in order to have opportunity to reflect on his African experience and share his insights more widely. *Christianity and Politics in Africa* (1957), *The Growth of the Church in Buganda* (1958) and *African Passion* (1958) were the fruit of his Geneva years.

Taylor became Africa Secretary of the Church Missionary Society in 1959 – a few months before Prime Minister Harold Macmillan's famous 'wind of change' speech in Cape Town – and immediately threw himself into the task of preparing the Anglican dioceses of East and West Africa for independence. He emphasized the need for the churches to become truly indigenous and later in his book *The Primal Vision* (1963) – another classic – evaluated the central features of African religion. He suggested that the African awareness of the universal presence of God was something from which Christians could learn, and to which they might add their own special insights, provided that these were disentangled from Western culture.

When Max Warren left the Church Missionary Society to become a Canon of Westminster in 1963, Taylor was his natural successor as General Secretary and during the next eleven years his perceptions of the Christian faith continued to broaden. While always bearing the marks of his evangelical origins, he recognized the valid insights of other traditions and of new developments in theological scholarship. He was an inspiring preacher and teacher, the growing liberality of whose thinking was generally expressed in biblical categories. This protected him from accusations of diluting revealed truth.

In 1975 Taylor became the first priest since the Middle Ages to be appointed directly to the senior bishopric of Winchester. He announced his arrival in the see with the publication of *Enough is Enough* – a small book which questioned the continuing acquisition of wealth by the rich at the expense of the poor – and he insisted on some modifications to his enthronement service to emphasize a bishop's servant role. He proved to be an excellent chairman of the Church of England's Doctrine Commission and after retirement his poetic gift found expression in books of poems and meditations which revealed the soul of a mystic and an artist.

# Martin Luther King

## (1929–1968)

Martin Luther King preached the century's most memorable sermon, 'I have a dream . . . ', and his powerful oratory was matched by his leadership of the American Civil Rights movement in the 1950s and 1960s. This leadership was marked by a commitment to non-violence, and also the reconciliation of blacks to whites as well as whites to blacks. This led to his assassination in 1968, for he had enemies on both sides of the racial divide. In the year before his death he was awarded the Nobel Peace Prize.

He was born in Atlanta, Georgia, where his father was the pastor of a black Baptist church. Although it was anticipated that he would follow in his father's footsteps, he came to believe during his high school years that the church was irrelevant to the needs of black people. At Morehouse College, however, where initially he intended to train either as a doctor or a lawyer, he came under the influence of its President and decided to become a pastor after all. He was ordained as an assistant pastor to his father when he was only eighteen. At the same time he continued his education at Crozer Theological Seminary in Pennsylvania where, through the experience of being refused admission to a white restaurant, he learned that racism was not confined to the South. A scholarship for post-graduate work took him to Boston University, where he completed a doctorate in the philosophy of religion.

At the age of twenty-five King became pastor of a Baptist church in Montgomery, Alabama, and it was in this town under his leadership, shared with his close friend Ralph Abernathy, that what has sometimes been called America's Third Revolution began. It was sparked off by an incident in a segregated bus when a black woman, Rosa Parks, refused to yield her seat to a white man. A policeman was called and she was arrested. The resentment of American blacks was already nearing explosion point, and on the day following Rosa Parks' arrest a meeting held in a room at King's church planned a boycott of public buses by black people. This went on for thirteen months and ended when the Supreme Court declared that segregation on buses was a violation of the Constitution.

Meanwhile King had been elected President of the Montgomery Improvement Association, and it was only a matter of a few weeks before a bomb was planted in the porch of his house. 1957 saw the formation of the Southern Christian Leadership Conference to co-ordinate Civil Rights activity, and during the next twelve months King, as its president, travelled 780,000 miles and made 280 speeches. In 1958, while autographing copies of his book on the Montgomery bus boycott in a New York shop, he was stabbed by a demented black woman, and only high-quality surgical skill saved his life.

On his return from convalescence in India he resigned from the pastorate of his church in order to devote himself fully to national and international campaigning. He was sent to prison for four months in 1960 after leading seventy-five black students into a segregated restaurant in Atlanta but was released after the intervention of President John F. Kennedy. In 1963 there were several days of demonstrations in Birmingham, Alabama, in the course of which King was arrested and sent to prison. He remained there for eight days, during which he wrote what was to become a famous 'Letter from Birmingham Jail' – a statement of the basis of his commitment to the struggle for justice and freedom.

Eventually a settlement was reached giving Birmingham's black people the modest concessions they demanded. This victory put new heart into the South's black communities and led to the passing of the landmark Civil Rights Bill a year later. 1963, the year of President Kennedy's assassination, was also the year of a march of 250,000 people to the Lincoln Memorial in Washington, where King delivered his 'I have a dream . . . ' speech. This did not bring peace and, following another prison sentence in 1964, he and his family moved to a black ghetto in Chicago to continue the campaign in the North.

By now, however, King had come to see that the plight of black people could not be separated from the plight of poor people generally. So he launched the Poor People's Campaign and began to denounce the Vietnam war, not only for its violence but also for its waste of money and resources needed by the poor. In March 1968 he went to lead a march in Memphis, Tennessee. While he was standing on the balcony of a motel before addressing a meeting in a church, a shot rang out and he fell to the ground mortally wounded.

S. B. Oates, *Let the Trumpet Sound,* Search Press 1982.

# Makarios III

## (1913–1979)

Makarios III became Archbishop and Head of the Orthodox Church of Cyprus in 1950 and the first President of Cyprus in 1959 – offices he held until his death. He first achieved international prominence through his advocacy of *enosis* – the union of Cyprus with Greece – and his involvement with EOKA – a terrorist organization which sought to bring about this union by force. The extent of Makarios's involvement with EOKA remains unclear. He claimed to be concerned only with hard political bargaining with the British government and tried to negotiate a settlement in 1955–56. It is also the case that when he became President and changed his mind about *enosis* he was twice the victim of assassination attempts by Greek extremists and found it necessary to proscribe EOKA. On the other hand the British government believed in 1956 that his support for terrorism was strong enough to require his deportation to the Seychelles.

At the end of the 1939–45 war the British, who had occupied Cyprus since 1878, following three centuries of Turkish rule, proposed either complete independence or Commonwealth status. This was unacceptable to the Greek Cypriots, who believed they would be secure only if the island were integrated with Greece; and it was also rejected by the Turkish Cypriots, who pressed for partition to safeguard their interests. The Orthodox archbishops always played an important political role, so the involvement of Makarios in the resolving of the island's future was not surprising, but the extent of his involvement and the methods he employed were redolent more of Byzantium than of the modern world.

The son of a poor shepherd, Mihail Christodoulou Mouskos was born in the Paphos area of Cyprus. At the age of thirteen he entered the Kylako monastery and on profession as a monk took the name Makarios (Blessed). He then studied for the priesthood at Athens University Theology School and, following his ordination in 1946, went to American to study sociology. Two years later, while still at Boston University, he was elected Bishop of Kition (Larnaca), and two years after this, at the age of thirty-seven, he became Archbishop. Immediately he began to speak out in favour of union with Greece, and after a meeting with the Greek Prime Minister in 1954 secured the support of the Greek government. He also travelled extensively in Greece and the United States, seeking support for *enosis,* and conducted an unofficial referendum in Cyprus which indicated that 95% of the population favoured union.

The terrorist campaign against the British, who rejected the *enosis* solution, began in 1955 and reached its climax under the leadership of Colonel Georgios Grivas in 1956, when the British army of occupation was depleted by the demands of the Suez crisis. Makarios was charged with sedition and support of terrorism and sent into exile. He was released in the following year, but banned from Cyprus, so he led the *enosis* movement from Athens, while the guerilla warfare in the island continued. A British government proposal in 1958 that Cyprus should have separate Greek and Turkish governments was rejected by him, but in February 1959 he met the British, Turkish and Greek Prime Ministers in London and signed an agreement for an independent Cypriot republic.

In December of that year Makarios was easily elected as first President and he immediately declared an amnesty for members of EOKA. He was also re-elected by huge majorities in 1968 and 1973, but during the 1960s there was much fighting between Greeks and Turks, and his attempts to secure the integration of the two communities failed because of Turkish resistance. A United Nations Peace-Keeping Force brought the warfare to an end in 1964, and in 1967 Makarios was obliged to accept a Turkish provisional administration for the Turkish community. Attempts on his life were made in 1970 and 1973.

In 1973 his own bishops tried to have him deposed from the Archbishopric on the grounds that his political and spiritual roles were incompatible, but his position was upheld by a synod of the Orthodox Churches of the region presided over by the Patriarch of Alexandria. In fact, church life was strengthened during his rule by considerable development of monasticism and better training of the parish clergy. Much more serious was a brief coup carried out in 1974 by Greek extremists in the National Guard who resented the fact that he had not pursued the policy of *enosis.* He was deposed and forced into exile, until civilian rule was restored a few months later. Meanwhile Turkey, believing the coup to be a prelude to *enosis*, had invaded Northern Cyprus and set up a zone under Turkish Cypriot control. Makarios opposed partition, but his negotiations with the Turkish government, designed to recover the island's unity, were unsuccessful.

Stanley Mayes, *Makarios,* Macmillan 1981.

# Josef Hromadka

## (1889–1969)

Josef Luki Hromadka was one of the most able theologians in Eastern Europe during the Communist era, and his Christian convictions led him to a positive evaluation of Communism and a readiness to collaborate with the Communist government of his native Czechoslovakia. Three factors in his life combined to bring him to this position, the first of which was the tradition of the fifteenth-century Czech Reformation, in which obedience to the Word of God was seen as requiring commitment to social justice and a readiness to embrace social and political change. The influence of Karl Barth's crisis theology was also considerable, and this led him to note the extent to which spiritualized Christian societies had bred social deprivation and economic injustice on a scale that required radical action of the Communist kind to put matters right. He concluded that it was the task of the church to seek to redeem Communism from within, rather than align itself with the prevailing Western anti-Communism.

One of the ways in which he sought to do this was through the Christian Peace Conference, which he and a few friends founded in 1958 shortly after he had received the International Lenin Peace Prize. During the next ten years, under his leadership, large-scale peace conferences, attended by delegates from the West and the Third World, were held in various Eastern European centres. A valuable dialogue ensued in which the differences of understandings between East and West of the meaning and conditions of peace were frequently exposed, but the statements issued by the conferences usually reflected the Russian position on peace. And even Hromadka's greatest admirers were from time to time driven to lament his apparent blindness to the ruthless character of the Soviet system – a blindness which certainly ended in 1968 when Russian tanks crushed the liberalism of Czech Communism, and Soviet intervention led to the dismissal of the General Secretary of the CPC. Hromadka was broken-hearted and died shortly afterwards.

He was born into a Moravian peasant family, but his high intelligence was quickly recognized, and he studied first at Prague, then at Vienna, Basel and Heidelberg. In 1910 he attended, as a student, the first World

Missionary Conference at Edinburgh, and in the following year he spent a year at the United Free Church College in Aberdeen. From 1912 to 1920 he was the pastor of three Czech Protestant congregations, and during this time completed a doctorate on President Thomas Masaryk's philosophy of religion. In 1920 he became Professor of Systematic Theology at the newly founded Jan Hus Theological Faculty in Prague, and in 1923 began to read the work of Karl Barth. By this time Communism was becoming well established in Russia and Hromodka, who had come to believe that socialism was an appropriate political expression of the Gospel, regarded the Russian revolution as likely to provide the basis for a more just society, though he was critical of some aspects of it.

In 1932, while quite unaware of Stalin's reign of terror in Russia, he went so far as to describe the revolution as 'perhaps a greatest positive development in the history of religion'. The rise of Nazism in Germany seemed to pose a greater threat, and shortly after Hitler's army marched into Czechoslovakia in March 1935 Hromadka emigrated to America. For the next eight years he was Professor of Christian Ethics at Princeton Theological Seminary. On his return to Prague in 1946 he once again became Professor of Systematic Theology, and was made Dean of the Theological Faculty of the Church of the Czech Brethren. He also played a prominent part in the foundation of the World Council of Churches, which he actively supported for the rest of his life.

He welcomed the Communist rise to power in Czechoslovakia, and advised the Protestant churches in other parts of Eastern Europe to share his optimism about the future. He never joined the Communist Party, because he believed that he must remain free to evaluate the political situation in the light of the Christian faith. He frequently criticized government policy, especially when it encroached on personal freedom, and during the severe repression in the 1950s tried to persuade the authorities to ease the pressure. But he always approached them privately, rather than by means of public pronouncements, and in the situation of his time this was the only way in which he could hope to exert influence.

Hromadka's initiation of a Christian-Marxist dialogue led to an international conference on the subject at Marienbad in 1967 and seriously challenged the atheism of leading Communist thinkers. His was a lonely and courageous role in Eastern Europe, and when the Prague Spring ended tragically his response was to plead for even deeper involvement by Christians in the building of democracy.

# Ted Wickham

## (1911–1994)

Edward Ralph Wickham was Suffragan Bishop of Middleton in the Manchester diocese from 1959 to 1982, but his greatest work and influence was as the pioneer of industrial mission and as a prophetic voice at a time when the gulf between the church and industrial society was widening rapidly. The Sheffield Industrial Mission, which he founded in 1944 and led until 1959, became a model for similar developments in many parts of Britain and also in the USA and Nigeria. Wickham's book *Church and People in an Industrial City* (1957) combined an analysis of church life in Sheffield from the seventeenth to the twentieth century with a theological evaluation of the evidence thus elicited and a series of specific proposals for mission strategy and church reform. Few of these were ever adopted.

Wickham was born in the East End of London and never lost his Cockney style. He left school when only fifteen and worked for some years in a thermoplastics factory, though he was unemployed in the 1930s and later claimed to be the only Anglican bishop ever to have stood in a dole queue. Feeling drawn to Holy Orders, he taught himself Latin, Greek and Hebrew and in 1937 obtained a London University external BD. He then spent a few terms at a theological college in Oxford and in 1938 became a curate in a poor parish on Tyneside. Three years later the parish was flattened by a single night's wartime bombing, and Wickham moved to become chaplain of the Royal Ordnance Factory at Swynnerton in Staffordshire. There he began to experiment with the small snap-break meetings that were to be developed later in Sheffield.

In 1944 Bishop Leslie Hunter invited him to see if it was possible to establish full-time chaplaincies on the shop-floors of major steel works. Access to a number of works was negotiated with management and trade unions, and visiting the men at work was seen as the main task. But soon fifteen- to twenty-minute meetings for the discussion of social and religious issues were being held in breaks between steel-making processes, and after a time regular Thursday evening meetings were established to enable issues to be taken further.

By 1950 Wickham's work had ceased to be regarded as experimental.

The Sheffield Industrial Mission was formed, more chaplains were recruited and Wickham was made a Canon Residentiary of Sheffield Cathedral to provide him with a church base, an income and a status. Steel works in nearby Rotherham, and eventually British Rail, also had their chaplains, and after 1955 the key projects were given stronger lay leadership in what Wickham described as 'the most audacious and creative mission experiment in recent years'. Its aim was 'to stain industry with Christian values'. Residential conferences, involvement in company training programmes and summer conferences for ordination candidates were added to the regular round of factory visits and meetings. Frontier groups provided a forum for lay people to work out the relationship of the Christian faith to the secular world, though partisan political stances were studiously avoided.

The developments in Sheffield coincided for a time with the priest-worker movement in France, and contact between the two groups led to useful discussion of policy and methods. But Wickham did not believe the French approach to be right for Britain as it was, in his view, too highly clericalized. The autonomy of the secular must be recognized and Christian leadership in industry could be exercised only by the laity. He believed the days of the parochial system were numbered and that a new kind of organization was needed to enable the church to engage with the secular world. Meanwhile, many other Anglican dioceses were taking up the idea of industrial mission, and eventually some degree of central co-ordination was required. Wickham became the half-time secretary of the Church Assembly Social and Industrial Committee. He also campaigned for the setting up of an Industrial Secretariat, with himself the most likely leader, and he was very disappointed when this proposal was stymied by the diocesan bishops.

By this time he was becoming somewhat detached from the work in Sheffield and the question arose as to what he should do next. The Bishop of Manchester, William Greer, provided an answer by having him appointed Suffragan Bishop of Middleton. No one ever pretended that this was a happy arrangement. Wickham himself said that he had been 'blackballed into the episcopate', and it was never conceivable that he would settle down to oil the wheels of an ecclesiastical machine that he believed to be incapable of moving in the right direction. He concentrated instead on serving local secular institutions and became deeply involved in the development of a new Salford University, serving as chairman of its Council, then as Pro-Chancellor.

# Thomas Roberts

## (1893–1976)

Thomas d'Esterre Roberts, a member of the Jesuit Order, was Roman Catholic Archbishop of Bombay from 1937 to 1950 and on his return to England achieved considerable notoriety for his outspoken questioning of the way in which papal authority was being exercised and of his church's opposition to contraception. Seen in the light of later wide-spread criticism of Roman policy, his views no longer seem particularly controversial, but at the time of their utterance they caused considerable alarm in official church circles and required considerable courage of Roberts. He was ostracized by many other bishops and forbidden to preach or lecture in some American dioceses and to conduct prayers at a CND/Christian Action peace rally in Trafalgar Square, London. His archiepiscopal title made him especially useful to the media.

Roberts had a Huguenot ancestry and was born in France, but his parents were English, and following the death of his father in 1901 the rest of the family moved to Liverpool. Thomas attended St Francis Xavier's College in Liverpool, and at the age of sixteen entered the Jesuit Novitiate at Roehampton in South London. Later he moved to the Society's college at Stoneyhurst and was ordained priest in 1925. He then taught in Catholic colleges until his appointment in 1935 as Rector of his old school. One day in 1937, however, he received a telephone call from the *Liverpool Post* enquiring how he felt about his appointment as Archbishop of Bombay. This was news to him and he immediately cabled the Vatican: 'Newspapers appoint me Archbishop of Bombay. Kindly comment.'

Confirmation of his appointment came in due course and, perhaps mistakenly, he accepted. Nonetheless, he achieved quite a lot during his thirteen years in India and began dramatically by having his cathedral pulled down. 'Why does a bishop need a cathedral? Outdoors is best for large crowds.' He established a seamen's centre in Bombay, and social services for the poor, the orphans and the prostitutes. He also initiated, against stiff opposition, a university hall for women students. But much of his time was devoted to the difficult task of reconciling the Portuguese and British Indian Catholics in the diocese. He persuaded Pope Pius XII to break the custom of alternating English and Portuguese Archbishops of Bombay and was succeeded in 1950 by an Indian who later became a cardinal.

Back in England he resumed the ordinary life of a Jesuit at Farm Street Church in London's West End. Soon he became known for his humanity and outspoken views, and in his *Black Popes: Authority, its Use and Abuse* (1954) he complained, 'A sadly crippled ship we have inherited'. In 1960 the Apostolic Delegate in London complained to the Vatican about his 'indiscretion'. This was illustrated by his association with Pax (an international Catholic peace movement), attendance at a conference on Christians and Nuclear Warfare held at St Paul's Cathedral, a letter to *The Universe* on liturgical matters, and the disclosure of confidential material relating to the forthcoming Council. The Vatican did not respond to the complaint, but Roberts deplored the fact that he had been falsely accused, probably libelled, and not officially vindicated.

He attended the Vatican Council where, although his deep involvement in the peace movement was widely recognized, he was not called to speak when this subject was debated. He did, however, influence a statement on the validity of conscientious objection to participation in war. He was not himself a pacifist and subscribed to the doctrine of the just war, but he believed that the United Nations and the church should condemn all weapons of mass destruction.

His views on birth control were also widely known, for he had said in *Black Popes* that the permissive view of the Anglican Lambeth Conference 'has force', but again he was not called to speak in the marriage debates. In 1964 he expressed his view of the matter in the Catholic newsletter *Search*, arguing that the Anglican position could not be refuted by reason alone and that decisions about contraception were best left to the consciences of the people concerned. His views were undoubtedly influenced by his Indian experience and the memory of millions living in abject poverty. The article attracted the attention of several national newspapers, and led to a long statement from the Catholic hierarchy, the gist of which was that God's law cannot be changed and that married couples with problems over birth control would do well to attend communion more frequently.

Roberts embraced a simple life-style and wore shabby clothes. He never put on episcopal purple and once likened lace vestments to 'ladies' underwear'. He said that he never felt really comfortable in St Peter's, Rome, since he could not forget that it was built largely from the sale of indulgences.

David Abner Hurn, *Archbishop Roberts, SJ*, Darton, Longman and Todd 1966.

# Benjamin Britten

## (1913–1976)

Benjamin Britten, the outstanding British musician of his time, was responsible for the revival of British opera. He was also a brilliant pianist – at his best when accompanying his lifelong friend and partner, the tenor Peter Pears. They lived together at Aldeburgh, Suffolk, where with Eric Crozier they founded the Aldeburgh Festival in 1948. This soon acquired an international reputation, for Britten was able to attract many of the best musicians, and it occupied much of his time for the rest of his life.

At an early age, and through the influence of his teacher, Frank Bridge, Britten became a pacifist. He and Pears registered as conscientious objectors during the 1939–45 war, and his hatred of war found powerful expression in the *War Requiem,* composed for the celebration of the dedication of Coventry Cathedral in 1962. It was also there in his opera *Owen Wingrave*, based on a Henry James story and written for performance, initially, on television. Pacifism and homosexuality combined to make him always feel something of an outsider, even though in the end he was the recipient of international acclaim and the highest honours, including a Peerage. This is discernible in what he called his church parables: *Curlew River* (1964), *The Burning Fiery Furnace* (1966) and *The Prodigal Son* (1968). Although these had biblical themes and made use of biblical imagery, they were in no sense liturgical works. They expressed the composer's deep concern for the plight of the innocent and his detestation of cruelty and war.

Britten was born in Lowestoft, Suffolk. His parents were musical, and from a very early age young Benjamin displayed unusual musical ability as a pianist and also as a composer. When only eleven years old, he was deeply affected by the performance of a work by Frank Bridge in Norwich Cathedral and three years later became Bridge's pupil. At Gresham's School, Holt, he continued to display his musical prowess and in 1930 won an open scholarship to the Royal College of Music, but the conservative atmosphere of the college did not suit him, and towards the end of his time there he found relief through association with left-wing theatre groups.

He also began to write music for a small film company in collaboration with the poet W. H. Auden and the film director John Grierson. About this time he began to acknowledge his homosexuality and in 1934 met Peter Pears. A song cycle *Our Hunting Fathers* (1934) with words by W. H. Auden was a satire against hunting and shooting, and a later *Ballad of Heroes* also consisted of social and political comment. National and international acclaim came in 1937 with *Variations on a Theme of Frank Bridge,* and in the following year he enjoyed success at the Salzburg Festival. He was now developing an original style that was in no sense avant-garde but had a freshness of approach that would in time offer something quite new for instruments and voices.

In May 1939, however, Britten and Pears decided to move to America. They were unhappy with the political situation in Britain, there had been discouraging reviews of their work in some London papers, and their friends W. H. Auden and Christopher Isherwood had already crossed the Atlantic. Britten continued to compose instrumental music while in America, but in 1942 he became nostalgic for East Anglia, so he and Pears returned to wartime England, where they were exempted from military service provided that they gave performances for the Council for the Encouragement of Music and the Arts.

During the war years he wrote a *Ceremony of Carols*, *Hymn to St Cecilia*, again with Auden's words, and *Rejoice in the Lamb*, a cantata in praise of the Creation based on the strange imagery of the mentally-disturbed poet Christopher Smart and including the memorable 'For I will consider my cat Jeffrey'. Britten was also much taken by the work of the Suffolk poet George Crabbe and a fisherman in one of Crabbe's poems became the principal figure in the opera *Peter Grimes,* which was first performed to mark the re-opening of the Sadlers Wells Theatre in 1945 and established its composer's international reputation.

Nine more operas followed. Britten himself conducted *Albert Herring* at the recently re-opened Glyndebourne Opera House, and he and some of his friends formed the English Opera Group for the performance of chamber operas, including his own. *Noye's Fludde*, a children's opera first performed in 1957, is a masterpiece which has given immense pleasure to young and old alike, but he was not very interested in church music. A *Te Deum* (1934) and *Jubilate* (1961) are still sung at cathedral Mattins and *Amor ego sum* (1949) is sometimes heard at weddings. A *Missa Brevis* (1959) was composed for the trebles of Westminster Cathedral.

Humphrey Carpenter, *Benjamin Britten*, Faber 1992.

# Georgi Vins
## (1928–1998)

Georgi Vins was a Russian Baptist pastor who witnessed heroically in the cause of religious freedom in the Soviet Union during the 1960s and 1970s. For virtually the whole of this time he was either in prison or on the run, and having served half of a ten-year prison sentence was released to America in 1979 in exchange for two Soviet spies. Following the collapse of the Soviet empire in the late 1980s, however, he had the joy of returning to his homeland, where he was able to exercise an open ministry.

Vins was a leader of the Reform Baptists who rebelled against the decision of the All-Union Council of Evangelical Christians and Baptists to issue in 1960 a set of new statutes, which severely restricted the church's activities. Among other things they required children to be excluded from public worship, discouraged and reduced to a minimum the baptism of people between the ages of eighteen and thirty, and curtailed evangelistic activities. This was in response to severe pressure from the Khrushchev government and ran counter to all that Baptists believed about religious freedom. Widespread opposition to the statutes resulted and Vins, together with two other determined men, formed an action group which called on the Council to rescind its decision or face expulsion from the Baptist Union. There was no response, so the action group sought to win as many congregations as possible to its side and organized activities, including meetings, and duplicated publications which violated the laws of the state. By the end of 1962 over 100 of these Reform Baptists, as they came to be called, had been imprisoned. This figure rose to 170 during the next eighteen months and as late as 1981 there were 95 of them in prison.

Vins was the son of an American Baptist missionary who went to Russia soon after the 1917 Revolution and, having been sent to prison for three years in 1930, was executed in 1936. Young Georgi was born and brought up in Siberia by his devout mother and, in spite of the anti-religious indoctrination at school, shared her faith. After training as an electrical engineer at Kiev he became an active layman in the Baptist Church, and during the crisis created by the New Statutes was ordained a pastor – retaining his secular employment as required by law.

The Reform Baptists met privately for worship and Bible study in members' homes and sometimes in the forests. By 1966 there were estimated to be 155,000 of them with their own Council, of which Vins was the General Secretary. He and Gennadi Kryuchkov, the President, were now the leaders of the first human rights movement to be organized on a national scale in any Communist country. At one point permission was sought for them to be released from secular employment in order to serve the Council full-time but this was refused, and thereafter they directed Reform Baptist affairs from underground. Before long most of the Council members were in prison. Vins was first arrested in 1966 after organizing, with Kryuchkov, a mass demonstration outside the Communist Party Central Committee building in Moscow. They demanded freedom to express their Christian faith, in accordance with Soviet law, and also the release of Baptist prisoners. Vins was invited into the building to discuss these issues and emerged three years later, broken in health, having undergone brutal treatment in prison for a year, followed by two years in a labour camp in the Urals.

Meanwhile a Council of Baptist Prisoners' Relatives had been formed, and this provided support for the families of those who were in prison, as well as collecting information about prisoners which was smuggled abroad to keep the West informed of the situation. Soon after his release in 1969 Vins was sentenced to twelve months' forced labour for 'parasitism', and he then went on the run until his capture in 1974, when he was sentenced to five years in a Siberian labour camp, to be followed by five years of internal exile.

It was at the end of the first five years of this sentence that he was released to America, having first been stripped of his Soviet citizenship. There he set up an organization 'International Representation', which raised funds and other forms of support for the persecuted Russian Baptists, whose corporate life he continued to direct through secret channels. Sadly, but perhaps not surprisingly, he found it difficult to adapt to life in the West, and trusted only his close friends. The promulgation in 1990 of new laws on freedom of conscience enabled Vins to return to Russia, and during the next seven years he played an important part in the renewal of Baptist witness there, preaching in churches, schools and colleges and at open-air meetings.

Georgi Vins, *Three Generations of Suffering*, Hodder 1976.

# Gleb Yakunin
## (1934–   )

Gleb Yakunin was one of the most courageous Russian Orthodox priests of the post-1945 era. He openly challenged the State policy of religious repression and his church's complicity in the imposed restrictions on its life. This led to his spending over eight years in prison, labour camps and Siberian exile, but he survived to become a member of Parliament and of the Supreme Soviet following the collapse of the Communist order. The church responded by deposing him from the priesthood.

Yakunin first came to national and international attention when in November 1965 he and another priest, Nikolai Elishman, addressed an open letter to Patriarch Alexi of Moscow. This accused the government of breaking Soviet law on the separation of church from state and of interfering in church affairs. It also accused the Patriarch of failing to stand up to the authorities and went on to ask for the monasteries and seminaries closed during Khrushchev's anti-religious campaign (1959–64) to be reopened, for children to be allowed to attend church, and for priests to be allowed to conduct services in the homes of parishioners. The letter was later circulated to all the diocesan bishops, and the two priests wrote on similar lines to the chairman of the Presidium of the Supreme Soviet.

The Patriarch immediately declared the circulation of such open letters to be contrary to canon law, and in May 1966 summoned Yakunin and Elishman to the Patriarchate to 'explain various points' in their letter. On the following day Alexi announced that they had been relieved of their appointments and were forbidden to exercise the priesthood until they had fully repented. He also warned that if they continued their 'evil activity' more severe action would be taken. They refused to accept this judgment, and Yakunin was thereafter employed in a series of menial jobs, including for a time that of night-watchman in a Moscow church.

He was born in Moscow and nurtured in the Orthodox faith by his devout mother. He entered the Moscow Theological Seminary and was ordained priest in 1962 when the Khrushchev assault on religious believers was at its height. After serving in a Moscow parish, he moved to another in the nearby city of Dimitrov, but his ministry there was cut short when he was suspended from the priesthood. In November 1975 a considerable stir was created when Yakunin and another priest, Lev Regelson, addressed an appeal to the Fifth Assembly of the World Council of Churches in Nairobi. In it they described the situation in the USSR and asked for the support of the world church. They noted the WCC's involvement in many other world problems – wars, race issues and breaches of human rights – but were unaware of its making any protests about the lack of religious freedom in the Soviet Union. In the ensuing debate the Russian Orthodox delegates attempted, with no great success, to defend their government's religious policies and, although the Assembly made no official pronouncement, its expressions of concern about the situation in the Soviet Union became noticeably stronger from that point onwards.

In June of the following year Yakunin was a signatory of an ecumenical appeal for greater religious freedom to the Supreme Soviet and six months later he was one of the founders of what became an important Christian Committee for the Defence of Believers' Rights in the USSR. This was basically Orthodox in composition, but it included some members of other churches and was equally concerned for the rights of these churches. Its aim was to collect, study and disseminate information about breaches of religious freedom, give legal advice to victims of religious repression, and appeal to state institutions about believers' rights. During 1977 Yakunin was warned that he would be arrested if he did not abandon his activities, but he continued to defend the rights of believers, and following a trial in August 1980 he was sentenced to seven years' imprisonment, to be followed by five years of internal exile. He responded: 'I thank God for this test he has sent me. I consider it a great honour and as a Christian I accept it gladly.' But, deprived of his leadership, active dissent declined.

Yakunin was among the political prisoners released by Gorbachev in early 1987 and was appointed to a parish near Moscow. In 1990, however, he was elected to the Russian Congress of People's Deputies and with two other priests founded the Russian Christian Democratic Movement, becoming joint chairman of its Parliamentary group. At the end of 1994 the Bishops' Council decreed that his political activities were contrary to canon law and when he refused to give up his seat in Parliament he was unfrocked, though he continued to wear his clerical robe and pectoral cross.

François Rouleau, *Un prêtre seul au pays de soviets*, Éditions Criterion 1984.

# Beyers Naudé
## (1915–   )

Beyers Naudé was an outstandingly courageous opponent of apartheid in South Africa during the 1960s and 1970s, when the Afrikaaner government's policy of racial segregation was at its most ruthless and repressive. During this time he occupied a unique position inasmuch as he was himself an Afrikaaner and had been a leader in the Dutch Reformed Church which provided religious support for apartheid. His rejection of racism as inconsistent with biblical truth therefore brought him into sharp conflict with his church as well as with the government. Naudé's witness was exercised mainly as Director of the Christian Institute, an ecumenical organization which he founded in 1963 with the support of some other Afrikaaners and leading figures in the English-speaking churches. It offered a constant challenge to racism until it was closed by the government in 1977.

The dissemination of ideas during a period when all the African political organizations had been repressed kept alight a flicker of hope in those who sought change. The Institute brought together the Independent African Churches and enabled them to communicate with the wider church in South Africa. It also helped to raise the awareness of the world church to a deteriorating situation in South Africa and became the main channel through which the World Council of Churches and the Dutch Reformed Church in the Netherlands provided aid to apartheid's opponents. During the latter part of its existence the Institute, through Naudé's work with the Independent African Churches, embraced and propagated the insights of the Black Consciousness and Black Theology movements, and following the publication of the *Message to the People of South Africa* by the South African Council of Churches in 1968, took this project forward and began to offer a radical critique of economic structures that condemned black people to poverty.

All of this cost Naudé a great deal. When, as the newly elected Moderator of the Southern Transvaal Synod of the Dutch Reformed Church, in 1963 he refused to resign from the editorship of the anti-apartheid paper *Pro Veritate,* he was dismissed from the church's ordained ministry. Ten years later, when he refused to give evidence to a parliamentary committee charged with investigating the affairs of the Christian Institute, he was put on trial and sent to prison. (He was released after twenty-four hours, following the payment of a fine by the minister of the parish in which he was living.) And when the Institute was declared unlawful in 1977, he and some of its other leaders were made subject to five-year banning orders. Between these events he was subjected to other government pressures and lost many of his friends and collegues in the Dutch Reformed Church.

Naudé was born at Roodepoort in the Orange Free State, where his father, who had fought in the Boer War, was a Dutch Reformed Church minister. Young Beyers was brought up to believe that the Afrikaaners were a 'chosen people'. At the age of sixteen he had a conversion experience and, having taken a degree at Stellenbosch University, entered a theological seminary to prepare for ordination. He was now a moderate nationalist and during his time as a trainee minister at Wellington, near Cape Town, he joined the Broederbond – a secret society which promoted Afrikaaner nationalism and had considerable political influence. In 1943 he became minister of Loxton – a small town in Cape Province – and during the 1939–45 war opposed South Africa's involvement, displaying some sympathy for the Germans. On the other hand, pastoral responsibility for a Coloured congregation in a separate township made him aware of the poverty endured by the people, and in 1948, by which time he had moved to become minister of Pretoria South, he and twelve other members of the church's regional Synod opposed a report which sought to provide a biblical justification for apartheid.

His leadership gifts were recognized by appointment to important churches in Potchefstroom and Johannesburg, but involvement in a Bible study movement and in the Cottesloe consultation, following the massacre of blacks at Sharpeville in March 1960, strengthened his questioning of apartheid. In 1962 he became editor of *Pro Veritate*, designed to stimulate theological and political debate among Afrikaaners, and in the following year he resigned from the Broederbond. Election as Moderator of the Southern Transvaal Synod soon after this was probably intended to tame him. But within six months the Christian Institute had been launched and his future lay in outright opposition to apartheid. When the banning order was eventually lifted in 1984 he became the caretaker Secretary of the South African Council of Churches, and in 1987 was ordained as a minister in the black Dutch Reformed Church. By the end of that decade the white leaders of the DRC had acknowledged their guilt for their church's support of apartheid.

Colleen Ryan, *Beyers Naudé: Pilgrimage of Faith*, Eerdmans 1990.

# John Robinson
## (1919–1983)

John Arthur Thomas Robinson was Bishop of Woolwich from 1959–69, then became Dean of Chapel at Trinity College, Cambridge, until his early death from cancer. His name will always be associated with the reform movements in the Western European and North American churches in the 1960s and in particular with his book *Honest to God* (1963). It was a modest volume of fewer than 150 pages, written while he was incapacitated by a long-standing back problem, and reflecting on the significance for Christian belief of the work of Bonhoeffer, Bultmann and Tillich. He concluded that the traditional image of God as ruling over the universe from a detached position was no longer tenable, and when an article summarizing his position was published in *The Observer* under the heading 'Our Image of God must Go', a controversy erupted.

He was denounced by many of his fellow bishops, and even the theologically literate Archbishop of Canterbury, A. M. Ramsey, felt constrained to censure him, though later he conceded that he had reacted too hastily. Over one million copes of the book were sold and it was translated into seventeen languages. Its author received over 4,000 letters reflecting strongly held opinions for and against his position. His position as a bishop was the main cause of the furore, since his views had been common currency in theological circles for some time. Three years before *Honest to God* Robinson found himself as the centre of another controversy when he appeared in court to defend the publication of an unexpurgated version of D. H. Lawrence's novel *Lady Chatterley's Lover*. His suggestion that the sexual relationship between the lady and her gamekeeper as portrayed by Lawrence was something akin to holy communion proved to be particularly offensive and this, too, earned him archiepiscopal censure.

Although Robinson had a strong academic background and a fine intellect, most of his thinking was governed by pastoral interests. When, to the consternation of many, he left Cambridge to become Bishop of Woolwich he overcame a shyness of personality and was soon recognized as a high-calibre pastoral bishop. He was a great encourager, forged links between the church and the secular community, was a gifted preacher and teacher, and pioneered the Southwark Ordination Course – the first, and very successful, attempt to train for the priesthood men who remained in their secular occupations.

Robinson was born in the precincts of Canterbury Cathedral, where his father – a member of a notable ecclesiastical dynasty – was a canon. After taking degrees in classics and theology at Cambridge, he prepared for ordination at Westcott House, Cambridge, and in 1945 became a curate at St Matthew Moorfields Church, Bristol, where the vicar was Mervyn Stockwood. Stockwood later became Bishop of Southwark and invited his former curate to become one of his suffragans. After three years in inner-city Bristol, where he completed a PhD on the thought of Martin Buber, Robinson became Chaplain of Wells Theological College and wrote his first book – a small volume on eschatology *In the End, God* (1950). In 1951 he was appointed Fellow and Dean of Clare College, Cambridge, where he also lectured in the university's Divinity School. During this time he became interested in liturgical renewal and his revision of the Clare College worship was described in *Liturgy Coming to Life* (1960).

As Bishop of Woolwich, he played a leading part in attempts to reform the Church of England, and in its Church Assembly strongly backed proposals for pastoral reorganization, the deployment and payment of the clergy, the ordination of women, synodical government and unity with other churches. *The New Reformation* (1965) enjoyed a wide readership, and he also wrote and lectured on new approaches to morality.

All of this might have been expected to be taken forward into a major diocesan bishopric, but his reputation (often grossly exaggerated) as a radical reformer stood in the way of this and eventually, in 1969, he returned to Cambridge to be Fellow and Dean of Chapel at Trinity College. Denied a university teaching post, he lectured frequently in many other parts of the world and wrote several more books. The *Human Face of God* (1973), arguably his best, was a notable essay in christology. *Truth is Two-Eyed* (1979) discussed the Buddhist, Hindu, Christian encounter, and *The Roots of a Radical* (1980) reflected on the basis for change in the church.

Increasingly, however, he began to explore some of the stranger by-ways of religious thought, including the Turin Shroud, which he thought might be authentic. Shortly before his death he completed his Bampton Lectures, which were published posthumously – *The Priority of John* (1984). His argument that the Fourth Gospel was essentially earlier than the Synoptics convinced few other New Testament scholars.

Eric James, *A Life of Bishop John A. T. Robinson: Scholar, Pastor, Prophet,* Collins 1987.

# Harry Williams

## (1919–    )

Harry Abbott Williams entered the Anglican Community of the Resurrection at Mirfield, Yorkshire in 1969, but he was most influential during his eighteen years as a Fellow of Trinity College, Cambridge. Initially employed to teach New Testament, he showed every sign of becoming a meticulous scholar, but a psychological breakdown, thought to have been caused by a sharp conflict between orthodox belief and personal need, drove him in another direction. In his autobiography *Some Day I'll Find You* (1982) he revealed his homosexuality and said of his Cambridge years: 'I slept with several men, in each case fairly regularly. They were all friends. Cynics, of course, will smile, but I have seldom felt more like thanking God than when having sex. I used in bed to praise Him there and then for the joy I was receiving and giving.' This would have surprised the former Master of Trinity, G. M. Trevelyan, who told him when he was an undergraduate: 'As a clergyman it will be your responsible duty to be a guardian of British culture and civilization.'

One consequence of the combination of psychoanalysis and an acute theological mind was the production of a deeply personal interpretation of the Christian faith. During the 1960s and 1970s many others found this helpful, and a volume of his sermons *The True Wilderness* (1965), preached in the chapel of Trinity College, Cambridge, became a best-seller and spiritual classic. At the end of his autobiography he wrote:

> As one fed by the Christian religion I find it necessary to distinguish between the historical Jesus and what could be described as the Christ Reality. I believe that the historical Jesus embodied the Christ Reality to a unique degree. But I don't believe that the Christ Reality was confined to him or that he monopolized it. And I see that if I had been fed by another religion I should call the Christ Reality something else.

Williams's early years were conventional. His father, a naval captain, had fought in the Battle of Jutland, but soon after the end of the 1914–18 war retired to the South of France. Harry was sent to Cranleigh School and went on to Trinity College, Cambridge, where he obtained a First in theology. Having from his school days felt drawn to holy orders, he went to Cuddesdon Theological College and in 1943 became a curate at St Barnabas Church, Pimlico, in London. This was followed by three years at the famous Anglo-Catholic Church of All Saints, Margaret Street, in London's West End, where he became experienced in counselling and hearing confessions. He then returned to Cambridge as chaplain of Westcott House, where he also taught New Testament. After three years there he was elected to a fellowship at Trinity College and in 1958 was appointed Dean of Chapel.

Willaims's early years in the college were marred by his breakdown, and for some two years he felt unable to preach in the chapel. Eventually he came through this, aided by analysis, pills and gin, then had twelve happy years in a place which, even after he had become a monk at Mirfield, he always regarded as home. 'Trinity was for me the scene of the most acute mental suffering it is possible for man to bear. My blood is mixed up with its stones, because it was there that I had to encounter the forces of destruction which I had either to fight and conquer or perish.' In *True Resurrection* (1972) he argued that the truth of Christ's resurrection could be deduced, not so much from historical enquiry as from resurrection experiences in normal human life.

It was about this time that he began to question ever more seriously orthodox Christian belief – a process that continued for the rest of his Cambridge years – and, although great surprise was expressed when he announced his intention of testing his vocation to the religious life at Mirfield, he found the life of a monk a great help in the search for his own identity. Sharing in the community's regular life of prayer also resulted in his coming to regard the events in the Gospels as being less and less important as historical happenings and 'more and more important as the externalized poetic or narrative representations of realities which occurred or were found in the depths of what I was – in what I've called the final me'. In spite of (possibly because of) his heterodox belief, Williams remained in great demand as a preacher and conductor of retreats. This provided opportunities to escape the rigours of monastic life and from time to time his rotund figure was to be seen in the best London restaurants. He enjoyed conviviality and, being a man of wide culture, and a lover of gossip, was always good company.

H. A. Williams, *Some Day I'll Find You: An Autobiography*, Mitchell Beazley 1982.

# Mark Gibbs

## (1920–1986)

Mark Gibbs was a passionate and persistent promoter of the ministry of Christian laymen and women in the modern world; a communicator who enabled pioneers in lay ministry in several countries, notably Germany and North America, to profit by shared experience; and an Anglican lay theologian whose thinking was enriched by wide ecumenical contacts. His particular concern was with the education of the great majority of the laity who are called to witness in the secular world, rather than through involvement in the institutional life of the church, and he was always highly critical of lay training programmes which emphasized the latter at the expense of the former.

Born in London and educated at University College, London, he found his spiritual home in the North of England when he went to Manchester in 1946 as history and economics master at Audenshaw Grammar School. His interest in the ministry of the laity was stimulated by early contacts with pioneering lay movements in Germany and with the Iona Community in Scotland, and he was much influenced by the thinking of Hendrik Kraemer and J. H. Oldham.

A visit to refugee camps in Germany and Austria led to his first enterprise – the Audenshaw Periodical Service – which sent used weekly and monthly publications first to the camps and later to colleges in the Third World. At the same time he made contact with the 'Lay Academies' which sprang up in Germany after the 1939–45 war, and with Reinhold von Thadden, who revived the National Lay-people's Rally or Kirchentag in 1950. Gibbs organized the international centre for English-speaking participants in the Kirchentag from 1954–85 and was for many years closely connected with the Association of Laity Centres in Europe. He also maintained contact with similar centres in Malawi and other African countries.

During the 1950s he had become involved in laity education with the Iona Community and he collaborated with its deputy leader, Ralph Morton, in the writing of *God's Frozen People* (1964) – a bestseller which declared the obvious but often disregarded truth that ninety-nine per cent of the responsibility for the church's witness and service in the world rests on the laity. The importance of new methods of clergy training to enable priests and ministers to serve the laity more effectively was strongly emphasized. This book was soon followed by *God's Lively People* (1966), which contained many constructive ideas about the form and content of lay training. Gibbs took an active part in the World Council of Churches Laity Department and its Ecumenical Institute and was the last secretary of the Christian Frontier Council.

He was a tireless worker, but by 1964 it had become evident that he could no longer combine his work as a schoolmaster with his many other activities, so he created the Audenshaw Foundation as an independent charity, financed to a limited extent by subscriptions, but mostly by his own earnings from lecturing and consultancy work in North America. His work in the North American churches led to the editorship of a number of publications concerned with lay ministry, and for more than twenty years his Audenshaw Papers, containing contributions by prominent lay people and clerics, were published on both sides of the Atlantic. Through these papers he continued the tradition of J. H. Oldham's *Christian Newsletter*, with personal comments on current events in which he frequently expressed his impatience with the radicals of the 1960s, whose excursions into the realms of economics and politics were, he believed, altogether too superficial and lacking in awareness of the realities of the secular world and the need for responsible compromise. Another special concern was the development of a spirituality suitable for lay people, to replace the monastic traditions which he accused the clergy of imposing on the church.

This extraordinary output of work was accomplished only by maintaining over thirty-five years a most punishing schedule which involved as many as a dozen flights to California a year, innumerable calls in American and Canadian cities on the way back, and frequent journeys in mainland Europe. Only a man of exceptional discipline and devotion could have accomplished so much with such limited administrative and financial support. His Christian commitment ran very deep and the final phase of his life, when he travelled in much discomfort and pain as cancer exacted its toll, was truly heroic.

He was unable to suffer fools gladly, however, and his influence in Britain might have been greater had he been endowed with greater patience and not come to regard laity education in the Church of England as a lost cause. But he believed passionately in the need for the church to be de-clericalized, so that it might become a more effective instrument of the Christian mission, and he was unwilling to compromise on this fundamental point.

# Eric James

## (1925– )

Eric Arthur James, one of the Church of England's most able and best known priests, devoted the greater part of his ministry to the reform and renewal of the church and society. He was a man of wide vision who had unusual skills as a communicator, and during the 1960s was a leading exponents of what became known as 'South Bank religion'. As Director of the Parish and People movement, he led a campaign which aimed at wide-ranging church reform, but, although the movement had upwards of 2,000 members, including many bishops, it was unable to make much progress and after five years of speech-making and organizing pressure groups James resigned.

In 1972, following the General Synod's rejection of an Anglican/Methodist reunion scheme, he also resigned from the Synod, having informed the Archbishop of Canterbury that a 45,000-mile journey through developing countries had convinced him that he should 'not waste further time in such a body'. Later he became Director of Christian Action, and for seventeen years, following in the footsteps of John Collins, sought to encourage the British churches to become more deeply involved in social and political activity. His main achievement during this period was the suggestion, taken up by Archbishop Robert Runcie, of a Commission on Urban Priority Areas, the administrative servicing of this Commission, and the widespread propagation of its report *Faith in the City* (1985). He was also responsible for Christian Action's financial support of many organizations concerned with housing, poverty, racism, sexuality and community development.

James was born at Dagenham, Essex. He left school when only fourteen to work at a wharf in the heavily bombed riverside area near London Bridge. Organ lessons took him into nearby Southwark Cathedral where he came under the influence of the Provost, and, having qualified for entry to King's College, London took a degree in theology after the war and in 1951 became a curate at St Stephen's Church in Westminster. Four years later he was appointed a chaplain at Trinity College, Cambridge, and was soon immersed in the questioning of orthodox belief and practice which was then exciting the university and spread more widely in the 1960s. When the vicar of the university church, Mervyn Stockwood, was appointed Bishop of Southwark in 1959, he invited John Robinson and other Cambridge priests to join him in an effort to bridge the wide gap between the church and the working class in South London.

James went to St George's Church, Camberwell – an inner-city area – where he stayed five years, experimenting with new forms of worship and pastoral ministry. But he became convinced that the renewal of the church's mission required the reform of many aspects of its organization at every level. This coincided with Parish and People's need for a full-time Director. After this he became a Canon Residentiary of Southwark Cathedral and devoted much of his time to the inner city riverside parishes of South London, but this ended abruptly when he had a serious disagreement with the bishop over another issue.

At Robert Runcie's invitation he became Diocesan Missioner of St Albans – a post which included concern for the church's mission in Hertfordshire's expanding towns and the development of specialised new area ministries, and also left him with time to pursue his national interests. These included Christian Action, of which he became part-time Director in 1979 before moving back to London as full-time Director in 1983. In addition to the *Faith in the City* project, James gave time to the editorship of the *Christian Action Journal* and produced sixty issues which displayed a range and depth of Christian social concern without equal in the church or in the more general field of social ethics. From 1978–97 he was also Preacher of Grays Inn, where he exercised a remarkable prophetic and pastoral ministry among some of Britain's leading lawyers.

For many years he was a frequent broadcaster in the BBC's 'Thought for the Day' slot, but there was a year's gap in 1989 when he had a major disagreement with the BBC over what he regarded, with justification, as undue editorial interference with his scripts. He declared his own homosexuality on television, and created some controversy in 1998 with a lecture in Westminster Abbey in which he called for a national debate on the possibility of monarchs being elected. The fact that he was a Chaplain to the Queen made this proposal specially interesting to the media.

Among many publications his biography of Bishop John Robinson (1987) was the most widely acclaimed. Many believed that he should have been given high office in the church, but he was content with his role as a gad-fly and probably made a greater contribution in that way.

# Nicolas Stacey

## (1927–   )

Nicolas David Stacey was one of the Church of England's most prominent priests during the 1960s and forsook a promising career in the Royal Navy and spectacular success on the athletics track in the hope of serving God in a reformed and renewed church. He believed that a combination of vision, imagination and radical change in the structure of England's established church would revivify it, and he sought to prove this in the large South London council house and flat parish where he was Rector from 1960 to 1968.

When he arrived at Woolwich the congregation at the parish church, designed to seat 700, was no more than 50. The interior of the building was dark and decaying, and the unused gallery was occupied by rats and mice. Two smaller daughter churches were attended by mere handfuls of people, and the church's involvement in the community was negligible. Over the next eight years Stacey did everything in his power to remedy the situation. A large team of able curates was recruited and a massive new ministry programme of pastoral care through house-to-house visiting and social work was developed. A discotheque in the crypt with a licensed bar attracted hundreds of young people; a branch of the Samaritans was formed; a housing association for homeless families was started and eventually became the largest in London; the aisles of the church became offices for local voluntary bodies and the gallery a coffee bar. The local Presbyterians closed their church and joined forces; Methodist and Baptist ministers and a Roman Catholic priest joined the staff, making the whole enterprise ecumenical. The worship was enlivened, the preaching was good, and enormous care was taken over preparation for marriage and baptism.

It was a remarkable example of renewal parish ministry, but after six years Stacey was not satisfied with its progress, and used his considerable journalistic skills to pen an article for the *Observer Colour Supplement* which he headlined 'A Mission's Failure'. His chief point was that although he and his team had 'pulled out all the stops', the congregation had risen to only 150 – they had hoped for at least 400, which would still have been only a small fraction of the population. When compared with the progress achieved in similar areas in South London and the rest of England, this represented notable success. But Stacey believed that his team's work at Woolwich demonstrated that no amount of inspiration and hard work stood any chance of significantly increasing congregations in working-class areas. A less formal kind of church life was needed, Christians must be encouraged to infiltrate their local secular organizations, and the clergy should seek employment in key secular occupations in the area.

The church did not like this message. The Archbishop of York accused him of 'rocking the boat', others accused him of 'defeatism', and his own bishop, Mervyn Stockwood, warned him that he must not expect to be given another appointment in the Church of England for many years to come. Two years later he left Woolwich to become Deputy Director of Oxfam, the overseas aid agency.

Stacey's parents had originally intended that he should be educated at Eton, but on the outbreak of the 1939–45 war he elected instead to go to the Royal Naval College, Dartmouth. There he became Chief Cadet Captain and was awarded the King's Telescope. As a midshipman, he sailed in a battleship to the Far East during the closing weeks of the war. The sight of the devastation caused by the atomic bomb at Hiroshima led him to resign from the Navy and seek ordination. He took a degree in modern history at Oxford, where he developed an unsuspected ability in athletics, and was not only President of the University Athletics Club but also represented Britain in the Empire Games and the 1952 Olympic Games. He completed his ordination training at Cuddesdon Theological College, and from 1953 to 1958 was a curate in Portsmouth.

He then became Domestic Chaplain to the Bishop of Birmingham, Leonard Wilson (of wartime Singapore fame), and founded and edited a tabloid newspaper *The Birmingham Christian News,* which had a circulation of 35,000. It later expanded to become *The National Christian News.* Appointment to Woolwich followed. After Oxfam, where he had pleaded without much success for greater emphasis on education and political lobbying, he became Director of Social Services, first in London, then in Kent. Ironically, although he and his ideas had been largely rejected by the church, his pioneering work in introducing professional fostering leading to the closure of every approved school in the country, care in the community tranforming the lives of hundreds of thousands of people, and 'mentoring' delinquent teenagers as an alternative to prison, all became national government policies.

Nicolas Stacey, *Who Cares?*, Hodder 1971.

# John XXIII

## (1881–1963)

John XXIII, by common consent the greatest Pope of the century, achieved in the space of five years what was generally believed to be impossible: he enabled the Roman Catholic Church to break out of the strait-jacket of entrenched conservatism and to embark on a process of reform and renewal comparable with the Protestant Reformation of the sixteenth and seventeenth centuries. The chief instrument of this *aggiornamento*, as he called it, was the Second Vatican Council, which he convened soon after his election, but even more important was the spirit and style he brought to the papacy – to which he was elected when he was seventy-seven. He radiated goodness, was warm-hearted and humorous, relaxed much of the stuffy formality of the Vatican, and used words like dialogue, openness and brotherhood. He often astonished groups he was addressing – Jews, socialists, prisoners and others – with the introductory greeting 'I am your brother, Joseph', and the leaders of other churches who anticipated a formal reception were welcomed with genuine affection.

Angelo Giuseppe Roncalli was born – the third of thirteen children – into a peasant farming family who lived near Bergamo, in Northern Italy. He attended the village school and went from there to the local seminary to train as a priest. A scholarship took him to the St Apollinare Institute where, in 1904, he was awarded a doctorate in theology for research into the life of St Charles Borromeo. From 1905–14 he was secretary to the Bishop of Bergamo and also lectured in church history at the local seminary. When war came he was conscripted as a hospital orderly, but soon transferred to the army chaplains' department. On leaving the army he was appointed by Pope Benedict XV as National Director of the Congregation for the Propagation of the Faith – a key Vatican post responsible at that time for the building up of an indigenous clergy and hierarchy in mission territory. After five years of this, Benedict's successor, Pius XI, appointed him Apostolic Delegate to Bulgaria and titular Archbishop of Areopolis. This marked the beginning of his special concern for the Eastern Orthodox Churches. In 1934 he became Apostolic Delegate to Turkey and Greece, and during the wartime German occupation of Greece was involved in relief work and sought to prevent the deportation of Jews to Germany.

Following the liberation of France at the end of 1944, Roncalli went to Paris as Nuncio, where he handled with firmness but sensitivity the problem of the many bishops accused of collaborating with the Vichy government, and supported the worker priests. In 1953 he was made a cardinal and expected to be recalled to a Vatican post, but the unexpected death of the Patriarch of Venice led to appointment as his successor. His five years there were marked by strong pastoral work, informality and firm resistance to the Communists, who exercised considerable power in Northern Italy.

Roncalli's election as Pope in 1958 owed everything to the fact that the College of Cardinals could not agree on either of the main Italian candidates and, after eleven inconclusive ballots, chose him as a caretaker Pope. The idea of a council came to him, he said, under the prompting of the Holy Spirit, and he prayed that it would be 'a new Pentecost' that would renew the church's life and bring about the reunion of the churches of the East and West. It was attended by all the Catholic bishops and by official observers from eighteen other churches, as well as some hundreds of specialist advisers, and at the opening session on 11 October 1962 Pope John urged the bishops to expound the truth positively and without recourse to anathemas. He did not himself attend the subsequent sessions but intervened in November 1962 when a draft schema on the Holy Spirit produced by the Curia was deemed too conservative. On 8 December the Council was adjourned for nine months, but before it could reassemble John was dead.

Among his other achievements were the setting up of a Secretariat for Christian Unity and a Pontifical Commission on Birth Control. He also issued three major encyclicals: *Ad cathedram Petri* (1961) said that truth, unity and peace should be promoted in the spirit of love, and greeted non-Catholics as 'separated brethren'; *Mater et magistra* (1961) updated Catholic social teaching and called on the richer nations to help the poor; *Pacem in Terris* (1963) pleaded for the end of colonialism and the arms race, for peaceful co-existence between East and West, and an improvement in the status of women. It was a short, hyper-active pontificate, and if unable to sleep, the 'caretaker Pope' would say to himself, 'Relax, Angelo, it's not you who runs the church but the Holy Spirit'.

Peter Hebblethwaite, *John XXIII. Pope of the Council*, Geoffrey Chapman 1984.

# Léon-Joseph Suenens

## (1904–1996)

Léon-Joseph Suenens, Cardinal Archbishop of Malines-Brussels and Primate of Belgium, was a leading figure at the Second Vatican Council and fought for the adoption of decrees designed to modernize the life of the Roman Catholic Church. In this he had some success, but his efforts to secure the implementation of these decrees when the Council ended brought him much disappointment, and he turned to the charismatic renewal movement as the most likely way of liberating the church for its mission in the world.

Suenens was an ardent disciple of Pope John XXIII. The two men liked each other, and the aged Pope saw in the able bishop from Belgium someone who would represent his views in the Council. He was given a share in the preparatory work and produced an outline of the form the Council should take which became official policy. When, soon after the opening of the Council in 1962, a document on the church, compiled largely under curial influence, was deemed too conservative, it was Suenens who proposed redrafting it. with greater emphasis on the church's role in the world. He was entrusted by the Pope with the task of presenting his Encyclical *Pacem in Terris* to the United Nations and gave the address at his Requiem Mass in St Peter's in 1963.

During the Council he secured approval for the appointment of permanent deacons, and after pointing out powerfully that the Holy Spirit – 'the principle of surprise in the church' – is present in the whole church, not just in the bishops, more lay people, including some women, were admitted to the Council as auditors. Although Suenens had a good relationship with Paul VI, who made him a Moderator of the Council, he was sometimes critical of his decisions. He complained that while the Pope had supported the concept of collegiality for the bishops, he was unwilling to accept it for himself. When the policy of clerical celibacy was reaffirmed, he said that the Pope had not taken account of the flexibility of the priesthood over the centuries, and on the issue of birth control he thought the encyclical *Humanae Vitae* gave insufficient weight to the non-procreative aspects of marriage.

These criticisms brought him many abusive letters and scurrilous attacks from certain sections of the Italian press.

Suenens was born into a poor family in Ixelles, a suburb of Bussels, and his father died when he was only three. His mother thereupon took him to live in the presbytery of an uncle who was a parish priest, but after a time they moved back to Brussels, where they lived in poverty. Young Léon-Joseph attended a good local school and having felt called to the priesthood was sent by Cardinal Mercier, the Archbishop of Malines-Brussels, to be trained at the Gregorian University. He was disappointed with the education he was offered there, complaining that the philosophy was too abstract and the theology too speculative. But following his ordination in 1927, he returned to Rome for a further two years in order to complete a doctorate in philosophy and theology and a degree in canon law. He then taught for six months in his old school in Brussels, but this did not suit him, and he was pleased to be appointed Professor of Philosophy at the Malines seminary. He was there for ten years and proved to be a good teacher. There was a Flemish bluntness in his style, and his spirituality was always down to earth and influenced by a deep feeling for nature.

On the outbreak of war in 1939 he served as an army chaplain until the German occupation of Belgium, whereupon he became Vice-Rector of the University of Louvain. This was a difficult assignment, involving negotiations with the German authorities over the conscription of students for forced labour, and for the final fifteen months of the war he had full responsibility for the university, the Rector having been imprisoned by the Gestapo. He found opportunity, however, to initiate a course of theological study for the laity.

In 1945 he became an auxiliary bishop to Cardinal Van Roey, the Archbishop of Malines-Brussels, and established the Legion of Mary as a lay movement in Belgium. His book *Theology of the Apostolate* (1953), a handbook for the movement, was translated into thirty languages. He succeeded Van Roey in 1961 and became a cardinal three months later. After the Council his international reputation took him on preaching and lecturing tours, often ecumenically sponsored, to many parts of the world, and it was during a visit to America that he first encountered the Catholic charismatic movement. His book *Co-Responsibility in the Church* (1968) expressed powerfully his understanding of the nature of the church and of hopes that remain unfulfilled.

Elizabeth Hamilton, *Cardinal Suenens,* Hodder and Stoughton 1975.

# Hans Küng

## (1928–    )

Hans Küng was the best-known Roman Catholic theologian of the second half of the century – and the most controversial. Although a prominent theological adviser at the Second Vatican Council, he was disappointed by its results and thereafter was a frequent critic of papal pronouncements and Vatican policy. His first book, in which he said there was no fundamental difference between the teaching of the prominent Protestant theologian Karl Barth on the subject of justification and that of the Council of Trent, caused considerable surprise and aroused the suspicion of the Vatican. Further books on the exercising of authority in the church led to official hearings and condemnations, and in 1979 his licence to teach as a Catholic theologian was withdrawn. Nonetheless he remained as Professor of Dogmatic and Ecumenical Theology at the University of Tübingen and stayed in the Catholic Church, occupying what he called a position of 'critical loyalty'.

Küng was born into a devout Catholic family in Sursee, Switzerland. As a boy he felt drawn to the priesthood, and after completing his early education at the cantonal school at Lucerne, went to study philosophy and theology at the Gregorian University in Rome. At this time he shared the conservative outlook prevailing in Rome during the pontificate of Pius XII and his thesis for the licentiate in philosophy was on the atheistic humanism of Jean-Paul Sartre. Turning to theology, however, he came under the influence of a leading biblical scholar, Stanislas Lyonnet, who was silenced and banned by the Holy Office in 1961. He also came to know Yves Congar – a prominent French theolgian who had also been banned. Encouraged by them and another Swiss theologian, Hans Urs von Balthasar, he explored Barth's teaching on justification and, having secured his licentiate in theology with a dissertation on this subject, went to the Institut Catholique and the Sorbonne in Paris to develop this into a thesis for a doctorate in theology.

From 1957 to 1959 Küng was engaged in pastoral work at the Hofkirche in Lucerne; then he went to Germany as a research assistant in the Catholic Faculty of Theology at Münster. There, foreseeing some of the issues to be faced by the coming Vatican Council, he wrote *The*

*Council, Reform and Reunion* (1960), which urged radical reform of Catholic institutions and attitudes. In the same year he was appointed Professor of Fundamental Theology at Tübingen and wrote two books, *Structures of the Church* and *That the World May Believe*, both of which appeared in 1962 at about the same time as he was made a Council adviser.

A lecture tour of America in 1963 which attracted huge crowds aroused considerable controversy, and he was banned from lecturing in some Catholic universities. On his return to Germany he was appointed to a newly-created chair of Dogmatic and Ecumenical Theology at Tübingen and Director of a new Institute for Ecumenical Research. At the same time he was summoned back to Rome, where proceedings against his *Structures of the Church* had started. Fortunately for him, these were presided over by Cardinal Bea, a leading Catholic ecumenist, and no action was taken.

The publication of his Council lectures *The Living Church* followed, and with some other reformist scholars he co-founded the international theological journal *Concilium,* which became an influential forum of Catholic thought for the rest of the century. In 1964 he left the Council early, disappointed with its progress, and thereafter concentrated on teaching, lecturing and writing. He protested publicly against the papal encyclical on clerical celibacy (1967), and went on Swiss television to criticize the encyclical on contraception (1968). His criticism of new Roman regulation on mixed marriages led to a rebuke from the German bishops.

Thereafter his name was never out of the spotlight for long. His literary output was prodigious. He worked long hours, employed a team of researchers, and produced a series of books of considerable length and erudition. *The Church* (1967) included some criticisms of the church's practices, but argued for staying within its life. Nonetheless, he was ordered by the Vatican to withdraw it from circulation, which he refused to do. *Infallible: An Enquiry* (1970) landed him in further trouble with the German bishops, and later with the Congregation for the Doctrine of the Faith in Rome, though it also won him a declaration of solidarity from 300 Catholic and Protestant theologians. *On Being a Christian* (1974) was seen by many as a superb introduction to the Christian faith, but drew three statements of criticism from the German bishops in 1977. The withdrawal of his licence to teach as a Catholic theologian followed. Later books were concerned with the relationship between Christianity and other faiths, and *Global Responsibility* (1991) marked the beginning of his concern for a global ethic.

# Alexander Men

## (1935–1990)

Alexander Men was one of the century's most remarkable Russian Orthodox priests, whose combination of learning, spirituality and pastoral skill enabled him to exercise very great influence during and after the Communist tyranny, not least among Moscow's intellectuals. Although not himself an open dissident, he provided friendship and strong spiritual support for Alexander Solzhenitsyn, Gleb Yakunin and other leaders of the heroic sruggle for human rights and religious freedom. His literary output was immense but, apart from a few important books published abroad under pseudonyms, his writings had to be circulated in duplicated form until freedom came in 1988.

Men's chief concern as a scholar was to bridge the gulf between the message of the Christian gospel and the modern scientifically trained mind. He tackled many of the intellectual problems facing Christians in the modern world, including the fact of evil, of which he and his fellow countrymen had experienced a great deal. He drew important lessons for both church and state from the twentieth-century Russian experience, and while always emphasizing the uniqueness of Christ, said, 'I am convinced that each of the founders of the world religions speaks truth to us'. His achievement was all the more impressive because for the greater part of his life he had no access to the contemporary theological work of the West. Having survived the persecutions of Stalin, Khrushchev and other tyrants, he was murdered by unknown men and for no apparent reason while on the way to conduct Sunday worship during the early days of freedom.

Men was born in Moscow. His father was an intellectual of Jewish origin, but his mother was a Christian convert, and the young Alik was brought up in the Orthodox faith during the harsh years of Stalinist repression, modified only when the Soviet Union was drawn into the Second World War. At school he displayed outstanding intellectual gifts and from the age of twelve was aware of a vocation to the priesthood. He was involved as a chorister and server in his local church but his Jewish background precluded entry to a university, so he went instead to a Moscow institute to study biology. In 1955 the Institute was transferred to Siberia, where he attended a nearby cathedral and undertook some work for the bishop.

After three years, however, when he was about to take his final examinations, these links with the church came to light and he was sent back to Moscow unqualified. It was then decided that he should be made deacon immediately, without seminary training, and he served in a southwest Moscow parish for two years before becoming a priest in 1960. At this point he moved to Alabino, about sixty miles from the capital, and in spite of Khrushchev's anti-religious campaign, achieved a great deal – winning the trust of his own parishioners and attracting to the church many others who admired his erudition and spiritual depth.

When he moved to another parish in north Moscow, the effect was the same and this was repeated when he became priest, then archpriest, of Novaya Derevnya, where he remained for twenty years until his death. A feature of his ministry was the formation of small Christian communities for Bible study and prayer, usually in defiance of government regulations. Many of those who joined them were Jewish converts, and young people flocked to his seminars. Over the years thousands came from all parts of Russia to be baptized by him – usually in secret – and throughout the 1970s he was frequently picked up for questioning by the KGB. He also experienced tension with the church because of his Jewish background, while others objected to his ecumenical outlook and his attempts to introduce Western spirituality to Orthodox believers. When some of his friends suggested that, for the sake of his own safety, he should leave Russia, he said that he must stay: 'All that can be done is to believe, to hope and to continue to live.'

After 1988 he was able to give public lectures on the Bible and Christianity, and frequently spoke on radio and television. He worked at a frantic pace and during the final period of his life gave as many as twenty-two lectures a month to overflowing meetings. He also founded an education society 'Cultural Renaissance', and on the day before his death delivered an inaugural lecture on Christianity at a new university named after him and of which he was to be the Rector. When the news of his murder became known, President Boris Yeltsin called a Supreme Soviet meeting to observe a moment of silence, and a group of friends wrote: 'He was a magnet attracting people's hearts . . . He had a great gift for love and he imparted it to all who were suffering.'

*Christianity for the Twenty-first Century: The Life and Work of Alexander Men*, edited by Elizabeth Roberts and Ann Shukman, SCM Press 1996.

# Daniel Berrigan
## (1921–   )

Daniel Berrigan was an American Jesuit priest who became a professor of theology, but abandoned academic life in order to become one of the leading opponents of the Vietnam War and later devoted equal energy to opposing nuclear warfare. He recognized the value of dramatic gestures for the securing of publicity for a cause and became internationally famous in 1968 when he was convicted of destroying the official registration records of future recruits for the Vietnam War at Catonsville, Maryland. For this he was sentenced to three years in prison, but went underground for several months until re-arrested. In 1980 he was again arrested and convicted of damaging three nuclear warheads which were under construction at a General Electric plant in Pennsylvania. At this court hearing he put up a spirited defence:

*Judge*:    Father Berrigan, regardless of the outcome of these hearings, will you promise the court that you will refrain from such acts in the future?

*DB*:    Your Honour, it seems to me that you are asking the wrong question.

*Judge*:    OK, Father Berrigan, what do you think is the proper question?

*DB*:    Well, your Honour, it appears to me that you should ask President Bush if he'll stop making missiles, and if he'll stop making them then I'll stop banging on them and you and I can go fishing.

The previous trial provided the subject for an off-Broadway play, *The Trial of the Catonsville Nine*, written by Berrigan when he was on the run in 1971.

   He was born in Virginia, the son of a militant socialist labour organizer, and became a Jesuit novice when he was 18. In 1952 he was ordained to the priesthood, then spent a year with the French worker-priests. He was radicalized by this experience, but on his return to America was allowed to teach only in Catholic preparatory schools. About this time he began to express his social concerns in poetry and in 1957 won a prestigious poetry prize with a collection *Time Without*

*Number.* In the same year he was appointed Professor of Theology at Le Moyne College, Syracuse, New York, where he proved to be an able biblical scholar and also encouraged the students to become involved in social work and political activities.

Recognizing, as he put it, that the Bible is concerned with life-and-death issues, he founded with his brother, also a priest, the Catholic Peace Fellowship and also, in 1964, Clergy and Laity Concerned about Vietnam. From this point onwards active opposition to the Vietnam War became his chief concern and in 1968 he went with Professor Howard Zinn of Boston University to Hanoi, in North Vietnam, to secure the release of three American Air Force pilots who had been shot down. Demonstrations, petitions and the organizing of a huge protest movement brought opposition and denunciation from the conservative elements in American society, including the church, and he was subject to the constant attention of the CIA. The Jesuit Order tried to solve the problem by sending him out of the country, but he quickly returned. Following his first arrest in 1967 he declared that the peace demonstrations were less about resistance than about celebration and that it was better to burn draft files than children.

In most of this witness he worked closely with his brother, Philip, who had seen active service with the US army in Europe from 1943 to 1945 before becoming a secular Catholic priest in 1955. After serving in a number of pastoral and teaching posts he too made the peace movement his chief concern. At the Catonsville trial he was sentenced to six years' imprisonment and, like his brother, went underground until captured by the police in a Manhattan church in 1970. This led to a book, *Prison Journals of a Priest Revolutionary*. In the previous year he had married a former nun, Elizabeth McAlister, and, having failed to resign from the priesthood, was excommunicated in 1973.

The two brothers mounted the first Plowshares Action against the General Electric plant, and many more demonstrations against nuclear weapons were held throughout the 1980s. These included attacks on the actual weapons, and Philip was indicted 100 times and spent over six years in prison between 1970–92.

Daniel based his work on the Jesus Centre, and besides anti-war demonstrations wrote over fifty books, produced several films and conducted retreats. He came to be regarded as one of the most original and profound thinkers in the Jesuit world and believed that Christ was calling the church to die to its past traditions and to be reborn to a mission of loving service to the victims of all forms of poverty.

Daniel Berrigan, *Autobiography*, Harper and Row 1987.

# Gustavo Gutiérrez

## (1928–    )

Gustavo Gutiérrez was the pioneer, and for many years the foremost exponent, of liberation theology in Latin America. He exerted great influence not only in his own part of the world but in other places where attempts were made to articulate the Christian faith from the standpoint of the poor and the oppressed. A half-caste (mestizo), he was born in poverty in Lima, Peru in 1928. He nonetheless managed to gain entrance to the Lima University School of Medicine, where he was also active in student politics. After five years, however, he felt called to the priesthood and began a course on theology and philosophy at Santiago, Chile. There his intellectual gifts were quickly recognized, and in 1951 he was sent to Louvain, Belgium, to study philosophy and psychology.

During the next four years he established a close friendship with a fellow-student, Camilo Torres, who, a few years after his ordination to the priesthood, joined the guerrilla forces in his native Colombia and was killed in the Andes in his first encounter with the Army in 1966. Gutiérrez chose the way of the theologian and after four years at the University of Lyons, where he took a doctorate in theology, and a brief spell at the Gregorian University in Rome, was ordained priest and returned to Lima. The post awaiting him was that of Professor of Theology at the Catholic University but, having been radicalized during his time at Louvain, he quickly discovered that the theology in which he had been trained did not fit the socio-economic situation of the people for whom it was intended, most of whom were living in desperate poverty and without any political influence in their communities. So he moved into Rimac, a slum area of Lima, and besides his teaching work at the university listened to what the people around him were saying. He also analysed their economic plight, using Marxism as one of his tools, and re-examined the Bible in the light of what he was discovering.

In 1964 Gutiérrez attended a meeting in Brazil to consider the pastoral work of the church in Latin America. At this meeting he put forward the idea that the true role of theology is not to hand down concepts of the truth received from the past and approved by the church, but rather to reflect on action taking place in the contemporary world, particularly the struggles of the poor and oppressed. Theology is always the 'second act', never the first. The following year saw armed groups in action in Latin America attempting to liberate the continent from its dependency on the USA and other Western trading nations, and this led Gutiérrez to the conclusion that European theology could not cope with Latin American problems. Whereas European theology starts from the question posed by Bonhoeffer, 'How are we to proclaim God in a world come of age?', the challenge in Latin America is, 'How do we proclaim God as Father in a world that is not human and what might be the implications of telling non-humans that they are children of God?'.

Later he argued that the church must be re-incarnated in new forms, including especially the establishing of what he called 'base communities', consisting of the poor and oppressed meeting in their own environment to consider and take action for political and economic freedom in the light of the Gospel message of liberation from social and institutional, as well as personal, sin. Eventually, many thousands of such groups came into being all over Latin America, and Gutiérrez believed that it was from these groups that a new and dynamic theology would one day emerge.

The publication of his insights and ideas in 1971 in *A Theology of Liberation* was a landmark in twentieth-century theology. By this time Gutiérrez was exercising considerable influence in the church. He was an adviser to the Latin American bishops who attended a post-Vatican II conference held at Medellin, Colombia, in 1968 and his hand could be discerned in the final documents of the conference which spoke of institutional violence, dependent and base communities. So much so, that he and other like-minded theologians were denied access to a follow-up conference attended by Pope John Paul II at Puebla, Mexico, in 1979. Nonetheless, they established a base outside the conference centre and fed material to sympathetic bishops.

Besides his teaching work in the university and involvement in local base communities, Gutiérrez was the Founder and Director of the Instituto Bartolomé de las Casas, established to undertake research and promote liberation theology. He wrote several more books and many articles on the subject. *The Power of the Poor in History* (1983) provides the most comprehensive account of the development of his thinking.

# Helder Camara

## (1909–1999)

Helder Passoa Camara, one of the greatest figures of the twentieth-century church, was Archbishop of Olinda and Recife in North East Brazil from 1964 to 1984. He had previously been an auxiliary bishop in the Diocese of Rio de Janeiro for twelve years and more than anyone else was responsible for taking the ideas of the Second Vatican Council to Latin America and for getting the Roman Catholic Church in Brazil to support the poor.

Standing no more than five foot tall and possessed of a gentle voice, he nevertheless had a most dynamic personality, and his warmth and love evoked a tremendous response wherever he went. He refused to live in the official episcopal palace at Recife, preferring to occupy three rooms in the outbuildings of a nearby church. He wore a simple black cassock and a pectoral cross of black wood. He had no car and travelled about his diocese either on foot or by begging lifts from friends or passing motorists. Long hours were spent in prayer, and he encouraged the formation of base communities in which groups of Christians, mainly poor, were encouraged to read the Bible in the light of their social conditions and consider what action might be required.

Camara was born in Fortaleza in the Brazilian state of Ceara. He trained for the priesthood in a local seminary and, although he possessed no great intellectual power, soon after his ordination he was appointed Secretary for Education in his state. This gave him considerable insight into the relationship between education and political aspiration. Moving to Rio de Janeiro in 1936, he became acutely aware of the vast gulf between rich and poor and also of the popular discontent simmering beneath the surface of national life, especially in the shanty towns of Rio, São Paulo and other cities.

Camara's pastoral ministry among the poorest was recognized by his appointment as auxiliary Bishop of Rio de Janeiro in 1952, and in the same year he founded the National Conference of Brazilian Bishops in the hope of developing a co-ordinated approach to missionary and social problems. He served as its secretary until 1964. In 1955 he helped to form a Conference of Latin American Bishops for the same purpose and in 1961 initiated a Movement for Basic Education Classes. These were intended primarily for the poorest areas of Brazil and he coined the slogan 'Educate to transform'.

His appointment in 1964 as Archbishop of Olinda and Recife, another desperately poor region, came at about the same time as a military coup which had the support of the middle classes, the leading state governors, some of the bishops – and the USA. It left the country in the hands of a military dictatorship until well into the 1960s and one of its first acts was to suppress the primer of the Basic Education Classes – *The Struggle to Live*. Soon after this it initiated a regime of torture, imprisonment and murder of political dissidents which Camara strongly denounced. As a result, according to a Belgian theologian who worked with him, he was 'treated by the authorities and the media as no bishop has been treated in the Western world in this century. Only he knows the details of the round-the-clock persecution.' From 1968 to 1977 he was banned from public speaking, his books were also banned and journalists were forbidden to mention his name. There were rumours of attempts to assassinate him.

After 1968 Camara certainly worked for the overthrow of Brazil's political and social structures, but only by non-violent methods. The militant guerrilla movements were wiped out in the early 1970s, but a Cost of Living Movement, formed largely on the initiative of church groups active in the shanty towns, began to make demands on the government, and in 1978 sent to the President a petition about price increases signed by 1.4 million people. It was partly in response to this and other signs of serious popular discontent that a policy of political liberalization was adopted from 1980 onwards.

Camara favoured what he called 'a line of socialization adapted to Latin-American needs . . . The world trend is towards socialism. At this time, Christians offer to it the mystique of universal brotherhood and hope.' He was awarded the Martin Luther King Memorial Prize and nominated for the Nobel Peace Prize. He was also nominated at various times as Mayor of Rio de Janeiro, Federal Minister of Education and Vice-President of the Republic. Although he declined political office, he said, 'Politics, in the grand and beautiful sense of concern with the great and serious human problems, is the human and Christian right and duty of all members of the church, including the bishops.' Following his retirement a conservative successor reversed most of his policies.

# John Hick

## (1922– )

John Harwood Hick, a philosopher of religion, devoted his life to making belief believable and often found himself involved in controversy for his views on the incarnation and on the relationship between Christianity and other religious faiths. He was a scholar of great erudition and first became widely known through his book *Evil and the God of Love* (1966), which attracted a good deal of attention and remains a classic survey of the Christian understanding of the enigma of evil and suffering. He supported the view, first propounded by St Irenaeus in the second century, that evil and suffering are necessary for the growth of souls. In the end evil promotes good. Unfortunately, this failed to take account of the Holocaust and the problems raised by genocide.

Altogether more controversial was the book *The Myth of God Incarnate* (1977) with which his name remains chiefly associated, but which was in fact a volume of essays edited by him. In it he and his eight theologian colleagues argued that, while Jesus undoubtedly has a special role in God's purposes, the concept of him as God incarnate, the second person of the Trinity, having a human life, is best thought of in mythological terms. The book had a hostile reception. The Moderator of the General Assembly of the Church of Scotland called on its authors to resign their offices in the church, but in thoughtful circles it was held that the chief problem lay in the book's title, rather than in its contents. And although it became a best-seller, it had little impact on the church's education work in the parishes.

It was an easy step from this understanding of the incarnation to the belief that salvation is not necessarily received exclusively through faith in Christ and that other religions have their own ways of expressing how God is at work in human life. Hick became a specialist in the non-Christian religions and pleaded for greater understanding and tolerance among all believers.

He was born in 1922 and on leaving Bootham School, York, served in a Friends' Ambulance Unit as an alternative to military service during the 1939-45 war. This brought him into close contact with the casualties of war and raised in his mind some of the questions that later engaged his attention as a philosopher and theologian. After the war he took a First in philosophy at Edinburgh University, then completed a DPhil at Oriel College, Oxford.

He trained for the Presbyterian ministry and in 1953 became minister of the church at Belford in Northumberland. After three years of pastoral work he moved to America to become Assistant Professor of Philosophy at Cornell University. In 1959 he was appointed Professor of Christian Philosophy at Princeton Theological Seminary and while there wrote *The Philosophy of Religion* (1964), which ran to four editions and many translations. Earlier, in *Faith and Knowledge* (1957), he had advanced the principle of eschatological verification as a way of supporting Christian belief, but few people found this convincing. In 1961 and 1962 he was indicted for heresy by fundamentalists in the United Presbyterian Church of the USA for not affirming belief in the Virgin Birth, but no action was taken against him.

In 1964 Hick returned to England to become a lecturer in theology at Cambridge and three years later was appointed Professor of Theology at Birmingham – a post he held until 1982 and which he combined, from 1979, with that of Professor and Director of Programmes in World Religion at Claremont Graduate School, California. A small book, *Christianity at the Centre* (1968), offered a moderately liberal interpretation of the Christian faith. Two further editions indicated by their changed titles – *The Centre of Christianity* (1977) and *The Second Christianity* (1983) – how his thinking developed during his Birmingham years. This was prompted in part by his involvement in race-relations work and a growing conviction that the minimal contribution of the churches to this work was not unrelated to their failure to understand the religious belief of the Asian community and to an exclusivist christology that did not permit growth towards understanding. 'There are many lamps but the same light,' he said, and pursued this further in *An Interpretation of Religion* (1989).

In 1997 Hick was attacked by Cardinal Ratzinger, Prefect of the Vatican Congregation of the Doctrine of the Faith, in a lecture to the doctrinal commissions of the bishops' conferences of Latin America. He described Hick as one of 'relativism's founders and eminent representatives' and went on to say that his theology 'sounds beautiful, but when it is considered in depth it appears as empty and vacuous'. Hick responded by pointing out the confusions and misunderstandings in the cardinal's use of his work.

# Jean Vanier

## (1928–  )

Jean Vanier, a French-Canadian Roman Catholic layman, abandoned his career as a naval officer in order to train for the priesthood, but before reaching ordination established a community, l'Arche, which pioneered a new approach to mental handicap and at the same time illuminated some often neglected Christian insights into human nature.

In 1964 Vanier, who was at the time teaching ethics at Toronto University, visited a number of French mental hospitals and was appalled by the conditions he found in them. He responded to this experience by purchasing a house in the village of Trosly-Breuil, north of Paris, and inviting three mentally-handicapped men to live with him. The basis of this arrangement was that they should live together as if in a family, sharing a common life, giving and receiving from each other according to ability and need, without any suggestion of superiority or inferiority.

Vanier saw this as providing better care for the handicapped but also as a way of bridging the gulf between the strong and the weak, the powerful and the vulnerable. The initiative sprang, he said, from a desire to live the Gospel and follow Christ more closely. It would be a sign of contradiction to the values of the modern world. Today the community at Trosly-Breuil has about 200 mentally handicapped members, with the same number of care assistants, and there are about 100 similar l'Arche communities in 26 other countries. Associated Faith and Light communities of mentally-handicapped people, with families and friends, are located in 70 countries. Vanier, a charismatic figure, relinquished the leadership of l'Arche in 1976, following a serious illness, but remains in great demand as a retreat conductor and spiritual guide in all parts of the world.

He was born in Canada, where his French-Canadian father was a distinguished diplomat and destined to become Governor-General. Service at the Candian High Commission brought the family to London in the 1930s and in 1942 Jean went to Dartmouth as a naval cadet. By the time he had completed his training, however, the war was over and in 1947 he transferred from the Royal Navy to the Canadian Navy. While on leave in Paris, where his father was now Canadian Ambassador, he consulted a Dominican priest, Thomas Philippe, about the future course of his life. As a result, he decided to leave the navy to train for the priesthood, and from this time onwards Philippe was a powerful influence. Instead of entering a traditional seminary, he studied at an educational community, Eau Vive, run by the Paris Dominicans. He then spent a year in a Trappist monastery and from 1956 to 1962 lived mainly alone, studying philosophy and theology, and working for a doctorate on the ethics of Aristotle at the Institut Catholique in Paris. By this time Thomas Philippe had become chaplain of a home and workshop for the mentally-handicapped at Trosly-Breuil, and it was in the course of a visit to his mentor that Vanier's concern for the poor in general and the handicapped in particular was aroused.

The name l'Arche was chosen for Vanier's Trosly-Breuil community because it could mean either ark or arch – the basic concepts of the experiment. From the outset the different approach aroused considerable interest and in 1965, just twelve months after its initiation, Vanier was buying additional houses in the village and one in the nearby town of Compiègne to accommodate those who wished to be involved. Volunteers were recruited to serve as care assistants, living on equal terms with the handicapped and usually committed for an agreed period of time. More than 50 of these subsequently became priests and over 80 joined women's contemplative religious orders. In 1968 there were 73 mentally-handicapped people at Trosly-Breuil and by 1972 the number had risen to 126.

Psychiatrists were employed to assist the community's medical work and the state made grants. Otherwise, money was raised from agricultural products grown by the community and by outside work undertaken by the handicapped and the care assistants. Some problems were encountered with the village people, mainly over the care assistants who came from all parts of the world and threatened to take over village life, and this stimulated Vanier to expand l'Arche's work elsewhere. In 1969 the Daybreak Community at Richmond Hill, Ontario, opened under the leadership of two Anglicans, and in the following year the first Indian community was started in Bangalore. Although l'Arche had Catholic origins and in many places had a Catholic ethos, only a minority of the handicapped and care assistants in India were Christians, and Vanier applied no religious tests to those who joined a community. His own distinctive spirituality transcended boundaries, and he believed that l'Arche provided a model for all true communities.

Kathryn Spink, *Jean Vanier and L'Arche: A Communion of Love*, Darton, Longman and Todd 1990.

# Edward Schillebeeckx
## (1914–    )

Edward Cornelis Florentius Alfons Schillebeeckx, a Belgian Dominican priest who spent most of his life in the Netherlands, was one of the outstanding theologians of the century, ranking with Karl Barth in breadth of learning and influence. His output in books, articles and actions was extraordinary, and the core of his thinking appeared in a massive trilogy *Jesus*, *Christ* and *Church*. At various times his ideas, particularly when these involved the questioning of aspects of the church's life, caused anxiety in the Vatican, and on three occasions his work was subjected to official examination by the Congregation for the Doctrine of the Faith. His basic position was that God is mystery and beyond the world; yet he reaches out to us in order to fulfil the humanity of those whom he has created and to fulfil the destiny of the world. The grace of God is therefore to be discerned primarily in and through the world, and human experience is the channel through which God normally reveals himself. Thus the church is a community of grace inasmuch as it is at work in the world; contemplation and politics are held together in 'political holiness'.

Schillebeeckx, the sixth of fourteen children, was born in Antwerp. After attending a strict Jesuit school he entered the Dominican Order in Ghent in 1934 and was sent to Louvain for three years of philosophy, to be followed by three of theology. In 1938, however, he was conscripted for a year's military service. This completed, he returned to Louvain, but on the outbreak of World War II in September 1939 was called back into the army. Belgium was so rapidly overcome by the German forces in 1940 that he saw no military action and soon completed his studies. From 1943 to 1945 he taught in the Dominican house in Louvain, then moved to the Dominican faculty in Paris. There, under the influence of Yves Congar and M.D.Chenu, he became involved in a new approach to theology which involved the historical study of the patristic and mediaeval periods, but also concern for and involvement in the life of the contemporary church.

In 1947 he returned to Louvain as a lecturer in dogmatics and also as chaplain to the local prison. His first book, *Christ the Sacrament* (1952), indicated continuing Thomist influence, but his exposition of the concept of Christ as the primordial sacrament, the other sacraments flowing from him and serving as a means of encounter with God, aroused wide interest and was translated into ten languages. In 1958 he became Professor of Dogmatics and the History of Theology at Nijmegen University in the Netherlands and remained there until his retirement in 1983. His arrival in the Netherlands coincided with a revival in the life of the Roman Catholic Church there, and a desire both for reform and for greater effort to relate the Christian faith to the needs of the modern world. Schillebeeckx became deeply involved in this, and played a significant part in the drafting of a letter issued by the Dutch bishops in 1960, which outlined a liberal agenda for the forthcoming Vatican Council. He accompanied the bishops to the Council as an adviser, but was not accorded official status, as the Vatican was suspicious of his views.

The publication of *God the Future of Man* (1969), based on lectures given in the USA, indicated that he had now moved away from Thomism as a framework for his thinking and had absorbed some of the thinking of the new hermeneutics of the Heidegger School and the social-critical thinking of the Frankfurt School. This led to a much deeper interest in social and political issues and led him to posit the question: how can one be faithful to both the church and secular reality? The discussion of this and other related questions took place in the influential journal *Concilium,* which he helped to found and edit.

In *Jesus* (1974) he argued that the early experience of the followers of Jesus, who regarded him as 'the eschatological prophet', was also the way for people in every age to come to recognize him as the Christ. And in *Christ* (1977) he continued to stress the importance of human experience, social as well as personal; the need for liberation from social suffering led him to embrace much of the thinking of the Latin American liberation theologians. Schillebeeckx was also attracted by their advocacy and experience of 'grass roots' churches and in *Ministry: A Case for Change* (1981) he advanced the controversial view that present forms, including celibacy, were not necessarily permanent. In 1982 he became the first theologian to be awarded the Erasmus Prize and soon afterwards was made a Commander of the Order of Oranje-Nassau – the highest civilian honour in Holland.

John Bowden, *Edward Schillebeeckx: Portrait of a Theologian,* SCM Press 1983.

# Jürgen Moltmann

## (1926–   )

Jürgen Moltmann, who was Professor of Systematic Theology in the University of Tubingen from 1963 to 1994, was the most influential Protestant theologian of the second half of the century, though much of his prolific work remains to be assimilated and even more translated into the social and political action which he saw as the essential concomitant of theological reflection.

Of his many books, the first two remain the most important. *Theology of Hope* (1965) made a considerable impact at the time of its publication and this extended far beyond Germany. In contrast with current discussions of demythologizing, death of God and secular Christianity, it offered a more positive interpretation of Christianity based on the rediscovery of biblical eschatology. 'Hope alone keeps life – including public, social life – free', he said, and practised what he taught through his political commitment and involvement in protest marches and demonstrations.

In *The Crucified God* (1973) he tackled the problem of suffering in the post-Auschwitz world and questioned the traditional view that God by his very nature is unable to suffer. On the contrary, said Moltmann, the crucifixion, which is the central point of the Christian revelation, shows Jesus expressing the anguish of God, since he is fully divine as well as fully human. The relationship between the suffering of the Son, who feels forsaken, and the Father himself, is necessarily mysterious, and is to be understood as a transaction within the Trinity. There will be no end to suffering in this world, but God stands with the sufferer, and at the end of history sorrow will be turned into joy. Meanwhile, this future hope must impel the Christian to strive for the elimination of the causes of suffering in the here and now. The book ends with a chapter on Ways Towards the Political Liberation of Mankind, which includes discussion of 'political religion' and 'a political theology of the Cross'.

In a series of books designed to present a coherent systematic theology, *The Trinity and the Kingdom of God* (1980) offered more on the theme of suffering and also sought to reconcile the churches of East and West as well as to encourage theological conversation between Christians and Jews. Another volume, *God in Creation* (1985), discussed the importance of the relationship between an adequate doctrine of creation and current ecological issues. None of Moltmann's books is easy reading. The depth of his thought is, as might be expected, expressed in the language of the German philosophical tradition, and most of his early books were intended for fellow professional theologians. Later, however, he wrote other volumes that were more accessible to lay people. One of these, *Experiences of God* (1980), contains a moving statement of personal faith which provides a valuable introduction to his thought.

Moltmann was born in Hamburg. His parents' religious life consisted of little more than the observance of Christmas, and during his late teens his own chief interests were mathematics and physics. During the early part of 1944 he was conscripted as an Air Force auxiliary, and in February 1945 was captured in Belgium by the Allied armies. He spent next three years in prisoner-of-war camps in Britain. This proved to be a formative experience. He had taken with him into the Air Force Goethe's poems and the works of Nietzsche, but these failed to meet his needs and he fell back on a copy of the New Testament given to him by an army chaplain, in which the Psalms were an appendix. The Psalms especially spoke to him in the desolation and hopelessness of his situation, and he wrote later of his prison camp experience: 'I cannot say I found God there. But I do know in my heart that it is there that he found me, and that I would otherwise have been lost.'

Following his release, he studied theology at Göttingen, and during his student years took part in protests against the re-armament of the German Federal Republic, the atom bomb and the willingness of the church to provide chaplains to the armed forces. He also worked for German-Polish reconciliation. In 1952 he became the pastor of a Lutheran church in a suburb of Bremen and in 1958, having completed a doctoral thesis on Christopher Pezel, a sixteenth century Reformed theologian, he became professor at a theological seminary in Wuppertal. He subsequently moved to the chair of systematic theology at the University of Bonn, and then until his retirement held a similar chair at Tübingen, where he exerted great influence on new generations of theologians and pastors. His wife, Elisabeth Moltmann-Wendel, was also a theologian and they wrote a stimulating joint volume *Humanity in God* (1983), which included a lively chapter on the role of women in the church.

# Joseph Tson

## (1934–   )

Joseph Tson, a Baptist pastor, was an outstanding Christian leader in Romania during the 1970s when the Communist regime of Ceausescu held that country in an iron grip. In 1955 the small Baptist Church was driven by the government to implement a series of restrictive regulations, and, although no one in the church was ever happy about this, it was not until 1973 that the policy was openly challenged. Tson had recently returned to Romania after studying theology in Oxford and become a teacher at the Baptist Theological Seminary in Bucharest. His challenge came in a lengthy essay on 'The Present Situation of the Baptist Church in Romania' and included a strong denunciation of its Congress for what he called a 'betrayal of Baptist principles'.

He pointed out that as a result of the 1955 agreement with the government the number of Baptist churches had been reduced; services held in the remainder had also been reduced and the forms of worship brought under central control, as also had the appointment of pastors; lists of candidates for baptism were submitted for approval by the local Inspector of Cults and the finances of the church were supervised by the Department of Cults. As a result, the church's life and mission had been seriously hampered. Tson had no difficulty in demonstrating that this was theologically unacceptable. The essay was translated into English and widely circulated in the West, to the grave embarrassment of both the Baptist Church and the Romanian government.

Nothing daunted, Tson published in 1974 a longer paper 'A Christian Manifesto: The Place of Christians in Socialism'. This was addressed to the Romanian people as a whole, and in particular to their Communist rulers. It argued that the government's atheistic propaganda and restriction of church activity was actually hindering the creation of a new socialist society, since socialism required men and women whose lives had been transformed by Christ. Again the paper was translated into English and sent to Britain and America. Swift action followed. The Baptist Union Council publicly dissociated itself from the two papers and dismissed Tson from his post in the seminary. The government charged him with propaganda against the state, but eventually the case was dropped and, following American pressure on Ceausescu, who was seeking US assistance, he was reinstated at the seminary. The Baptist Church was also given some legal rights under state law.

Tson was born in Transylvania, near the Hungarian border, where his parents' home was used as the place of worship for local Baptists. He went from a state school to the University of Cluj and took a degree in philology. Feeling called to ordination, he enrolled at the Bucharest Theological Seminary in 1955 but left after two years because of doubts about his faith. He then taught for ten years in Cluj, and while on a tourist visit to England in 1968 was attracted by Oxford and secured a place at Regents Park College to read theology. On his return to Romania in 1972 he was ordained as a pastor and besides his teaching post was given oversight of the Baptist Church at Ploesti at the centre of the Romanian oilfields. After the problems arising from his critical papers had been resolved, he was soon in trouble again when in the spring of 1977 he and five other pastors issued 'A Call to Truth: The Neo-Protestant Denominations and Human Rights in Romania'. This led to harsh interrogations and harassment by the security police, and he moved to become pastor of the church in Oradea, in Northern Transylvania.

There his powerful preaching and energetic ministry built up a congregation of 1,700 members, 1,000 of whom attended his weekly Bible schools. He continued to be subjected to personal harassment, however, and, after he had written a paper on the right of Baptist churches to use money as they thought best, he was summoned to the Ministry of the Interior in 1981 and given a one-way passport to leave the country. He then spent several years in America until the overthow of the Ceausescu regime in 1990, when he returned home to become Head of the Romanian Missionary Society.

The task of the Society was to rebuild Baptist life in the country, and Tson embarked on a massive scheme at Oradea which included a cathedral-scale worship centre, with 2,300 seats (the largest Baptist church in Europe), a medical centre for the needy, an orphanage, a Bible Institute, and a teacher training centre. Approval was then given for the opening of a business school and for the educational side of the project to be called the Emmanuel Christian University. It was the fulfilment of an idea that came to Tson in 1986, and he became its President.

# Don Cupitt

## (1934–    )

Don Cupitt, who taught at Cambridge for over thirty years, worked on the frontier between religion and philosophy. His approach was primarily that of a philosopher rather than that of a theologian. He came to believe that religion was essentially a human invention and that the word God had no objective reality. It was, he said, 'a necessary myth', and his position was best described as a form of Christian atheism. His attacks on the church and theologians were often savage. In *Taking Leave of God* (1980) he accused the church of exercising 'psychological terrorism' and saw his own role as that of 'rescuing Jesus from dogmatic captivity and God from metaphysical captivity'. None of this won him many friends among church leaders or indeed among his fellow academics and in 1996, after twenty-three years as a lecturer in the Cambridge Divinity School, he resigned because he felt that his colleagues were not taking him sufficiently seriously.

Cupitt was, in fact, a brilliant communicator and this was recognized when in 1977 he presented a television documentary *Who was Jesus?* This encouraged the BBC to engage him for an expensive series of programmes with the title *Sea of Faith,* in which all the world's main religions were brought under critical survey. Large audiences watched the series and, following the publication of a book based on it, a 'Sea of Faith Movement' came into being. Membership of the movement was never large, but a young priest who declared himself to be a follower of Cupitt and wrote a book encapsulating the thought of his master was dismissed from his clergy training post in Chichester.

Don Cupitt was educated at Charterhouse School and Trinity Hall, Cambridge, where he began by reading natural sciences; he then switched to theology, in which he gained a First. In 1959 he became a curate in a working-class parish in Salford, Manchester, where the experience of life in the back streets of an industrial city convinced him of the need for a reinterpretation of the Christian faith and a radical reformation of the churches. In common with Bishop John Robinson and other theologians of that time, however, he did not question the basic premise of traditional Christianity.

After three years as a curate he returned to Cambridge as Vice Principal of Westcott House theological college, then became a Fellow of Emmanuel College, serving as Dean from 1966 to 1991. There he remained for the rest of his teaching career, and was revered by successive generations of students who enjoyed his revolutionary thinking and at the same time greatly valued his high-quality pastoral care. Curiously, as it seemed to some, he was very conservative on liturgical matters.

His first book, *Christ and the Hiddenness of God* (1971), was welcomed as a valuable contribution to christology, but his next, *The Crisis of Moral Authority* (1972), raised a number of awkward questions about the doctrine of original sin and the concept of atonement. In *The Leap of Reason* (1976) he was still able to argue for the reality of God, but asserted that much Christian dogma ran contrary to religious experience. *The Worlds of Science and Religion* (1976) marked a change of interest from doctrinal matters to the relationship between religion, philosophy, psychology and sociology and this was to occupy his thinking for the rest of his life. About this time he was much influenced by Derrida and other French deconstructionist philosophers. He also acknowleded debts to Nietzsche, Wittgenstein and Heidegger, and became very interested in Eastern philosophy, acknowledging the attraction of Buddhism.

The development of Cupitt's thinking could be charted in his books which appeared at regular twelve-month intervals, and of which *The Long-Legged Fly* (1987) was specially important. They often seemed more akin to work in progress than to substantial summas, and they tended to be somewhat repetitive, but they were eagerly awaited by a significant number of readers who were hovering on the edges of faith. They constituted an important challenge to theologians who claimed to be radical in their thinking. The philosopher-novelist Iris Murdoch greatly valued his work.

At various times it was suggested that Cupitt's beliefs were incompatible with his position as a priest in the Church of England, but he never accepted this and believed it to be the task of the clergy to encourage exploration of the unknown. His own faith was summed up in *After All: Religion without Alienation* (1994): 'We should live as the Sun does. The process by which it lives and the process by which it dies are one and the same. It hasn't a care. It simply expends itself gloriously, and in so doing gives life to us all.'

# Dorothee Sölle

## (1929– )

Dorothee Sölle was a German radical theologian with an original mind who exercised considerable influence both in Germany and in America, where she taught at the Union Theological Seminary in New York. Coming from a liberal, non-Christian background, she began to study theology through the influence of her religious education teacher, who had been a pupil of Rudolf Bultmann, the radical New Testament scholar. She was subsequently much influenced by her reflection on the significance of Auschwitz for the Christian doctrine of God, then by liberation theology, and most recently by feminist theology. 'God's Spirit is not blowing in the faculties of theology,' she declared, 'He long ago emigrated from them, and is now blowing among the women and men who block the transporting of nuclear waste or do other things that are necessary in our world.' She was a leading figure in the German peace movement.

Sölle's first major book *Christ as Representative* (1965) was subtitled 'An Essay in Theology after the Death of God'. This death was of the monarchical God who sits on a throne receiving the homage of human beings. Such a God is redundant in the modern world, so Jesus Christ – the poor homeless man – has become God's representative. This 'representative' concept required a new approach to the doctrine of the atonement, replacing the theory that at the crucifixion Jesus was offering himself as a substitute for human beings whose sin had provoked the wrath of God and required a propitiatory sacrifice to put matters right. Sölle argued that this theory left man doing nothing himself and without responsibilities. If, however, Christ is seen as representative, rather than as substitute, this means that he holds a place open before God for man to step in himself: 'Like every other representative, Christ depends on our assent, otherwise he would be merely a replacement.'

In *Thinking about God* (1990) she described the doctrine of God's omnipotence as a male delusion – a projection of male wishes on to God – and in a television interview in 1996 she said of Auschwitz, 'I think that God was very small. God had no friends at this time; God's sun, righteousness, did not shine; and the Spirit had no dwelling in our land.'

A different concept of power is therefore needed, and this is better expressed by 'empowerment – good power is what makes others powerful, empowers others, makes us capable of love'.

Sölle was born and brought up in Cologne. During her final years at school she was concentrating on classics until a gifted teacher, Marie Veit, introduced her to the thinking of Heidegger, Sartre, Kierkegaard and Pascal and demonstrated that there was no need to abandon intelligence when entering a church door. She continued to have problems with the church, however, regarding it as 'a boring enterprise'. She was attracted to study theology at Göttingen University by the presence of Professor Friedrich Gogarten, who, she said, 'taught me to ask questions', and also Ernst Käsemann, who 'opened up the New Testament world for me'. She continued her studies at Cologne University, where she belonged to an ecumenical group which engaged in reflection on the consequences of Auschwitz. This led to what she called 'the politicization of conscience', by which she meant the moving away from an individual to a corporate understanding of sin: 'What separates me from God is not my sexuality or the fact that I have always been rejected, but the way in which I am destroying my grandchildren's water supply.'

After Cologne, marriage and the bringing up of children occupied several years until she returned to university life, first as a student counsellor, then as a teacher. Journalism and television also occupied much of her time. Several visits to Latin America, including a spell of teaching at a theological school, introduced her to liberation theology – an experience which, she said, caused scales to fall from her eyes. In an account of one of her visits, *Celebrating Resistance* (1993), she gave a graphic account, based on brief interviews and vignettes, of how the poor are not only suffering but also finding spaces for hope and joy. This confirmed for her something she had learned from her study of Marx, namely that knowledge and hope need to be combined with one another: knowledge is not to be recognized as knowledge if it contains no perspective of hope.

*Suffering* (1973) was arguably the best book on its subject to appear during the century and drew heavily on some of the era's worst horrors of sadism. She concluded that much suffering, especially that caused by social factors, can be avoided through change. But not all, and in these circumstances the only way forward is 'by sharing the pain of the sufferers with them, not leaving them alone and making their cry louder'.

# Henri Nouwen

## (1932–1996)

Henri Nouwen was a Dutch Roman Catholic priest. He became one of the best known spiritual guides of the century and had a world-wide following who found uniquely helpful his particular insights into the relationship between emotional need and life in the Spirit. He wrote more than forty books, of which the most widely read was *The Wounded Healer* – first published in 1972 and never out of print. The title was an accurate description of his own life, for he was afflicted with serious psychological problems. He was a homosexual who longed for a deep and permanent relationship, but although he had some important friendships, these were not lasting, and in the end he found the greatest acceptance and peace within the life of the L'Arche community.

Nouwen was a hugely gifted man – a compelling speaker, a fluent writer, a creative liturgist, a loving and caring pastor, and a talented painter and musician. His magnetic personality attracted large audiences, and gave him cult status and a host of devotees, but he could be obsessive, manipulative, selfish and impossible to deal with. He craved for affirmation and approval, yet never got enough of either, and beneath the confident, successful public figure was a lonely, depressed man who endured the agonies of self-doubt and believed rejection.

He was born into a wealthy family in Nijkerk in Central Holland, and from his earliest years felt drawn to the priesthood. At the age of twelve he wanted to go to a junior seminary, but his parents insisted on his waiting until he was eighteen before taking this decisive step. After six years at a seminary in Rijsenberg, he was ordained in 1957 at Utrecht, then went to the Catholic University at Nijmegen to study psychology.

This led to a particular interest in the relationship between psychology and spirituality, and when his course at Nijmegen was completed he went to America for further study. During his time there he became more conscious of his homosexuality; in addition to his growing reputation in the fields of psychology and spirituality, he was known as a priest who held progressive opinions about social and political matters. He attended the Second Vatican Council, and on returning to America was appointed

Visiting Professor of Pastoral Psychology at the University of Notre Dame in Indiana.

His impact there was considerable. Although he was essentially an individualist and not over-concerned about church structures, he recognized the importance of the Council, and was largely responsible for introducing its revolutionary ideas into the university. His integration of psychology and theology startled many of his colleagues on the teaching staff but it fascinated the students, and his lectures, which started with human experience, were always crowded. He took part in Martin Luther King's historic march to Selma in 1965, though the local bishop forbade Catholic priests to be involved in it. He returned to Holland in 1968 to teaching posts in Amsterdam and Utrecht, followed by further study at Nijmegen, but although appreciated in America he was regarded with some suspicion in the Dutch Church. He, in turn, was unhappy with the post-Vatican II radicalism, which seemed to him to be neglecting the church's spiritual roots.

So he went back to the United States, where in 1971 he and a nun became the first Roman Catholics to be appointed to the teaching staff of Yale Divinity School – he to the post of pastoral theologian. By this time he had written two books, including *Creative Ministry*, which argued that theology could not be properly studied as an academic subject, since theology had to do with God and this involved prayer, community and ministry. He left Yale in 1981 and spent the next twelve months in Bolivia and Peru, where he lived for a time in a slum in Lima and came under the influence of Gustavo Gutiérrez, the liberation theologian. On his return to America he took up a part-time teaching post at Harvard and undertook a six-weeks speaking campaign denouncing the American-backed Contra war against the poor in Nicaragua.

In 1985 he responded to an invitation from Jean Vanier to live with the handicapped members of L'Arche community at Trosly in France. This proved to be very successful, and after nine months there he moved to L'Arche Daybreak in Ontario, Canada. There he served as the community's pastor, but eventually had a psychological breakdown which necessitated his temporary withdrawal. When he returned he resumed his pastoral work in and beyond the community, wrote several more books, and conducted retreats in Canada and the USA. This led in 1995 to exhaustion, and in the following year he died while on a visit to Holland.

Michael Ford, *Wounded Prophet,* Darton, Longman and Todd 1999.

# Leonardo Boff

## (1938–   )

Leonardo Boff was a Franciscan friar and a leading Latin American liberation theologian. He held the chair of systematic theology at the Petrópolis Institute for Philosophy and Theology in the Brazilian state of Rio de Janeiro and wrote a number of stimulating books which attracted a good deal of international attention. Among these, *Church, Charism and Power* (1984) incurred the displeasure of the Vatican Congregation for the Doctrine of the Faith and led to his being silenced for a year.

The book applied liberation theology to the life of the church and concluded that a new model for the church was needed. This would embrace the primitive elements of community, co-operation and change and thus open the door to the free movement of the Holy Spirit. The comparison between this model and the life of the contemporary church was obviously marked, and Boff did not shrink from calling attention to the chief distinctions. Soon after publication Boff was summoned to Rome by Cardinal Ratzinger, the Prefect of the CDF, for what was described as a 'colloquy'. He was accompanied by two Brazilian cardinals to demonstrate the strong support he enjoyed at home.

The colloquy turned out to be a grilling, and in May of the following year a Vatican document was issued, answering and condemning some of Boff's theology. Two months later he received an official notice from Rome ordering him to observe an 'obsequious silence' for a period. He observed this for about ten months and during this time wrote another book, *Trinity and Society*. Meanwhile in Brazil he became a national hero, akin to a famous footballer, and ten of the Brazilian bishops criticised the Vatican's handling of the case. His younger brother Clodovis was also a prominent liberation theologian who wrote, among other books, *Feet-on-the-Ground Theology* (1987).

Boff came of Italian stock and was born in Concordia, Brazil; he studied philosophy and theology at Curitiba and Petrópolis. One of his professors was Constantino Koser, who later became Superior General of the Franciscan Order, and Boff himself became a friar. Moving to Europe for further study, he completed a doctorate at Munich on 'The Church as a Sacrament in the Context of Events in This World', and also took courses at Würzburg, Louvain and Oxford. He was immediately in demand for teaching posts, and was also appointed to the theological commission of the Brazilian National Episcopal Conference and to the Latin American Confederation of Religious. He edited a number of theological journals and was the Director of the religious division of a publishing house in Petrópolis.

A major book, *Jesus Christ Liberator* (1972), broke new ground by interpreting christology in terms of oppression in Latin America, rather than in the classical language of orthodoxy, and later in *Trinity and Society* (1986) he argued that the monarchical structure of the church – 'a single church body, a single head (the Pope), a single Christ and a single God' – was based on an inadequate doctrine of the Trinity. This created inequality in the church, with power coming down through descending orders of hierarchy, whereas the Trinity seen as a community of divine persons was both the source and the model for a human society based on universal collaboration and equality. Political, economic and social justice is therefore to be seen as intimately linked to trinitarian faith, 'for we seek to change society because we see, in faith, that the supreme reality is the prototype of all other things . . . Furthermore we wish our society to be able to speak to us of the Trinity through our egalitarian and communitarian organization.'

In an article in the journal *Concilium* in 1988 Boff outlined what he believed to be liberation theology's important insights for the study of theology as a whole. These included putting the poor at the forefront of the theological agenda, recapturing the Christian vision of transforming the world, and locating theology not in the university but in the Christian community in its experience of identifying with the cause of the poor. He regarded St Francis of Assisi, about whom he wrote a book, as a model for human liberation, and emphasized that socio-political liberation is not the only form of liberation, for without prayer and meditation no liberation is truly Christian. In *Way of the Cross – Way of Justice* (1980) he wrote:

> Wherever an authentically human life is growing in the world,
> Wherever justice is triumphing over the instincts of domination,
> Wherever grace is winning over the power of sin,
> Wherever human beings are creating more fraternal mediations in
> their social life together,
> Wherever love is getting the better of selfish interests and wherever
>     hope is resisting the lure of cynicism or despair,
> There the process of resurrection is being turned into reality.

# Ernesto Cardenal

## (1925–    )

Ernesto Cardenal was a priest, poet and politician who devoted his considerable gifts to the service of the poor in Nicaragua, Central America, and abandoned his pacifist position in order to support the overthrow of a right-wing repressive regime by the Sandinista Front Liberation Movement. Against the wishes of his church he became a minister in the succeeding revolutionary government.

He first became widely known through his foundation in 1966 of a lay community at Solentiname. This was located on one of thirty-eight islands of an archipelago on Lake Nicaragua, the total population of which was about 1,000 – mainly poor fishermen and farmers. The community was about ten strong and included the children of a married couple. Attached to the monastery was a fishing and agricultural co-operative, an artists' centre which became famous for its naive painting, a medical clinic and a library. The Sunday Mass drew people from all parts of the archipelago, and on some occasions Mass was celebrated outdoors on one of the other islands.

A distinctive feature of the worship was the sermon: copies of the gospel for the day were distributed to those who could read, a younger member of the congregation read it aloud, and this was followed by a discussion of the content in which all were invited to share. Many did, and the results, published in four volumes of *The Gospel in Solentiname*, offered startling new insights into the meaning of the gospel, especially the declaration of Jesus that he had come to preach good news to the poor. This involved denunciation of the dictatorial government and in October 1977 the National Guard arrived on the island and razed all the buildings to the ground. It was this event that caused Cardenal to join the Sandinista Front and he declared: 'Every authentic revolutionary prefers non-violence to violence, but he does not always have the freedom to choose.'

He was born in Granada, Nicaragua, and in 1957 went to the USA to become a novice at the Trappist monastery at Gethsemane, in Kentucky. There he had Thomas Merton as his spiritual director and, although ill-health required him to leave after two years, Merton remained a friend

179

and guide, helping him to recognize that his vocation was not contemplation but communication with God through people. After spending some time in Cuernavaca, Mexico, he returned to Nicaragua and was ordained priest in 1965.

A year later he founded the community at Solentiname, and by this time his poetic meditations had been translated into many languages. His holiness was also widely recognized, and he became increasingly involved in the struggle of the poor for justice and freedom. The activities of the community and his own public utterances, which included a denunciation of President Somoza's misuse of aid funds provided by the US Treasury after a devastating earthquake in 1972, brought him into serious conflict with the authorities. His name was on the death list of the Anti-Communist League of Nicaragua.

When the Sandinista Front, which had become a very broad coalition, achieved victory in 1979, it owed a great deal to the support provided by the church. The bishops, for the first time ever in the history of the Catholic Church, declared a revolutionary insurrection with left-wing policies to be legitimate. Cardenal was appointed Minister of Culture in the new government, and two other priests, one of whom was his brother, were given office. But by 1981 the Nicaraguan Conference of Bishops had become disenchanted with the Sandinista government's totalitarian tendencies and issued a statement, with, they said, 'the total support and authority of the Holy See', demanding that all priests in government office should 'return to their vocations'. It added that those who continued in office would be forbidden to celebrate Mass.

Cardenal refused to comply, for he was now deeply involved in the organizing of a National Literacy Crusade in which 60,000 secondary school children from the cities worked as literacy instructors in the rural areas, while another 40,000 volunteers worked in the shanty towns and nearby communities. By the end of 1982 1,258 new schools had been built. In March of the next year Pope John Paul II arrived at Managua airport during an official visit to Central America and Cardenal was in the government welcoming party. The Pope appeared to raise his fingers as if to admonish the disobedient priest, and when Cardenal tried to kiss his ring he withdrew his hand. It was an unhappy and embarrassing incident.

The Sandinistas lost the 1990 election and soon afterwards Cardenal joined the former President in founding a breakaway Movement for Sandinista Renewal – made necessary, it was said, by the 'corruption' which attended the hand-over of power to the new government. He remains suspended from the priesthood.

# Paulo Freire

## (1921–1997)

Paulo Freire was a Brazilian Roman Catholic educationist who achieved world-wide fame by his insight that true education liberates an individual not only from intellectual ignorance but also from social, economic and political forces of oppression. Education is the means to social revolution, and this is achieved through the process of conscientization, or consciousness-raising, which creates an awareness of what it means to be wholly liberated and of what obstacles stand in the way of liberation.

Freire's insight came initially through his involvement in adult literacy programmes in North East Brazil, where a high proportion of the poverty-stricken population were totally illiterate. He discovered that by relating reading and writing to the day-to-day experience of pupils, particularly to their poverty, literacy could be reached in just over six weeks. In 1963 he was put in charge of a national literacy programme, and by the following year had organized 20,000 'alphabetization' groups for two million illiterate adults. The revolutionary implications of this development were quickly recognized by the leaders of a US-backed right-wing military coup later that year. Freire was accused of being 'a traitor to Christ and to the Brazilian people' and was driven into exile in Bolivia, then to Chile, and finally to Geneva. He remained there, supported by the World Council of Churches and UNESCO, until an amnesty was declared in Brazil in 1979. Meanwhile his ideas had spread to Catholic grass-roots communities throughout Brazil, and also to Chile, Peru and Central America.

Freire was born in Recife and studied law before turning to education and completing a doctorate at the University of Pernambuco. During the 1950s he began experimental work in the field of literacy, and in 1962 he headed a programme that taught 300 illiterate workers to read and write in only forty-five days. His experience of working at this level led him to ask questions about the nature of education. He pointed out that all educational methods have an ideology behind them, and that most educational systems are 'domesticating' in the sense that they help people to come to terms with the political and economic *status quo*. Instead of being encouraged to explore their own experience of the world, they are simply told what the world is like and how best they can fit into it. However, a truly liberating education will lead to the asking of questions and a demand for change. It can never be purely theoretical, and it involves an interaction between teacher and pupil that leaves both open to change. The process is nothing less than death and resurrection, and Freire spoke of the need to 'make one's Easter'.

Before long he was addressing the same questions to the church which, in its traditional form, he believed to be part of the 'domesticating' process: it encouraged its members not only to accept the *status quo* but also to be dependent on the clergy. A prophetic church would be engaged in a constant struggle to transform the world and to enable individuals to realize their full potential as human beings.

Much of his thinking was expressed in his most widely read book, *Pedagogy of the Oppressed* (1970), which included the dictum: 'No one frees anyone. No one achieves freedom alone. Human beings achieve freedom in communion.' It ended with a profession of his faith 'in human beings and in the creation of a world in which it will be less difficult to love'. He wrote twenty-five other books, lectured in all parts of the world, and had a considerable following in India. But paradoxically the brilliant educationist was not always easy to understand, and Western Europeans complained that the experience of North East Brazil could not readily be translated to more affluent societies, though few of them ever attempted to do so.

Following his return to Brazil he became Education Secretary for the city of São Paulo, and within six months had organized 960 basic education classes in schools, churches and trade union centres. He also encouraged local communities to become involved in the running of their schools and introduced regular evaluation of teaching. Since then, however, public elementary education has been neglected by the government, and Brazil's literacy rate is lower than elsewhere in Latin America, except Bolivia. At another level he taught in the Catholic University of São Paulo until a week before his death and was a visiting Professor at Harvard. A lifelong friend of Archbishop Helder Camara, through whose influence much of his thinking and experience reached the agendas of the Latin American Catholic bishops, Freire was often called 'the father of popular education'. At his funeral requiem his life was described as 'a hymn to human dignity'.

# Pedro Casaldáliga

## (1928–   )

Pedro Casaldáliga became bishop of the missionary area of Sáo Felix in Brazil in 1972 and thereafter was one of Latin America's most courageously outspoken church leaders. The territory in which he ministered is among the poorest in Brazil and its Indian and peasant populations have endured long years of exploitation and repression at the hands of European invaders and military dictatorships. Casaldáliga, who identified himself closely with the people, had no doubt that the only answer is revolution: 'I believe that nowadays the only way to live is to live rebelliously. And I believe that you can only be a Christian by being a revolutionary, since there's no more use in pretending that we're going to "reform" the world.' Besides his vivid prose he was also a considerable poet, and his understanding of the role of a bishop was outlined in a souvenir which accompanied the invitation to his consecration:

> Your *mitre* will be the straw hat of the backlander; sunlight and
>     moonlight; rainy and clear weather; the glance of the poor
>     with whom you walk and the glorious glance of Christ, the Lord.
> Your *crozier* will be the gospel truth and the trust of your people
>     in you.
> Your *ring* will be fidelity to the new covenant of the God who frees
>     and fidelity to the people of this land.
> You shall have no other *shield* than the power of hope and freedom
>     of the children of God.
> You shall wear no other *gloves* than the service of love.

Casaldáliga was born in Spain and brought up on a cattle-raising farm in Catalonia. After a year at the diocesan seminary he joined the conservative Claretian Order and was ordained to the priesthood in 1952. During the next nine years he undertook youth work and pastoral work among poor immigrants from southern Spain, and from 1961 to 1964 he was responsible for training at a Claretian seminary in Aragon. He went to Madrid to edit the *Iris* magazine, which brought him into contact with Latin Americans and Africans, and this led to his volunteering in 1968 to go as a missionary to Brazil.

At Sáo Felix do Araguaia he and another Claretian began pioneering work in a 100,000 square mile area which was entirely lacking in infrastructure and services, and where the population lived in deep poverty. Priority was given to the training of leaders, the creation of communities, and the provision of health care and education services. The people were also encouraged to organize and struggle for their rights. In 1972 he was appointed bishop of the area, and on the day of his consecration he published clandestinely a 120-page Pastoral Letter on the church in the Amazon and the land problem. This was a hard-hitting document: 'To "Catholic" large landowners who enslave the people of our region – who themselves are often alienated by the self-seeking or comfortable contrivance of certain ecclesiastics – we would ask, if they are willing to listen to us, to choose simply between their faith and their selfishness.' The Letter was banned in the region and condemned elsewhere in Brazil.

Throughout the 1970s he was heavily involved in a combination of pastoral and political work and faced increasing conflict with the landholders and the government, leading in some instances to violence against his mission and threats of deportation. One of the Brazilian archbishops also made a series of public accusations against his mission. During the 1980s he made three controversial visits to Nicaragua to support those of its bishops who were in conflict with their government. All this activity prevented him from joining the other Brazilian bishops on their regular five-yearly visits to Rome, and when in 1986 he was requested by the Vatican to make a personal visit he wrote a remarkable letter to Pope John Paul II which combined loyalty, affection and extreme candour about what he believed to be the serious failings of the Roman curia. The long delayed visit was finally made in June 1988 when Casaldáliga, dressed in borrowed clothes, was given a severe grilling by two cardinals and had a fifteen-minute audience with the Pope. Warnings and a request for penitence and amendment followed. He responded with a poem which included the words:

> I, sinner and bishop, confess
>    that I dream of a church
>    wearing only the gospel and sandals;
>    that I believe in the church
>       despite the church sometimes,
>    that in any case I believe in the Reign,
>       journeying in the church.

He was nominated for the Nobel Peace Prize in 1989.

Pedro Casaldáliga, *In Pursuit of the Kingdom*, Orbis Books 1990.

# Oscar Romero

## (1917–1980)

Oscar Arnulfo Romero was Archbishop of San Salvador in Central America from 1977 until his martyrdom on 24 March 1980. At 6 p.m. on that day he began to say Mass in the chapel of the cancer hospital where he lived, but at the end of his homily a shot rang out and he died instantly. His murderers were never arrested, and at the outdoor funeral, attended by over 250,000 people, the explosion of a bomb and the firing of shots claimed the lives of another forty people who died in the ensuing stampede. Thereafter Romero was the symbol and inspiration of all who were engaged in the struggle for justice, freedom and peace in Latin America.

He was born in the small town of Ciudad Barrios in a mountainous region of El Salvador where his father worked for the postal service. At the age of thirteen he left the local school to be apprenticed to a carpenter, but he was a devout and studious boy who felt called to the priesthood. His father was opposed to this, but eventually he went to a seminary and was ordained in Rome in 1942. He spent the next twenty-five years as a parish priest in El Salvador, where he was valued as a diligent pastor and a fine preacher. The Second Vatican Council's proposals for change in the church troubled him somewhat, but in 1967 he was appointed Secretary General of the national Bishops' Conference and soon after this was given a similar post with the Central American Bishops' Secretariat. Inevitably he was deeply involved in the Council of Latin America bishops held in Medellin, in Colombia, in 1968, but he was not happy with the Council's decision that the church must play a much greater part, alongside the poor, in the securing of a more just society.

When Romero became an auxiliary bishop in the Archdiocese of San Salvador in 1970 his appointment was welcomed by conservatives, and his consecration was attended by the President and other leading right-wing figures in the government and the army. He exercised the ministry of a traditional Latin American bishop and when in 1974 he was made Bishop of Santiago – the diocese of his birth and upbringing – he still believed it was not the task of the church to take sides in the developing conflict between the poor and their rich rulers. As the pressure for change increased, he became more and more worried about the political involvement of some of his clergy and the new liberation theology that inspired them. He counselled caution and expressed the hope that more goodwill on all sides would solve the country's problems. His appointment as Archbishop in 1977 was hailed by the Press as a great conservative victory and it dismayed the progressive elements in the church and in society generally.

Just over a fortnight after Romero had become Archbishop the situation in El Salvador deteriorated sharply. The election of a new President marked the beginning of a renewed and more savage attack on those who opposed the corrupt, authoritarian regime. This led to a popular uprising, and to twelve years of bitter civil war in which 75,000 people of all ages, including priests and nuns, lost their lives. The first of these priests – Father Rutilio Grande – was a close friend of the Archbishop and was shot while travelling in a jeep with an old man and a sixteen-year-old boy. This was a turning point in Romero's life and in the witness of the Catholic Church in El Salvador. He saw clearly that there was no possibility of not taking sides in the struggle – one was either with the poor or against them. An explanation from the authorities was demanded, those responsible for the murders were excommunicated, and, apart from an open-air Mass attended by 100,000 people, church services on the following Sunday were cancelled.

A crisis in church-state relations could no longer be avoided, and the activists in the church became the target of increasing violence and murder. 'Be a patriot – kill a priest' was the slogan on a widely distributed handbill, and many priests were killed. The situation became desperate, but, said the Archbishop, 'We don't want peace at any price. Peace is not the product of terror or fear. Peace is not the silence of cemeteries, the silent result of violent repression. On the contrary, the only order and the only peace God wants is one based on truth and justice.' For the next three years he exercised a heroic ministry on behalf of the poor and the oppressed. He became the arch-enemy of the government and was often threatened with death, but he was supported by only one of the four other Salvadorean bishops.

Jon Sobrino, *Archbishop Romero: Memories and Reflections,* CIIR 1990.

# Bede Griffiths

## (1906–1994)

Bede Griffiths was a monk who went to India in 1955 to help found a new Benedictine community and spent the remainder of his life in India pioneering ways of monastic life which combined the classical Benedictine tradition with Hindu mysticism and some of its culture. He came to believe that Christianity had no exclusive claim on the truth, and in an important book, *Return to the Centre* (1976), which remained in print for twenty years in many translations, he said, 'I have to be a Hindu, a Buddhist, a Jain, a Parsee, a Sikh, a Muslim and a Jew, as well as a Christian, if I am to know the Truth and to find the point of reconciliation in all religion'.

The ashram at Shantivanam, in South India, over which he presided for a quarter of a century, attracted huge numbers of visitors and he himself travelled widely, becoming an international figure renowned both for his holiness of life and for his concern to unite the religions of East and West. But he was criticized by conservative Roman Catholics in India and Rome. In response he described Catholicism as 'an extremely decadent religion, a kind of fossilization of what was once a great tradition', and denounced the Roman Curia as 'rigid and disgusting'.

Born Alan Richard Griffiths, he was brought up in a traditional Anglican, middle-class family and was educated at Christ's Hospital school. Towards the end of his time there he had a mystical experience while walking alone near the playing fields, and this inspired his life-long quest for the reality that lies behind and beyond all human experience. At Oxford he studied English literature under C. S. Lewis, with whom he established a deep and abiding friendship, and on leaving the university he and two other friends lived together for a year in a cottage in the Cotswolds, exploring the world of faith.

This was followed, for Griffiths, by a period of uncertainty until in 1932 a priest introduced him to the Benedictine Priory at Prinknash, Gloucestershire. He was immediately attracted to the community, entered it as a novice, became a Roman Catholic, was professed as a monk in 1937 and ordained to the priesthood three years later. In 1947 he was sent with twenty-four other monks to revive Farnborough

Abbey, where he served as Prior until 1951, when the Abbot at Prink-nash removed him summarily to Pluscarden in North East Scotland. There he wrote an autobiography, *The Golden String* (1954), which became an immediate best-seller and is now regarded as a spiritual classic.

During the 1930s he had become interested in Eastern religions, so he welcomed the opportunity to go with another monk to found a Bene-dictine community in the village of Kengeri, ten miles from Bangalore. They adapted a bungalow for this purpose, with an emphasis on the con-templative life, and anticipated enrichment by Hindu spirituality. But the new foundation was not approved by Rome and Griffiths moved 300 miles south to Kurisumala in 1956 to join a Cistercian monk in founding a new community there. This time full approval was given by the Indian archbishop and by Rome, and within eighteen months sixteen new mem-bers had been recruited. The community identified itself closely with the poor, adopted a very simple life-style, and used the ancient Syrian litur-gy, rather than the Latin Mass. Griffiths began to wear the saffron-coloured robes of an Indian holy man, though at this point he still saw the Eastern religions as preparatory to Christianity.

In 1968 he moved with some of his fellow monks to Shantivanam, in the southern state of Tamil Nadu, to revive a community originally founded by two French monks who had been seeking to link Christian and Hindu spirituality. After some initial problems the new community became established, attracted new members, and became a meeting place for Christians and Hindus. The Benedictine tradition was the model, but there was two hours of meditation at dawn and sunset, and the Christian cross was enclosed by a circle representing the wheel of law of the Buddhist and Hindu traditions. Hindu elements were also incorporated into the liturgy. By the mid-1970s the ashram was attracting large num-bers of visitors, and several thousand Hindus attended the silver jubilee of its foundation.

Griffiths had now come to recognize other faiths as complementing Christianity and said, 'To me Eastern wisdom gives the key to Christianity. I cannot conceive of Christ now except in terms of Vedanta.' None of this pleased the local Vicar General, who described the ashram as un-Christian and a scandal to the diocese. But Rome did not seek to inhibit its leader, who addressed 100,000 young people in Milan, and continued to travel until disabled by a severe stroke shortly before Christmas 1992.

Shirley du Boulay, *Beyond the Darkness*, Rider 1998.

# John Stott

## (1921–    )

John Robert Walmsley Scott was one of the Church of England's most influential clergymen during the century. He was an evangelical churchman who became Rector of All Souls Church, Langham Place, in the heart of London's West End in 1950, when it seemed that evangelicalism was a spent force and would never again exercise significant influence in mainstream English church life. But Stott stood firm in his conservative convictions, turned All Souls into a showplace for evangelical preaching and worship, wrote more than thirty books, and formed a group of young and able clergymen – The Eclectics – who helped to bring a deeper social concern to the tradition and later occupied positions of leadership in the church. By the end of the century there was an evangelical Archbishop of Canterbury, many diocesan and suffragan bishops of similar convictions, and evangelicalism had replaced liberalism as the dominant force. While it would be an exaggeration to attribute all of this to Stott, it is hard to believe that it could have happened without him.

He was born in London, where his father Sir Arnold Stott was a distinguished physician. As a child he was taken by his mother, who had been brought up as a Lutheran, to All Souls Church, where he was destined to become Rector, and went from Rugby School to Trinity College, Cambridge, to read modern languages. He intended to enter the diplomatic service but came under evangelical influences and, with a First in French and a Second in German, stayed on at Cambridge to take a First in theology. He prepared for ordination at Ridley Hall, Cambridge, and in 1945 became a curate of his home parish church which was then out of action, owing to wartime bombing, the congregation meeting in another church nearby. He made a considerable impact and, following the death in 1950 of the Rector after a long illness, the leading laity petitioned for Stott to succeed him. This was opposed by the Bishop, but after much negotiation the twenty-nine-year-old curate took charge of one of London's leading churches.

Although there was a strong congregational life, there was need for new vision and the building was in urgent need of repair. Stott more than made up for his lack of experience with a combination of vision, dedication and skill. He believed the local church to be the chief agency of evangelism, with every member involved in some way in its mission. He also demanded the highest standards in worship and all other elements in the church's life, and made a special point of creating a welcoming atmosphere. This made All Souls particularly attractive to London's many students and young professionals living alone in bed-sits. Overseas students were specially wooed, and vocational groups for doctors, lawyers and the like were soon established. It tended to be middle-class in its appeal, but some work among the underprivileged and the young people living in the back streets was initiated. Chaplains were appointed to the big West End stores. And it proved to be highly successful in terms of very large congregations and a vigorous church life.

Stott soon became recognized as one of the leaders of the Church of England's small evangelical wing. He was in demand as a preacher and lecturer, and accepted responsibility in the main evangelical organizations. As a preacher, he had a powerful, distinctive style, but unlike many evangelists, he spurned histrionics and emotion was balanced by regard for the intellectual aspects of faith. This did not extend, however, to the forsaking of a fundamentalist interpretation of the Bible, and although later he spoke and wrote of the importance of hermeneutics and of what he called 'cultural transposition', his approach to the Bible remained essentially conservative.

Still, marked changes in the evangelical outlook were noticeable at a National Evangelical Anglican Conference organized by Stott and his young 'Eclectic' disciples in 1967. This displayed a new concern for worship and the sacraments, a radical approach to social and political issues and, above all, a desire to become influential in the Church of England, rather than to remain an introverted sect. They could hardly have been more successful in this aim. The radical movement of the 1960s ran out of steam, the traditionalist Anglo-Catholic wing continued to decay and the door was wide open for enthusiasts who answered, rather than raised, questions and provided strong leadership in local churches.

Stott's own future became uncertain. The Church of England had not changed sufficiently for him to become a bishop, and after twenty-five years at All Souls he needed greater freedom to pursue his rapidly developing national and international ministry. The problem was solved by appointing a vicar to lead the church and parish, while Stott remained titular rector. He continued to preach, teach and write and to exercise enormous influence world-wide.

# Janani Luwum

## (1922–1977)

Janani Luwum was Archbishop of Uganda from 1974 until his martyrdom at the hands of President Idi Amin – one of the most ruthless tyrants
of the century, who seized power in 1971. With the aid of his own trib-
al soldiers Amin quickly established a reign of terror against the other
tribes and during the first two years of his rule nearly 100,000 Ugandans
were murdered. Luwum was killed for protesting against the massacre.

He was born in the province of East Acholi – on Uganda's border with
the Sudan. His father taught in a local church, where the memory of
Uganda's late nineteenth-century martyrs was still very much alive. The
family was poor and lived mainly off the produce of a smallholding, and
Janani did not attend school until he was ten. He did well, however, and
after attending a teacher training college returned to his home territory
as a primary school teacher. When he was twenty-six he had an evangelical conversion experience, and went about preaching with great fervour. After a time he gave up teaching in order to become a missionary
and went to Buwalasi Theological College to prepare for ordination. He
became a priest in 1956 and, perceived to have leadership qualities, was
sent to St Augustine's College, Canterbury for further training.

On his return to Uganda he was put in charge of one of the country's
toughest parishes with twenty-four churches scattered over forty miles of
scrubland and only a bicycle for transport. After five years in this post he
became Vice-Principal, then Principal, of his old theological college, and
in January 1969 was consecrated as Bishop of the newly-formed Diocese
of Northern Uganda. Luwum spent the next five years travelling in his
diocese, engaged in evangelistic work and founding churches, schools
and clinics. His election as Archbishop of Uganda came three years after
Amin had seized power and Christians were being persecuted on a large
scale. The aim was to turn Uganda into a Muslim state, though 70% of
the population were Christian.

In 1976 the churches began to make formal protests, but to no avail.
Plans for celebrating the centenary of the arrival of missionaries in
Uganda included a pageant depicting the early martyrs, but shortly after
one of the rehearsals the six actors were found murdered. The Anglican

and Roman Catholic bishops then convened a conference to which they invited leaders of the Orthodox Church and the Muslim community. Archbishop Luwum chaired the conference and a message was sent to President Amin requesting an interview to discuss the country's problems. This was met by an angry rebuke and it seemed that the Archbishop was now in grave danger. Yet he frequently said, 'We must love the President. We must pray for him, for he is a child of God.' Some of the other bishops thought he was being too generous towards the tyrant, but he told them, 'I don't know for how long I shall be occupying this chair. While the opportunity is there, I preach the gospel with all my might . . . I have been threatened many times. Whenever possible I have told the President the things the churches disapprove of. God is my witness.'

In February 1977 there was a further crack-down. The Archbishop's house was attacked by gunmen and on 14 February Idi Amin sent for Luwum and six other bishops. His wife begged him not to go, but he said, 'Even if he kills me my blood will save the nation.' The Archbishop and his colleagues were summoned to an open space near the international conference centre in Kampala where they were kept standing for two hours in the intense heat while someone read out a statement accusing Janani Luwum of being involved in an arms deal with a neighbouring government.

All the bishops, apart from Archbishop Luwum, were then sent home, but he was ordered to stay behind to see the President. As he said good-bye to his fellow bishops he told one of them that three days earlier he had been advised by a girl messenger that he was now No. 1 on the security forces death list and that he would do well to flee the country. But he told the girl, 'I cannot go. I am the Archbishop. I must stay.' His final words to the bishops were, 'I can see the hand of the Lord in this.' Whether or not the interview with the President ever took place is unknown, but the next morning it was announced that Janani Luwum had been killed in a motoring accident while trying to escape. No one believed this, and he was in fact shot in a prison cell after praying with the other prisoners and for his captors.

# Desmond Tutu

## (1931–    )

Desmond Tutu was the Anglican Archbishop of Cape Town from 1986 to 1996 and one of the world's outstanding religious leaders, admired for his heroic commitment to justice and reconciliation in a country where for the greater part of his life black people were oppressed. He played a leading part in the ending of apartheid and of white rule, and afterwards was chairman of a Truth and Reconciliation Commission which sought to heal past wounds by requiring those, black as well as white, who had engaged in oppression and violence to acknowledge their misdeeds. He was awarded the Nobel Peace Prize in 1984 and became the first South African citizen to receive the Order for Meritorious Service (Gold), which was presented to him by President Nelson Mandela when he retired from the Archbishopric.

Small of stature, full of gaiety and endowed with a high-pitched voice, Tutu held audiences spellbound, and although his central message was always of love and reconciliation, he never hesitated to speak in forthright language. Soon after his election as archbishop he told an audience of students: 'If Christ returned to South Africa today he would almost certainly be detained under the present security laws, because of his concern for the poor, the hungry and the oppressed.' P. W. Botha, the President at that time, regarded him as a traitor, but dare not have him arrested because of his international status and strong following among the black population.

Tutu's father was headmaster of a Methodist primary school in the Western Transvaal, but the family lived in poverty. Nonetheless young Desmond was sent to a high school in Johannesburg and during a long spell of tuberculosis Father (later Archbishop) Trevor Huddleston often visited him and exerted great influence on him. On completion of his high school education he trained as a teacher, took an external degree at the University of South Africa, and taught for two years at a high school in Krugersdorp. Frustration with the government's restrictive education policy for black education drove him to prepare for the priesthood, and he was ordained in Johannesburg in 1960. After two short curacies he was sent to King's College, London, for further theological education, and on his return joined the teaching staff of the theological seminary at Alice in Cape Province.

A protest strike by the students involved him in his first action against apartheid, but he soon moved away to become a lecturer at the University of Botswana, Lesotho and Swaziland; this was followed by three years as Director of the Theological Education Fund – based in London and travelling widely in the Third World. In 1975 he was appointed Dean of Johannesburg and chose to live in the black township of Soweto rather than in the official deanery, located in a white suburb. Before he could accomplish much at the cathedral, however, he was elected Bishop of Lesotho – a mountainous diocese involving much travel by air and on horseback. Eighteen months later he was persuaded to become General Secretary of the South African Council of Churches and for the next seven years offered inspired leadership in an organization which had a key role in the struggle against apartheid. When he left to become the first black Bishop of Johannesburg in 1975, he was the most widely recognized leader of South Africa's black community. Once again his stay was short, for in the following year he was elected Archbishop of Cape Town and Primate of the Anglican Church in South Africa – the church having recognized that it could no longer witness effectively under white leadership.

The government found him a formidable opponent, and after the leaders of the Dutch Reformed Church had acknowledged their error in supporting apartheid, he became the spokesman of the entire Christian community in South Africa. He also travelled widely to enlist the support of the world church and foreign govenrments, and contributed to the political movement with considerable skill, though the extreme wing of black activists sometimes complained that he was not moving fast enough. When a new multi-racial government established a Truth and Reconciliation Commission in an unprecedented move to avoid destructive recrimination and Nuremberg-style trials, Tutu was acknowledged to be the only person able to preside over it. Over 10,000 people attended its hearings and although difficulties were experienced with some, notably Winnie Mandela, the estranged wife of the President, and P. W. Botha, a former President, the work was carried out sensitively and maintained a balance between justice and compassion. Its report was critical of the conduct of some members of the black African National Congress as well as the much larger number of white oppressors. When this work was completed, he remained a world-wide ambassador for justice and freedom.

# James H. Cone

## (1938–   )

James H. Cone was the pioneer of black theology in the USA, his insights and subsequent work having been stimulated by the American black revolution during the 1960s. Martin Luther King's non-violent witness contributed much to this revolution, but in 1966 the National Conference of Black Churchmen declared their solidarity with Black Power and James Cone, who was one of their number, saw the need for theological reflection on the issues involved.

He was well equipped to do this, since he combined first-hand experience of oppression at the hands of white Americans with an acute, well-trained theological mind – one good enough for him later to be appointed Professor of Systematic Theology at the Union Theological Seminary, New York. At the time of his first book, *Black Theology and Black Power* (1969), he was virtually unknown, but its appearance made him famous overnight. It was couched in provocative, polemical language which succeeded in expressing the anger of America's black community, and at the same time presented God as the champion of the oppressed and Jesus as the liberator of black humanity. This, he asserted, was not one of many interpretations of the gospel: it was the gospel itself.

Inevitably the book drew criticism from orthodox white theologians, some of whom suggested that it was no more than an emotional outburst, and some black theologians objected to Cone's use of the insights of Barth, Bonhoeffer and Moltmann, at the expense of the historical experience of blacks. Another book, *A Black Theology of Liberation* (1970), soon followed and developed further the question: what has the gospel to do with the black struggle for liberation? This time Cone used the insights of Paul Tillich and aroused the same criticisms.

*The Spirituals and the Blues*, published in the same year, was different. In it Cone drew on the experience of his early years in the South when the songs and hymns had come from the days of slavery and often expressed the belief that just as God had delivered Moses and the Israelites from bondage in Egypt, so one day he would deliver black people from their bondage in America. This rather than the doctrinal disputes of the fourth and fifth centuries, Cone argued, is the proper material of contemporary religious discourse, and action.

He was born in Fordyce, a small town in Arkansas, but his parents moved to Bearden, about fourteen miles away, when he was a year old. This was a community of 800 whites and 400 blacks. The schools, cinemas and churches were segregated and the white population regarded the blacks as their servants. Those who objected were beaten by the police or gaoled. Cone never forget the experience of this time. He attended the Macedonia African Methodist Episcopal Church, became a member when he was ten, and entered its ministry when he was only sixteen. Involvement in the black church was, as he put it, 'a way of remaining physically alive in a situation of oppression without losing one's dignity'.

In due course he went to Garrett Theological Seminary and North Western University, Evanston, where he studied classical theology and completed a PhD on Barth's anthropology. He then began to lecture at Philander Smith College, Little Rock, but his teaching did not meet the needs of the black students who had come from the cottonfields – and some of them told him so. In 1966 he moved to another teaching post in Adrian, Michigan, and the outbreak of rioting in Detroit, seventy miles away, led him to ask: what has this to do with Jesus Christ? Finding no immediate answer in his own, apparently bankrupt, theology, he went back to the Bible and, having looked at it afresh in a black perspective, discovered new meanings. These he then started to teach, with strong emphasis on the themes of the Exodus and Jesus the liberator. It was at this point that he identified himself with the Black Power movement and said there was a Christian obligation to break laws that stood in the way of the exercise of human dignity.

In *God of the Oppressed* (1975), which is the most comprehensive statement of Cone's beliefs, he said that the Christian theologian, starting from the life, death and resurrection of Jesus, knows that 'the death of the man on the tree has radical implications for those who are enslaved, lynched and ghettoised in the name of God and country'. Theologians must therefore ask the right question: what has the gospel to do with the oppressed of the land and their struggle for liberation? And they must go to the right sources for the answers, which include imagining their way into the environment and ethos of black slaves.

# Una Kroll

## (1925–    )

Una Kroll was a medical doctor, and during the 1970s and 1980s the most courageous, colourful and outspoken campaigner for the ordination of women to the priesthood of the Church of England. She became world famous in 1978 when, in the silence that followed the General Synod's rejection of women priests, she cried out from the public gallery, 'We asked for bread and you gave us a stone.' This moment was captured by television cameras and shocked both the opponents and some of the advocates of women's ordination. 'I didn't want to do it,' she said later, 'but for over two hours God kept saying, Go on, get up there.'

Kroll's own concern for the matter went back almost fifty years, to the time when she was a medical student in Cambridge and in the course of a religious conversion felt that God was calling her to the priesthood. The daughter of a distinguished soldier, she was educated at St Paul's Girls' School in London and, following the outbreak of war in 1939, at Malvern Girls' College. On coming down from Girton College, Cambridge, she completed her clinical training at the London Hospital, where she remained as a house officer until 1953.

She was then professed as a Sister of the Community of the Holy Name and went to work as a missionary in Liberia and in Namibia, where she met Father Leopold Kroll, an American monk, who renounced his vows in order to marry her, though he remained a priest. She ceased to be a nun and returned with him to England in 1960, becoming a general medical practitioner in South London. Seven years later she saw an advertisement for the newly created Southwark Ordination Course – designed for training men who would exercise their priesthood in their secular employment – and applied for admission. No one had envisaged women being involved in this experiment but she persuaded the bishops to allow her to join, and on completion of her training in 1970 became a deaconess in the parish of St Helier, Morden, in Surrey.

For the next ten years she combined her parish responsibilities with those of a family doctor, and became increasingly involved in the Women's Liberation Movement. In 1972 she formed a Christian Parity Group, claiming that men as well as women needed to be liberated from the oppression of sexism. The Group, never large, organized petitions, took part in protest marches and demonstrations arranged by other women's liberation groups, and urged men, for their own sakes, to join the campaign. Kroll herself stood for Parliament in the 1974 General Election but attracted few votes.

Her style was a mixture of the forthright campaigner, calling her followers to the barricades, and the sensitive reconciler seeking to heal wounds. Her first book, *Transcendental Meditation: A Signpost to the World* (1974), indicated the spiritual basis of her vision and in *Flesh of My Flesh: A Christian View of Sexism* (1975) she wrote: 'I have learnt that I can oppose only those I have first learnt to love.' As the campaign began to gather momentum Kroll suffered considerably, for she came to be a hate figure for many of the opponents of women priests. She was also involved in a fierce battle with some of her friends in the General Synod and a new Movement for the Ordination of Women, who believed that the best way forward was through a gentler approach.

Throughout the 1970s, Leo Kroll provided Una and their four children with a strong emotional and domestic anchor, but by 1980 he was becoming old and frail, so they moved to Sussex where she became a clinical medical officer in the local health district. The Movement for the Ordination of Women was now increasing in size and influence, and she was content for others to take the lead. In 1987, soon after the General Synod had refused to let women priests ordained overseas minister in England, her husband died and, 'bruised and battered' as she described herself, she withdrew to an Anglican house of contemplative prayer in South Wales. In 1991 she was professed by the Bishop of Monmouth to the life of a religious solitary as a Sister of the Society of the Sacred Cross. The decision of the General Synod in 1992 that women might become priests gave her great joy, and her many friends and admirers were even more joyful when, soon after her seventy-first birthday in 1997, she was herself ordained to the priesthood. She said then: 'For anyone who has waited so long as I have it is a wonderful fulfilment of a personal vocation, so it feels like coming home. But after all the opposition over the years, I find it hard to accept. It doesn't feel possible, but I'm living by faith.'

# Kosuke Koyama

## (1929–    )

Kosuke Koyama was a Japanese theologian who served as a missionary in Thailand before his appointment to academic posts in New Zealand and the United States. His special concern, the subject of many books, was the expression of the Christian faith in the thought forms and language of South East Asia. In his first major book, *Waterbuffalo Theology* (1974), he pleaded for what he called a 'rice-roots theology' that would come out of the everyday experience of the farmers of Northern Thailand. One possibility he explored was that of merging the circular and linear images of history to form the image of an ascending spiral view of one unified history-nature. This would, he thought, bring the presence of God closer to the people of Thailand, since life in that country is strongly influenced by the circular movement of nature.

He strongly favoured getting rid of mission boards and complained, 'I do not think that Christianity in Asia for the last 400 years has really listened to the people. It has ignored the people. It has ignored the spirituality of the people. It has ignored the people's deepest aspiration and frustration.' He was also highly critical of Western idols of speed and efficiency, and in *Three Miles an Hour God* (1978) expressed his belief that God works slowly in the conversion process. 'Love has its speed. It is a spiritual speed. It is a different kind of speed from the technological speed to which we are accustomed. It goes on in the depth of our life, whether we notice or not, at three miles an hour. It is the speed we walk and therefore the speed the love of God walks.' He thought that the Buddhist philosophy and life-style of detachment and peace could do much to 'season' the Jewish and Christian religions.

Koyama was deeply influenced by the experience of his early years in Japan during and immediately after the 1939–45 war, and he spoke of the 'pain of God' caused by the intense evil and suffering of those days. He was born in Tokyo of Christian parents, his grandfather having been converted to Christianity by an Englishman who made a great impression on him because he was able to confess Jesus as Lord without ever making derogatory comments about Japanese culture or Buddhism. After studying at Tokyo Theological Seminary, Koyama went on to

Drew University in the USA, then to Princeton University Theological Seminary, and finally to the Ecumenical Institute at Bossey, near Geneva. He obtained a doctorate on Luther and taught theology at the Thailand Theological Seminary (1960–68), followed by six years as Director of the Association of Theological Schools in South-East Asia. He then spent five years lecturing at Otago University in New Zealand, before his appointment in 1980 as Professor of Ecumenics and World Christianity at the Union Theological Seminary, New York.

He had a sound background of modern biblical scholarship and wide learning in patristics and Lutheranism, but his chief concern was to interpret the Bible in various Asian contexts, and he discovered some surprising links with modern situations. In speaking and writing about these links he was assisted by a gift for striking, vigorous imagery unusual in a professional scholar, and he sometimes used this gift to deflate pompous Western theologians.

Self-consciously Asian, Koyama's work had three main themes. In *Mount Fuji and Mount Sinai* (1984) he studied the place of idols in Japanese and Christian spirituality and found many similarities. The extension of this to other religions provided him with a rich vein of comparison and contrast. His second main theme was the encounter between Christianity and Buddhism. 'How is the mercy shown in the name of Buddha related to the mercy shown in the name of Jesus Christ?' he asked. Much of his subsequent writing was devoted to answering this question and in his book on the cross he spoke of 'the broken Christ healing the broken world' and accomplishing this not by ruling from the centre but by going to the periphery of life. There was, he said, something distinctively Christian in this, and he contrasted the open hand of Buddha and the closed fist of Lenin with the pierced hands of Jesus, 'painfully neither open nor closed'.

Koyama's third special concern was with human greed. The relationship between Buddhism and Christianity, he averred, was not between 'true religion' and 'false religion', but between two different, yet intertwined, understandings of human greed, and he thought that Buddhism, with its spirit of detachment, had a special contribution to make to the overcoming of greed. The contrast between the Christian and Buddhist attitudes to history – one attached, the other detached – led him to assert that the truth is always to be discerned through two eyes.

# Elisabeth Schüssler Fiorenza

## (1938– )

Elisabeth Schüssler Fiorenza was a Roman Catholic biblical scholar who examined the New Testament in a woman's perspective and concluded that women had a prominent place in the life of the earliest Christian communities but, through the influence of St Paul, this was gradually reduced and eventually eliminated by the introduction of patriarchal structures imported from secular society. Thus women came to be subordinated to men in the life of the church – a position from which they have yet to recover.

This reconstruction of Christian origins, first made in her book *In Memory of Her* (1983), aroused considerable interest among New Testament scholars, as well as among feminists, for it was presented with formidable exegetical and theological skill and called for a totally different approach to the Bible. The task, she said, 'involves not so much rediscovering new sources as rereading the available sources in a different key. The goal is an increase in historical imagination.' This could be neither ignored nor dismissed simply as feminist rhetoric, and Schüssler Fiorenza's approach had lasting influence on New Testament studies. Translated into many languages, it is now regarded as a classic, but in common with her other writings, its style does not make for easy reading.

She was born at Täsnad, in north-west Romania, where she belonged to the German-speaking Catholic element in a mixed community. As the Russian army advanced through Romania in late 1944 her parents fled with her across Hungary and Austria to Southern Germany. She recalled the sight of dead bodies piled by the roadside during their journey and at the end of the war the family was living with other families in a barn near Munich. Subsequently they moved to Frankfurt, and after attending local schools she spent six years at the University of Würzburg studying religion. Her application for a scholarship to support her doctoral studies was rejected on the grounds that it would be a waste of money, since it was impossible for a woman to be appointed to a chair of theology. Nonetheless she went ahead, and obtained a doctorate for an analysis of the involvement of women in the church's ministry across the centuries. This was published in German as *Der vergessene Partner* (The Forgotten Partner) in 1964.

In 1967 she married Francis Fiorenza, an American theologian who was studying in Germany, and three years later they both secured teaching appointments at the Catholic University of Notre Dame in the USA. This enabled Elisabeth to attend meetings with feminist theologians, which had not been possible in Germany, and during a sabbatical at the Union Theological Seminary she became involved with the New York Feminist Scholars in Religion. From then on she began 'to do theology consciously as a woman and for women'. Later she co-founded and became co-editor of the *Journal of Feminist Studies in Religion*.

Appointment as the first Krister Stendahl Professor of Divinity at the Harvard Divinity School followed, and at the same time her husband became the School's Professor of Roman Catholic Studies. She regarded Catholicism as part of her culture, rather than as membership of an institution to whose discipline she was bound to conform. Her opposition to the ordination of women to the priesthood was based on the belief that in a male-dominated church the ordained ministry had become so grievously distorted from its orginal purpose that women should have nothing to do with it. They should instead pioneer new forms of ministry modelled on those described in the New Testament.

Schüssler Fiorenza acknowledged that it is not possible to be absolutely certain what happened during the time of Jesus or in the early years of the development of the Christian communities. Even so, she argued, it is evident that Jesus accorded an important place to women in his movement, and inasmuch as the gospel texts were subject to what she called 'patriarchal editorializing' it is reasonable to suppose, on the tip of the iceberg theory, that they had a place of even greater significance than is actually disclosed. Thus St Mark records an incident in which, not long before his death, Jesus was anointed by a woman and responded, 'Truly I say to you, wherever the gospel is preached in the whole world, what she has done will be told in memory of her.' Yet the woman's prophetic sign, with its messianic implications, never became an integral part of the Gospel and even her name was forgotten – 'because she was a woman'. Likewise in the Pauline writings it is apparent that women held positions of leadership in the early house churches, but their role was subsequently played down. Readers of the New Testament should therefore always apply to its text the 'hermeneutics of suspicion'.

# David Jenkins

## (1925–    )

David Edward Jenkins was Bishop of Durham from 1984 to 1994, and until his appointment to the fourth senior bishopric in the Church of England was virtually unknown to the general public. His career had been spent largely in the academic sphere and his theological position was moderately liberal; politically he was to the left of centre. None of his utterances and writings had aroused unusual interest, though his Bampton Lectures, published as *The Glory of Man* (1967) were well received. He was Joint Editor of *Theology* from 1976–82.

All this changed when, at the age of fifty-nine, he became a bishop. Soon after his appointment was announced he was interviewed on television and in response to a question said that he did not believe in the virgin birth and the resurrection of Jesus as historical events: 'I wouldn't put it past God to arrange a virgin birth if he wanted, but I very much doubt if he would.' This created a storm in the church and among others who felt that the basis of the Christian faith had been denied. A call to the Archbishop of York (John Habgood) that he should refuse episcopal consecration to the alleged heretic was refused, but three days after the ceremony had taken place in York Minster the building was struck by lightning and a large section of its roof was destroyed by fire. This was seen by some as a sign of divine disapproval.

The Jenkins saga was only just beginning. The enthronement of the new bishop in Durham Cathedral took place during a prolonged and bitter coalminers' strike and in the course of his sermon Jenkins, clearly siding with the miners, described the chairman of the National Coal Board as 'an elderly imported American whose withdrawal to leave a reconciling opportunity for some local product is surely neither dishonourable nor improper'. This was greeted with another storm of protest – this time from Conservative political quarters – and so, within a matter of weeks, the name of the new Bishop of Durham had echoed around the world and he was generally thought to be a dangerous radical.

Not so in the Diocese of Durham, where he quickly came to be seen as a deeply caring pastor who had interesting things to say and who, at a time when the right-wing policies of the Conservative government led by Margaret Thatcher were exacting a heavy toll from individuals and communities in North East England, was evidently a friend of the poor and the unemployed. Speaking about this work in 1987 he said, 'I love preaching to ordinary congregations, and the whole business of confirming people and trying to put them into the context of the love of God, and draw things out of them. I love teaching people to say their prayers. I'm not very good at it myself, that's what makes me good at teaching it, I think.' Courses of lectures on the Christian faith, which he gave from time to time at different centres in his diocese, always attracted large crowds.

Jenkins was equipped with a fine brain and an engaging personality. Born of Welsh parents, he was converted at an evangelical crusade class when he was twelve years old and during his mid-teens, spent in South London, he felt drawn to holy orders. First, however, it was necessary for him to serve in the wartime army. Notwithstanding this break in his education, he did brilliantly at Oxford, where it became clear he was destined for an academic career.

His fifteen years as a Fellow of Queen's College, Oxford (1954–1969), earned him the reputation of a stimulating teacher and a sensitive pastor, and his theological views were actually much less radical than those of some of his academic colleagues. But he was a fast talker, much given to the use of parenthesis, slang and the vivid phrase, and deliberately provoked his students to think for themselves. This gadfly approach, also employed successfully when he was a Professor at Leeds University (1979–84), was unusual in a bishop, and it was this as much as anything that brought him notoriety when he was appointed to Durham. Jenkins was not greatly troubled by publicity and was content to note that the reports of his sermons and speeches caused religious faith to be discussed in pubs and market places. Inevitably he was often misrepresented by the media, and the subtleties of his arguments did not always lend themselves to newspaper headlines. Thus he was often portrayed as a 'political' bishop, whereas he was in fact one of the few professional theologians among the bishops of his time. His criticisms of the church and other institutions were often fierce but his utterances were never without an element of hope.

# Jerzy Popieluszko
## (1947–1984)

Jerzy Alfons Popieluszko was a young Polish priest who became chaplain of the trade union Solidarity and strongly supported the campaign which led to the ending of forty years of Communist rule in Poland. However, his public criticisms of the government led to abduction by the security police and he was brutally murdered. The national shock created by this event administered the *coup de grâce* to the system, Popieluszko became Poland's liberation hero, and steps have already been taken in Rome to secure his eventual canonization as a saint.

He was born into a peasant family in Okopy, near Svchowola, in the immediate aftermath of the 1939–45 war and his early years were spent in conditions of extreme poverty and hardship. Inspired by the example of his compatriot Maximilian Kolbe, the priest who gave his life to save that of a fellow prisoner in a German concentration camp, he was ordained and shared in the conservative outlook of the Catholic Church in Poland. In 1980, however, following Pope John Paul's visit to Poland in the previous year, Solidarity was born and the Warsaw steelworkers went on strike in support of the striking shipyard workers of Gdansk. They asked for a priest to celebrate Mass at the steelworks and Popieluszko, being available, volunteered to undertake this.

He saw the task solely in sacramental and pastoral terms, but the experience of celebrating Mass for the workers against the background of a huge cross which they had erected made him realize that their struggle for justice was a spiritual struggle. He obtained his bishop's permission to serve as their chaplain, and said:

> The mission of the church is to be with the people and to share their joys and sorrows. To serve God is to seek a way to human hearts. To serve God is to speak about evil as a sickness which should be brought to light so that it can be cured. To serve God is to condemn evil in all its manifestations.

In 1981, faced by increasing strike action and other forms of dissent, the Government declared martial law, and over 1,000 members of Solidarity were arrested. Popieluszko visited them in prison and organized support for their families. The church of Stanislaw Kostka in Moscow attracted huge congregations to hear his fiery anti-Communist sermons at 'Masses for the Country', and as organized dissent became more difficult and dangerous – Solidarity was banned – he helped to keep alive the quest for freedom.

This brought an immediate reaction from the Government, which tried first to silence him by means of harassment. There were frequent interruptions whenever he celebrated Mass and on one occasion a bomb was thrown at the door of his flat. Then came more formal action, and between January and June 1984 he was arrested and taken in for questioning by the police on thirteen occasions. In July of that year he was charged with 'abusing the freedom of conscience and religion to the detriment of the Polish Peoples' Republic'. This led to widespread public protests, as a result of which he was given an amnesty.

At this point the workers became anxious about Popieluszko's safety and suggested to the bishop that he should be sent abroad for further study, but he refused to go. By this time the Polish bishops were themselves concerned about his activities. They shared the Government's belief that widespread expressions of dissent would lead, as it had done elsewhere in eastern Europe, to an invasion by the Soviet Union. Cardinal Glemp, the Primate of Poland, argued that martial law was a lesser evil than Soviet intervention, and in common with many others in the country could not foresee the end of Communist rule.

Popieluszko believed, however, that the truth about the Communist regime should be clearly and publicly stated and in his diary recorded a particularly difficult meeting with Cardinal Glemp: 'His charges against me completely knocked me off balance. Even the secret police during their interrogation showed me more respect.' During the summer of 1984 he became aware of the increasing danger he faced, now that he lacked official church support, and in one of his sermons said:

> If we must die, it is better to meet death while defending a worthwhile cause than sitting back and letting injustice take place . . . The priest is called to bear witness to the truth, to suffer for the truth and if need be to give up his life for it.

On October 19 his car was stopped by the security police on a country road. He was forced into the boot of the police vehicle, and when later he tried to escape was savagely beaten, tied up, and with rocks attached to his body thrown into a reservoir. His grave and church are a place of national pilgrimage.

Roger Boyes, *The Priest Who Had to Die*, Victor Gollancz 1986.

# Tissa Balasuriya

## (1924–   )

Tissa Balasuriya was a Sri Lankan theologian who became world famous in 1997 when he was excommunicated from the Roman Catholic Church following his refusal to sign a profession of faith compiled by the Vatican Congregation for the Doctrine of the Faith. This was designed to test his conformity to current Roman doctrine following the publication in 1990 of *Mary and Human Liberation,* in which Balasuriya questioned traditional Marian doctrine and, in the context of inter-faith dialogue, rejected orthodox christology. The excommunication aroused considerable concern among many Roman Catholics, including some who were unsympathetic to Balasuriya's views. It was the first time this discipline had been imposed since 1988 and the action was seen as the heavy-handed exercising of pre-Vatican II authoritarianism.

Balasuriya was an exponent of liberation theology in an Asian context and had a deep concern for the poor and the exploited, particularly those whom he believed to be the victims of colonial exploitation. He founded and became the Director of a Centre for Society and Religion in Colombo, and two other books, *The Eucharist and Human Liberation* (1979) and *Planetary Theology* (1985), indicated a radical stance on political and social matters, but no suggestion of theological heresy.

He was born into a Catholic family in a village in a central province of what was then known as Ceylon. His father was an apothecary in government service, and after attending St Patrick's College, Jaffra and St Joseph's College, Colombo, the young Tissa studied economics and political science at the University of Ceylon. In 1946 he was professed as a member of the Congregation of Oblates of Mary Immaculate and sent to the Gregorian University in Rome to study philosophy and theology. He was ordained priest in Rome in 1952 and on his return to Sri Lanka became a lecturer at Aquinas University College. This was followed by periods of further study at Oxford, where he took the diploma in agricultural economics, and at the Institut Catholique in Paris. Back in Sri Lanka in 1964 he became Rector of Aquinas College and remained there until the foundation of the Centre for Society and Religion in 1971.

By now he was becoming increasingly concerned to apply the insights of Latin America liberation theology to the Asian situation, and he was a founder member of the Ecumenical Association of Third World Theologians which held its first meeting in Tanzania in 1976. *Mary and Human Liberation* was first published as a double number of *Logos* – the house journal of the Centre for Society and Religion. It consisted of 170 pages and the original print run was 600 copies. Balasuriya expected it to be only of specialist interest and in the Preface acknowledged that in common with all theology, it was exploratory, fallible and 'open to criticism and correction in a climate and context of genuine search for the truth'.

The book itself was hardly a substantial work of theology, and drew heavily on the work of other Third World, and some European, theologians. It was written, however, in a lively and sometimes provocative style which helped to emphasize the unorthodox character of many of the things he was saying. Thus he wondered why Mary, when appearing to Bernadette at Lourdes, did not say anything about the conditions of the exploited working class in France of the day. He believed that Mary, 'as a woman of the working class, should have felt these social evils to be a grave injustice'. He added, 'This Mary, who comes to us in apparitions, and who is accepted by the dominant establishment, is not a liberating Mary', and went on to note that 'services at Marian shrines are usually dominated by male clergy'.

It was, however, his questioning of the orthodox doctrines of original sin and of christology which alarmed, first the Sri Lankan bishops, then the Vatican. Original sin had, he believed, been invented and used by male theologians and clergy as a way of denigrating women through the centuries. Much of Christian theology, not least that relating to the person of Christ, was, he asserted, the result of the imposition of ideology and imagination on the Jesus of the Gospels and had been used to devalue other religions. But 'different religious traditions are paths to God and to salvation'. He saw 'no reason why there cannot be a black, brown, white or yellow female Pope'.

In the light of this, and much else of a highly controversial character, the excommunication of Balasuriya was less surprising than his subsequent statement of reconciliation in January 1998 in which he appeared to retract much of what he had written. The Vatican responded by lifting the excommunication and announced later that in future the trials of alleged heretics would be conducted with 'greater transparency'.

# Jacques Gaillot

## (1935– )

Jacques Gaillot was Bishop of Evreux, sixty miles west of Paris, from 1982 until his dismissal in 1995. He claimed to be neither a militant nor a radical, but his departure from official Roman Catholic teaching included advocacy of the use of condoms to defeat AIDS, greater tolerance towards homosexuals, an abortion pill, and open debate on the possibility of ordaining to the priesthood women and married men. He was rarely off French television screens and the last straw for the church's hierarchy came with his appearance on a 'girlie' show answering questions about sex and drugs from scantily dressed interviewers and the audience.

His dismissal caused a great outcry. Thousands of supporters, including several other French bishops, attended his farewell Mass in Evreux cathedral, and there were demonstrations outside bishops' palaces in France, Belgium and Switzerland. Gaillot, bereft of a geographical diocese, thereupon created one of his own on the Internet and proclaimed this to be a modern way of carrying the gospel to the ends of the earth. On his website he offered, in the main European languages, comment on current issues in church and society, a forum for discussion, teaching on specific Christian doctrines and themes, and counselling. All became widely used and were served by a team, which enabled Gaillot to travel the world in support of the poor and the oppressed.

Gaillot, the son of a wine merchant, was born in Saint Dizier. He attended a strict seminary at Langres to prepare for the priesthood, but in 1957 was required to undergo twenty-eight months' military service. This was spent mainly in Algiers where he was greatly disturbed by the hatred and violence which attended the final phase of French colonial rule. On leaving the army, and shortly before the Second Vatican Council, he studied in Rome and became a priest at Saint Dizier in 1961. He then returned to Rome for a further period of study, after which he was appointed as a Professor at the seminary in Reims.

The ending of Vatican II and the eruption of Paris student riots in 1968 caused him to rethink the whole of his faith, and he became a Professor at the Liturgical Institute of Paris. He was then made Rector of the Reims seminary, followed by appointment as Vicar General of the diocese of Langres. In 1982, to his great surprise, he was made Bishop of Evreux. Later he confessed, 'It was there I realized that a bishop was not only for Catholics but for everyone – I think I realized that before vaguely, but it was at Evreux that my mission to non-Christians became clear.'

This mission took Gaillot into involvement with the marginalized in society – AIDS victims, criminals, drug addicts, immigrants and the homeless – and he was very open to the media, which took great interest in both his activities and his opinions. He in turn valued media attention, for he believed there should be open debate about controversial issues. In his diocese he was immediately confronted with a problem common to the whole of France – an acute shortage of priests. He tackled this by establishing an extensive programme of laity training to enable lay people to take responsibility for the church in their parishes – conducting non-sacramental worship, becoming pastoral visitors, and organizing parish life – leaving visiting priests to administer the sacraments. Synods were held at which the laity were encouraged to suggest initiatives for pastoral care, mission and social action, and by the time he left the diocese about one third of the parishes were run by lay people.

However, not everyone was enamoured by their bishop's actions and opinions. There were frequent complaints that he spent too much time on prison visiting, secular schools, regular meetings with the Communist Mayor of Evreux, and even flying to South Africa to see a political prisoner. All this, it was alleged, was at the expense of accompanying pilgrimages to Lourdes and attending major church events in the cathedral. It was also suggested that he did not speak often enough about God. Specially sinister was the attitude of the right-wing Minister of the Interior, whose harsh immigration policies were frequently attacked by Gaillot. A few days before the dismissal of the bishop this Minister was received in audience by the Pope in Rome.

Gaillot was in fact warned about his behaviour on a number of occasions by Cardinal Lustiger of Paris and also by the Pope. A few months after the announcement of his dismissal he was called to Rome and told by the Pope that if he changed his ways he could resume the leadership of Evreux, but he refused to accept this and returned to the hostel for the homeless in Paris where he was now living.

# Index